ASIAN AMERICAN SPORTING CULTURES

Asian American Sporting Cultures

Edited by
Stanley I. Thangaraj,
Constancio R. Arnaldo, Jr., and
Christina B. Chin

Foreword by J. Jack Halberstam
Afterword by Lisa Lowe

NEW YORK UNIVERSITY PRESS
New York and London

For our mentors

NEW YORK UNIVERSITY PRESS
New York and London
www.nyupress.org

© 2016 by New York University
All rights reserved

References to Internet websites (URLs) were accurate at the time of writing. Neither the author nor New York University Press is responsible for URLs that may have expired or changed since the manuscript was prepared.

ISBN: 978-1-4798-4016-8 (hardback)
ISBN: 978-1-4798-8469-8 (paperback)

For Library of Congress Cataloging-in-Publication data, please contact the Library of Congress.

New York University Press books are printed on acid-free paper, and their binding materials are chosen for strength and durability. We strive to use environmentally responsible suppliers and materials to the greatest extent possible in publishing our books.

Manufactured in the United States of America

10 9 8 7 6 5 4 3 2 1

Also available as an ebook

CONTENTS

Foreword: Success, Failure, and Everything in Between   vii
   J. Jack Halberstam

Acknowledgments   xi

Introduction: You Play Sports? Asian American
Sporting Matters   1
   *Stanley I. Thangaraj, Constancio R. Arnaldo, Jr., and
   Christina B. Chin*

PART I. ASIAN AMERICAN SPORTS IN HISTORICAL CONTEXT

1. From Perpetual Foreigner to Pacific Rim Entrepreneur:
The U.S. Military, Asian Americans, and the Circuitous
Path of Sport   23
   Ryan Reft

2. Reflections on Sport Spectatorship and Immigrant Life   53
   Shalini Shankar

PART II. ASIAN AMERICAN SPORTING CELEBRITIES

3. Everybody Loves an Underdog: Learning from Linsanity   75
   Oliver Wang

4. Manny "Pac-Man" Pacquiao, the Transnational Fist, and
the Southern California Ringside Community   102
   Constancio R. Arnaldo, Jr.

PART III. COMPLICATING "MODEL MINORITY" MYTHS,
ORIENTALISM, AND GENDERED STEREOTYPES

5. Indian Americans and the "Brain Sport" of Spelling Bees   127
   Pawan Dhingra

6. Mixed Martial Arts, Caged Orientalism, and Female
Asian American Bodies   152
   Jessica W. Chin and David L. Andrews

7. The Continued Legacy of Japanese American Youth
   Basketball Leagues　　　　　　　　　　　　　　　　　180
   Christina B. Chin

PART IV. REFUGEES, PACIFIC ISLANDERS, AND SPORT

8. Hmong Youth, American Football, and the Cultural Politics
   of Ethnic Sports Tournaments　　　　　　　　　　　　199
   Chia Youyee Vang

9. Lin, Te'o, and Asian American Masculinities in Sporting Flux　221
   David Leonard

   Afterword: "Competing against Type"　　　　　　　247
   Lisa Lowe

   About the Contributors　　　　　　　　　　　　　　253

   Index　　　　　　　　　　　　　　　　　　　　　　257

FOREWORD

Success, Failure, and Everything in Between

J. JACK HALBERSTAM

Sporting events are testing grounds for all kinds of assumptions about race, class, gender, and sexuality. And indeed, most people have a story to tell, when the topic of sports comes up, about their successes or failures in instances of intense competition or about losing their sense of power and strength in relation to all kinds of scenarios in team sports that favor the big, the tall, the strong, the normative. Sport, indeed, offers fertile ground for the crafting and sustaining of racial and gendered stereotypes and it offers a language or a grammar even for thinking about competition and bias. We adapt phrases from sports to describe fairness—"a level playing field," for example—and we go to sports to single out the disastrous effects of cheating—professional cycling, for example. Sport offers us a seemingly endless supply of inspirational narratives of the underdog, evolutionary narratives of size, strength, and the survival of the fittest, and surprising narratives about performance and play. And far from offering a neutral terrain for individual competition, sport has, in the last century, provided an arena for a whole array of contests within which national identity, race, sexuality, and gender hang in the balance.

In my work I have tried to understand the dynamic relation between winning and losing, succeeding and failing that make up any sporting event. As I argue in *The Queer Art of Failure* (2011), a culture oriented to only very narrow models of success relegates entire groups of people to stigmatized failure. But, as sporting competitions reveal, the distance between winners and losers is often only inches or seconds. Sport, more than most arenas of popular culture, offers us a chance to experience both the joy of victory and the agony of defeat. Indeed, even to play sport one must accept defeat as a likely outcome and must fold failure into the experience of competition itself. But of course these notions of success and failure are not value free and not neutral. Racial difference marks our relations to success and failure and even to what we understand these terms to mean in ways that have massive consequences for all who play sport, all who watch sport, and all who recognize sport as allegorical terrain for other kinds of contestations.

For example, historians like Gayle Bederman have used sport, boxing specifically, to highlight the contested arena of racialized masculinity at the turn of the last century. And so, in her book *Manliness and Civilization: A Cultural History of Gender and Race in the United States, 1880–1917* (1996), Bederman opens with the famous boxing match between African American champion Jack Johnson and the so-called "Hope of the White Race," Jim Jeffries, in 1910. Cast as a struggle between white and black manhood, this fight led to white riots when Johnson emerged victorious and Jeffries was beaten to the ground. Black fighters from Jack Johnson to Muhammad Ali to Mike Tyson have rarely been allowed to enjoy their success and instead they have been hounded, policed, punished, and demonized.

For women, sport has offered another kind of test. As we saw in the last few years in relation to the runner Caster Semenya, strong, muscular female athletes, particularly those who are nonwhite or non-Western, have been suspected of gender transgressions and subjected to repeated and confusing tests to "determine their sex." While the various athletic boards that have tested athletes over the years have used a myriad of methods from cheek swabs to genital examinations, most of these boards have failed to come up with clear guidelines for gender norms in relation to the athletic female body. More recently, calls have been made to bring such testing to an end.

Obviously, sport competitions—whether running, weightlifting, swimming, gymnastics, team sports, or tennis—offer a setting and an opportunity for all kinds of cultural contests to play out. And while the most visible such contests in the last century have involved black versus white bodies (as in boxing) or East versus West (as in gymnastics in the Cold War era), little attention has been paid to other modes of racial formation that unfold quietly and without much fanfare in sporting arenas around the country. As a few of the essays in this collection mention, the "Linsanity" that greeted the surprising rise and fall of Asian

American basketball player Jeremy Lin in the NBA in 2012 revealed a wealth of unexamined narratives about Asian and Asian American bodies within the national imaginary of sport and competition. As Oliver Wang writes: "The stock story of Lin's rise becomes a seductive affirmation of the American Dream's attainability (despite the fact that it's called 'a dream'). However, as Lin is also Asian American, the framing of his accomplishments within the American Dream narrative aligns all too well with another deeply embedded stock story around American race relations: the Model Minority Myth (MMM)." As Wang shows clearly in his analysis of the media coverage of Jeremy Lin, as much as stereotypes of Asian American masculinity and athletic ability were challenged and reconsidered in this moment of high visibility, so other stereotypes of conformity and docility were imposed within a wide array of coverage.

Increasingly in contemporary media, sport serves as a shorthand for long standing myths about the nation. Whether we are watching Serena Williams being booed at a tennis competition for yelling at a lineswoman, or listening to some supposedly neutral sports commentator deploy well-worn racial epithets to describe an athlete of color, we can see clearly how sport allegorizes race and buttresses narratives of racial difference. This volume on *Asian American Sporting Cultures* makes an incredibly important intervention into the current marketplace of ideas about athleticism, race, gender, and performance. It helps us to locate the nexus of assumptions about race and gender as they play out in sport competitions and these essays allow us to grasp the complex histories of racialization that are swept up into banal narratives about uplift or sinister narratives about ability and aptitude.

There were a few very welcome surprises in these essays for me as a reader. One in particular was the mention of the Mei Wahs in Ryan Reft's chapter on the histories of Asian Americans in sports. The Mei Wahs were two separate Chinese American women's basketball teams in California, active in Chinatowns in Los Angeles and San Francisco in the 1930s. These teams have been credited with popularizing women's amateur sports and sports historian Kathleen Yep has suggested that sport offered these women a site for Asian American mobilization against exclusion and discrimination.

Yep's insight that sport can be a place to contest, oppose, and even transform popular conceptions of Asian Americans is important because we are so used to thinking of political change in terms of the law and policy. And, as the editors remind us: "Sport has a special and important place in the processes of citizen-making and in the policing of national and diasporic bodies." This collection makes an important contribution to current thought on recreation, leisure, ideology, pleasure, politics, and race. There is much here to debate, to ponder, and to dispute. And rather than just waiting for the next version of "Linsanity" to break out in order to bring Asian American sporting cultures to our attention, this volume allows us to think race, gender, and sports together on the way to a much more complex understanding of competition and embodied cultures.

ACKNOWLEDGMENTS

There are many people who played major roles in the formation and completion of this book. We apologize in advance for any names we have forgotten. The error is solely ours. As Stan Thangaraj was working through *Desi Hoop Dreams: Pickup Basketball and the Making of Asian American Masculinity* (New York University Press, 2015), Martin Manalansan asked him to consider putting together an anthology on Asian American sporting practices. He encouraged and inspired the birth of this book. If it were not for Martin's continual support and wisdom, this book would have never become a reality. We owe much to Martin for his generosity, intellectual depth, and mentorship. Shortly after Stan started working on the early stages of the proposal, he met with Constancio and Chris while touring through the Midwest with Dan Burdsey. The conversations among the four of us set the foundation for the book. We are grateful to Dan for assisting us at a moment's notice and for offering nonstop support. He has provided wonderful insights and helped us polish up the chapters. The generosity of J. Jack Halberstam and Lisa Lowe is infinite, unexpected, and most gratifying—we are grateful for their time, energy, and scholarship, which is foundational to the conceptualization of this project. What great fortune and luck for us to have them on board! In fact, we attribute our own growth as junior scholars to Lisa Lowe's and J. Jack Halberstam's analytical toolkits. Their seminal works have been foundational to how we approach sporting cultures.

We owe many thanks to the contributors of this anthology. Without their professionalism, cooperation, and patience, we would not have had the critical insights and analysis that this book provides. They have also provided so much enthusiasm and excitement for the project, which have inspired us. Each chapter adds complexity and nuance to thinking about the fields of Asian America, ethnic studies, sport studies, and gender studies. Thank you Ryan, Chia, Pawan, Jessica, Dave, Shalini, David, and Oliver. In addition, we are grateful to some key scholars who have been instrumental in sharpening the theoretical and empirical claims of the book. Their own scholarship has had a profound influence on us and the honor has been ours to share time and space with them: Mimi Nguyen, Scott Brooks, Kimberly Hoang, Kemi Balogun, and Linta Varghese. Shilpa Davé's critical work on popular culture and her continuous support of our work enriched the project. Linda España-Maram met us at the 2013 Association for Asian American Studies (AAAS) conference and worked through the intricacies of this project. We admire, respect, and cherish Linda. She means the world to us. At various conferences and talks, our conversations with Junaid Rana, Fa'anofo Lisaclaire Uperesa, Robert Ku, Sameer Pandya, Maryam Kashani, Ben Carrington, Daryl Maeda, Seema Sohi, Umayyah Cable, David Roediger, Richard T. Rodriquez, Brian Montes, Maggie Whitten, Daya Mortel, Alex Gurn, and Sarah Gualtieri have been fantastic. Ryan Reft supported us through his various articles and Tropics of Meta. He and Alex Cummings have been great scholars and friends. They publicized and brought great visibility to the project in its earlier stages. Rachel Buff has been a tireless supporter who has always been there. Rachel Endo amazes us with her continued support of Illinois grads and we are most grateful to her; she makes the academy a great place for us. The early stages of this book were received well at the Association for Asian American Studies and the American Studies Association annual conferences. Northwestern University's Asian American Studies Program provided us with a venue to present our work; we thank Shalini Shankar and AAS for the opportunity.

We appreciate the faith, support, and continued guidance given to us by New York University Press. The comments by the anonymous reviewers were most helpful and productive. Jennifer Hammer believed in our project from the very start and has been instrumental in the structure and form it has taken. She has read many versions of our proposal and been there at a moment's notice to answer questions, problem shoot, and provide innovative solutions. Her incredible team at NYU Press, with Constance Grady, Dorothea Halliday, Dan Geist, Jodi Narde, Mary Beth Jarrad, and Betsy Steve, provided many resources and insights while making this process of publication seamless, smooth, and FUN. Thank you.

Stanley I. Thangaraj: I thank Arthur Spears for the leadership and guidance. Arthur inspires me with his breadth of knowledge, his humor, and his honesty. Lotti Silber affirms me and wows me with her generosity, brilliance, creativity, and support. She makes City College of New York feel like home. Kamilah Briscoe, Michael Busch, and Wanda Mercado are pivotal to my happiness at CCNY; they have always been there to hear me out on many things. Thank you Cheryl Sterling and Adrienne Petty for making multidisciplinary work riveting. Syd Steinhart has been a tireless supporter; I appreciate him. My partner, Alena, and my daughter, Jeya, make me laugh and give joy to every little thing in life. They are the love for which I am always, forever grateful. Working on this book with Constancio and Chris has been pure joy; they are intellectual powerhouses with such a great sense of compassion and humility.

Constancio R. Arnaldo, Jr.: It has been a true pleasure working with Stanley Thangaraj and Christina Chin. I appreciate Stan and Christina's collegiality, humor, and generosity. I deeply value their friendship and look forward to working with them on future projects. I would also like to thank Norma A. Marrun for asking me questions about sport that I often take for granted.

Christina B. Chin: I would like to extend my deepest appreciation to Min Zhou, Mimi Nguyen, Erica Morales, Anthony Ocampo, Noriko Milman, and Logan Tam for all their endless feedback, support, and encouragement. I am especially grateful to have the support of my co-editors who made this collaboration a labor of love and inspiration.

Introduction

You Play Sports? Asian American Sporting Matters

STANLEY I. THANGARAJ, CONSTANCIO R. ARNALDO, JR.,
AND CHRISTINA B. CHIN

African American baseball player Jackie Robinson entered the national discourse on race and citizenship when he joined the otherwise entirely white major Leagues in 1947. Although some athletes of color may previously have passed as "white" and played (Burgos 2007), Robinson was the first African American to publically integrate professional baseball in the twentieth century. There were two thriving Negro Leagues at the time, but the rules of segregation—de jure and de facto—affirmed in the Supreme Court's 1896 *Plessy v. Ferguson* decision limited opportunities for multiracial, male-on-male professional sporting venues.

Robinson's entry into white professional baseball was important in shifting some of the racial dynamics at play in America. Sport, in the mid-20th century, was a bastion of white supremacy and it embodied such U.S. national bodily ideals as white, heterosexual, respectable, Christian, muscular, and male.[1] Long histories of racial exclusion, racist violence, gendered policing, and sexual regulation positioned black men as outside the normative abilities of white men.[2] In this respect, sport was a microcosm of the racial nation, with the language of citizenship and racial resistance coded within black-white discourse. This black-white dichotomy failed to account for the long histories of Asian Americans in the United States (Chan 1991; Bow 2010; Bald 2013). As this volume shows, Asian American sporting cultures trouble the current racial synchronicity between sport and nation while illuminating multiple performances of "belonging."

Sport has a special and important place in the processes of citizen-making and in the policing of national and diasporic bodies.[3] Since the 1800s in the United States, recreation and sporting activities have been instrumental to the representation of respectable national bodies (Bachin 2005; España-Maram 2006). As recreational facilities and college sports took off in the late 1800s, the expansion of U.S. Empire through institutions like the YMCA explicitly linked Christian muscularity to national subjectivity and colonial dominance.[4] With stringent anti-Chinese and anti-Asian immigration acts and local legislation, citizenship was already coded as black-white while Asian Americans were in the category of "perpetual foreigner" (Lowe 1996; Prashad 2000; Yep 2009). Asian Americans were not intelligible within the dominant racial logic. The exclusion of Asian Americans within the discourse of United States sporting culture is informed by larger societal marginalizations outside the field of sport as well.[5] As Caribbean scholar C.L.R. James reminds us, sport is constructed in real life and real time and closely reflects larger social phenomena (James 2003). While the exclusions in sport are informed by broader societal marginalization of Asian Americans, Asian American communities can also use those very sporting cultures to stake their own claims to belonging while manifesting their versions of American identity.[6] The appropriation of sporting cultures is what sociologists Ben Carrington (2010), Douglas Hartmann (2003), and Michael Omi and Howard Winant (1994) deem as a "racial project" through which communities interpret and reinterpret racial dynamics while attempting to reshape racial realities.

Unfortunately, scholarship on race and American sport has itself been a racial project that perpetuates the ideology of racial life as determined through black-white diametric oppositions. Mainstream and academic understandings of sport in the United States frequently uphold the same racial logic they try to complicate. While Reuben May (2007) ethnographically investigates Atlanta's black basketball community, he does not account for either the large Asian American or Latina/o community in the city, which could productively complicate notions of race. The study of race and sport often involves contending with the black-white racial dichotomy without acknowledging how many racial Others are part of the process of "racial formation" (Omi and Winant 1994). The sociology of sport barely touches the surface of racial others with a few exceptions, such as Kathleen Yep's (2009) work on San Francisco's Chinatown playground. When the literature on sport in the U.S. does not account for Asian Americans and other communities of color, the black-white dichotomy is tautologically reaffirmed. In particular, the focus on black-white dynamics elides the racialized experiences of Asian Americans in American sport and does not attend to the multiply inflected racial parameters of national and diasporic belonging.[7] This volume recovers important narratives about Asian American sporting cultures as a way to complicate the simplistic U.S. black-white racial logic while showing the multiple ways in which Asian American communities stake national claims and diasporic belonging through sport.

While most recognize Jackie Robinson's entry into professional baseball as historically significant, a contemporaneous historically important sporting moment was met with virtual silence. Wataru "Kilo Wat" Misaka's entry onto the New York Knicks basketball team that same year received little public coverage, while African Americans Earl Lloyd and Nate "Sweetwater" Clifton were seen as integrating white professional basketball three years later (Farred 2006; Lloyd 2011). Most Asian American studies and history books pay minimal to no scholarly attention to Misaka's legacy. Misaka's erasure from the narrative of racial progression in American sport sheds light on how Asian Americans have been situated outside the contours of "race" and "national belonging."[8] Japanese American basketball players like Misaka, as well as Chinese American basketball players, like Willie Woo Wong and Helen Wong, and Filipino boxers, like Ceferino "Bolo Puncher" Garcia, and horse jockeys like Japanese American Yoshio "Kokomo Joe" Kobuki have not been adopted as part of the national narrative.[9] Asian American studies has minimally and sometimes somewhat uncritically engaged with sport. Rather, evaluations of Asian American consumption of U.S. popular culture and subsequent practices of cultural citizenship have foreground certain types of culture at the expense of dismissing the prevalence of sport within Asian America.

Critical work by Davé, Nishime, and Oren (2004), Nguyen and Tu (2007), and Desai (2004) has encouraged nuanced understandings of the ways in which Asian Americans negotiate their relationships to U.S. popular culture by emphasizing the different sets of attachments that heterogeneous Asian American and Pacific Islander communities have to popular culture, and the many contradictions within power structures. However, missing in this research is attention to how Asian American communities generate affinity, find symbolic and emotional attachment, and form a sense of identity through sport. Only recently has work by scholars like España-Maram (2006), Yep (2009), and Regalado (2012) made evident longer Asian American historical connections to sport. This volume follows this latter trajectory while also highlighting the ways in which "Asian America" is disrupted and disjointed as it accounts for various "Others." In the process, it examines mainstream sports in addition to nontraditional sports like spelling bees and mixed martial arts. Through multiple sporting practices, communities of color challenge the relationship between race and ability while expanding the parameters of American citizenship (España-Maram 2006; Gilbert 2010).

As we look back on Wat Misaka's entry into U.S. professional sport, we have to set the context to fully understand the significance of his sporting history in relation to the larger U.S. society. As the first Japanese American man to join the Basketball Association of America (BAA), the precursor to the NBA, Misaka's presence in the quintessentially American game of basketball was the product of a long engagement with sport.[10] He was an active participant in basketball culture from an early age and carried that passion through two collegiate championships with the University of Utah in 1944 and 1947. However, such expressions of American identity were overshadowed by the legacy of Executive Order 9066 and the Japanese internment camps during World War II, which promoted notions of Japanese Americans as dangerous and unfit American subjects. Yet even in this climate, Misaka and other Asian Americans demonstrated intimate engagement with many U.S. popular cultural practices such as sport.[11]

Misaka's ascendance through the professional basketball hierarchy might seem exceptional, but Asian Americans' engagement with sport is not. Sport is an everyday practice in Asian American communities and one stage for performing renditions of (Asian) American identity. There is a rich history of Asian American sporting cultures. By participating in American sports, Asian Americans have crafted American popular cultural forms into Asian American sites. Through an investigation of how these communities shape their identities, we can see how Asian Americans utilize sport as a racial project that changes the meanings of nation and diaspora in relation to race, gender, sexuality, class, and ability.

This volume draws upon insights from a diverse spectrum of scholars and showcases how sport is a key terrain in which national, diasporic, racial, gendered, and sexual identities are created while at the same time challenging various racializations of Asian Americans. As sport has always had particularly intimate ties to nation and respective practices of citizenship, looking at sporting cultures and celebrities offers a means to understand the performance of belonging, as marginalized populations enact their claims to citizenship, diasporic nationalism, and everyday modes of living in bodily ways.[12] Different Asian American and Pacific Islander communities have varying relationships to U.S. Empire (Burns 2012; España-Maram 2006), late capitalism (Hong 2006; Lowe 1996), and the ongoing "global war on terror" (Afzal 2014; Alsultany 2012; Naber 2012; Rana 2011), which in turn create multiple and different relationships to sport. Concurrently, sporting cultures challenge the very parameters of Asian America.

The term "Asian American" is a U.S.-based, politically charged, racial designation for a pan-ethnic Asian population that emerged out of the 1960s Civil Rights Movement.[13] Formed as a response to the racist designations placed on Asian ethnic groups, the term was given new meaning through the coalitional efforts of activists to claim Asian Americans' legitimate place in U.S. history and society.[14] The racial formation of "Asian American" involved various racial projects intended to invert and resist the racializations of Asian American communities. Asian American lives, however, are not always lived or shaped uniformly and equivalently at the grassroots level. The term "Asian American" implicates certain processes of racialization that are simultaneously expansive and restrictive, inherently contradictory, and subject to contestation as a result of geopolitical changes, contemporary transnational labor flows, and the tendency to rely upon particular narratives that privilege middle-class, heterosexual, masculine subjects.[15] It is in this spirit that we draw on the work of scholars Lisa Lowe and Martin Manalansan, who argue for acknowledging and prioritizing the diversity of Asian American lives, including differences in gender, class, sexuality, religion, and nationalism, within the category "Asian American."[16] Therefore, the scholars in this volume do not take for granted the category of "Asian America"; they refuse to conceptualize it as singular and cohesive.

Sport constitutes one compelling stage on which to talk about difference within the category of "Asian America" and it illuminates corresponding tensions, conflicts, and disruptions. This book highlights the heterogeneity of Asian American communities, which include, but are not limited to, Filipina/o, Chinese, Japanese, Korean, Laotian, Hmong, Vietnamese, Samoan, Cambodian, Thai, and South Asian Americans. These communities construct notions of self and community in relation to whites, African Americans, Latina/os, and other Asian American communities, among others. The differing times of immigration among Asian American groups, their multiple and different attachments to the U.S. nation and to mainstream sport, and their disparate social locations render Asian American identities heterogeneous, multiple, and always "in process" (Hall 2003).

The experiences of Asian American athletes like Wataru Misaka and Jeremy Lin in basketball can provide compelling insights into how Asian American sporting cultures take shape in relation to dominant racializations. In the process, we see how U.S. Empire and Asian American renditions of (ancestral) "home" shape experiences of sport and "Asia" in the United States. However, Lin's and Misaka's stories alone cannot speak for the complex social formations and disruptions within Asian America. The chapters in this volume draw on historical archives, media texts, quantitative data, and qualitative social scientific research to complicate these social formations. They critically investigate the relationships between racializations of Asian and Pacific Islander American communities at particular moments in U.S. history, the various Asian American responses and consumptive practices of sport, and the ways in which these communities transformed American sport into Asian American and Pacific Islander places. Through these sporting cultures, the categories of Asian America and U.S. identity are put in flux, driven by what immigration studies scholar Lisa Lowe (1996) deems as "heterogeneity, multiplicity, and hybridity."

When accounting for the sporting cultures of Asian American communities, one can decipher through their sporting narratives a metanarrative about U.S. society. The arrival on the sporting field/court of each community is accompanied by particular cultural baggage that includes different experiences of capitalism, many encounters with U.S. Empire, and multiple interpretations of race, gender, sexuality, class, and citizenship. Filipina/o Americans, Cambodian Americans, Hmong Americans, Laotian Americans, Pacific Islanders, and Vietnamese Americans bring stories of U.S. occupation and colonialism.[17] South Asian Americans today experience sport at the height of the "global war on terror" discourse, which often imagines them as threats to national security and yet also the "model minority."[18] Similarly, Korean Americans experience a particular relationship of their diasporic community to their homeland(s) at a time when the U.S. state vilifies North Korea as part of the "axis of evil."[19] Instead of seeing the differences within Asian America as disparate and separate phenomena, the volume highlights the contradictions of identity formation and larger structures of power. In the process, it centers how Asian American identities always take shape in relation to other peoples, times, and spaces. By incorporating studies of "comparative racializations" (Hong and Ferguson 2011) across a heterogeneous Asian American community, this volume foregrounds how the underresearched realm of Asian American sporting cultures can productively interrogate place-making in diasporas and nation(s).

This volume presents the fluidity and contradictions in Asian American identity formation through a careful exploration of quotidian and spectacular engagements with sport. It offers a combination of the everyday practices of sport and the spectacular moments of iconicity to decipher how the ordinary practices of sporting cultures can offer extraordinary knowledge about U.S. society and global phenomena. In order to elucidate the complex manifestations of Asian American sporting cultures, the chapters in this book are organized around the following questions:

What can Asian American participation in sport tell us about the heterogeneity of Asian American lives?
How do Asian American communities lay claim to sport? How does this claim simultaneously complicate their conceptualizations of U.S. society and of Asian American communities?
What is the relationship of participation in sport to mainstream racializations?
How do the inversions and negotiations of racializations through sporting cultures meaningfully reinterpret nation and diaspora?
What are the relationships of race, gender, and sexuality to racialization and corresponding sporting practices of identity?

How is place-making tied to identity formation in these various sporting circuits?

How do Asian American communities provide a critique of and expand the contours of the category of "Asian America" and American national identity through sport?

These governing questions serve a twofold purpose. First, they contextualize sociohistorical contexts in order to capture the particularity of dominant racializations and respective Asian American sporting cultures. Instead of stressing equivalence, the work of this volume explicitly and subtly takes up key tenets of women of color feminist theory (Lorde 1984; Davis 1985; hooks 1999; Hong 2006), which stresses difference within and outside of categories. Second, the chapters illuminate both the complexity of Asian America and the messiness of identity formation within U.S. sporting cultures. Asian American communities perform their ideas of identity and express ways of being a certain type of citizen on sports' uneven terrain while illuminating various types of antiessentialist projects. In this process, the boundaries of nation, diaspora, and identity are concurrently loosened. However, not all Asian American communities have the same capital, bodily recognition, resources, and spaces to perform normative conceptions of sporting identity within the pan-ethnic category of Asian America in particular and in U.S. society in general. This volume underscores how Asian Americans' participation in a variety of sporting practices can serve as acts of resistance to the multiple mainstream stereotypes that characterize them as the weak, passive, overly feminine, or the exotic "Other"; their athletic performances create alternate vistas for claiming American and Asian American identities.

Yet, as cultural studies scholars Mimi Nguyen and Thuy Nguyen Tu remind us, consumers of popular culture produce various meanings; appropriating popular culture can create new sets of pleasures while also allowing for another set of exclusions.[20] For example, although Bruce Lee stands as a key figure of tough masculinity in Asian America (Prashad 2001), the celebration of such hypermasculinity serves to ingrain and naturalize the differences between masculine-feminine, female-male, and straight-gay. Since power operates alongside pleasure in the realm of popular culture, one has to be attentive to how popular culture can create desirable, utopian, but also problematic social arrangements. When we return to the case of Jeremy Lin, his presence on the international basketball landscape inverts the racialization of Asian Americans in some ways, but we must not overlook his emphasis on Christianity, swagger, and respectability, which further marginalize Asian American communities that cannot similarly claim such "model minority" status (see Wang's and Leonard's chapters in this volume). Asian American celebration of Lin's sporting performance cannot be read in isolation; rather it must be read in relation to African American athletes and the corresponding racializations of black communities which often figure black men as aggressive, uncontrollable, and innately (and undeservingly) built for sport (King and Springwood 2001; Farred 2006; Brooks, 2009). Furthermore, Lin's racial legibility in this moment of U.S. sporting history is based on an overemphasis of muscularity that justifies sport as masculine to the exclusion of women.[21]

The narrative of Jeremy Lin's success and subsequent metonymic representations of both Asian America and U.S. society, while celebrated, problematically constrains expanding Asian American identity and U.S. belonging by narrowing the possible gendered and sexed categories of identification—as male-female—instead of allowing for an embodiment of a variety of intersex, transgender, gender nonconforming, and queer subjectivities.[22] Although Lin's story has opened up space for Asian American men in sports, his presence also serves to consolidate sport as an arena primarily for and by men. Thus, celebrating attempts at normative masculinity without allowing for a multitude of viable queer, masculine, and feminine practices leads to other projects of exclusion.[23] Here we see one of the contradictions of Asian American identity formation that simultaneously regulates boundaries of belonging in both Asian America and America. Inverting racializations through sporting practices and claiming sport as an Asian American place does not mean that Asian Americans refrain from using the same problematic categories of race, gender, sexuality, and class that initially marginalized them in U.S. (sporting) society.[24] However, it is this very discourse of meritocracy within sporting practices that occludes attempts at discussing the political realm of sporting cultures.

In many cases, sport constitutes an intriguing realm of voluntary organization as well as mandatory practice; it serves to build communities in ways that are mostly unexplored within Asian America.[25] Although several of the communities and characters we meet in this volume take to sport voluntarily, the force of U.S. Empire and required sport/physical education classes in school illustrate how sport also operates outside of individual choice. Highlighting these practices and their subsequent contradictions in Asian American sporting arenas conveys important information about identity formation through sporting practices. This book additionally moves beyond the mainstream discourse of Asian Americans, which vacillates between epithets including "coolie," "sexually deviant," "exotic," "terrorist," "thug," and "nerd," by showing the instrumental role of sport in nurturing alternate visions of American identity that allow for women and racialized men, and nonnormative sporting practices to exist as new sites of "cultural citizenship" (Maira 2009).[26] These alternate visions showcase explicit practices of place-making that collapse Americanness and Asianness while challenging monolithic representations of Asian America. Each Asian American group and their sporting cultures claim different places in the American symbolic and material landscape; sport becomes a medium through which to perform their sense of place and communal self.

Playing across Time, Space, and Asian America

To understand how Asian American participants of sporting cultures attribute particular meanings to leisure activities and express their identity through such practices, the chapters in this book shift between the past, present, and future to illuminate specific cultural processes at work. This text is structured to allow the reader to move through various historical points and gain a sense of how sporting practices have changed over time. Moreover, the ways in which different sporting cultures have come to take on particular meanings for a wide spectrum of Asian American communities will become clear.

We emphasize that there are no essentialist, monolithic readings of Asian American sporting cultures. Accordingly, the book's structure encourages various types of reading practices. One does not have to follow a linear trajectory when engaging with the foreword, chapters, and afterword in this volume. J. Jack Halberstam's foreword and Lisa Lowe's afterword offer distinctive ways of reading, conceptualizing, and analyzing the role of sport, popular culture, and racialization. Readers may start with either of these pieces and may read the interior chapters in any order. The scholarship found here enables us to center taken-for-granted realms of popular culture while complicating the category of Asian America.

Part I. Asian American Sports in Historical Context

Asian American communities have a tangled relationship to sport. In many instances, Asian communities are not encountering American sports for the first time when they arrive on U.S. shores. Rather, Asian American participation in sports including baseball and basketball has had longer ties to U.S. imperialism, the Cold War, and the American corporate entry into new markets (Thomas 2012; Gurn 2014; Thangaraj 2015). In the opening chapter, Ryan Reft demonstrates the long, uneven, and unpredictable connection between Asia, Asian America, U.S. Empire, and sport. His historical project contextualizes the intricate terrain of Asian American sporting cultures with multiple relationships of persecution, subjugation, and resistance. Reft's work illustrates shifts between relationships of dominance, resistance, and pleasure, looking at both macro- and micro-level implications. He extrapolates the relationship between sport, empire, and late capitalism, dismissing the hegemonic discourse of sport as "neutral" and structured through meritocracy by demonstrating the role of U.S. militarism in creating disjointed and contrapuntal zones of sporting contact.

As Reft's chapter provides a historical backdrop of Asian and Asian American sports participation and their entanglements with imperialism, war, and economic markets, Shalini Shankar uses memoir to demonstrate how intimate family and personal histories across generations shape a different sports landscape. Using a creative and nontraditional form of academic writing, Shankar compels us to rethink the histories of South Asian American consumption of mainstream sports. Her work centers memoir as a form of critical analytic, self-reflexive practice, and offers a call to reshape how we understand the social world. She reconceptualizes immigrant family life by centering sporting practices of spectatorship, social interactions, and community building. Shankar offers a view of her family's experience and her own experience as an immigrant child. This approach enables a micro-level examination of the quotidian experience of U.S. sports and the tensions within enculturation and assimilation for South Asian American communities. In the process, Shankar delves into the changing landscape of New York City from the 1970s to the present to provide an engaged exploration of desi life that is always in conversation with larger sporting cultures.

Part II. Asian American Sporting Celebrities

While the first section provides insight into different aspects of Asian and Asian American sporting history, the second section moves to the contemporary period and teases out the construction, management, and celebration of Asian (American) celebrity athletes. Sporting celebrities play an important part in engendering sporting pleasures and desires, which in turn influence identity formation. This section interweaves discussions of famous Asian American athletes and the ideological, symbolic, and material force of their iconicity. Instead of conceptualizing Asian American celebrities as existing in a social vacuum devoid of value and affect, Oliver Wang and Constancio R. Arnaldo, Jr., explore how Asian American communities are made and remade through Asian American sporting celebrities and subsequent spectatorship.

Oliver Wang critically examines the "Linsanity" phenomenon to decipher how race structures and serves as the background to the production, reception, and appropriation of Jeremy Lin's iconicity. His work analyzes how pundits/critics, commentators, and lay people sought to frame Lin—the person/player—and Linsanity—the phenomenon—using a recurrent set of themes related to masculinity, race and race relations, and the American Dream. The chapter is part media analysis but also a critical, self-reflexive exercise, as the author wrote extensively on Linsanity as it was "happening."

Constancio R. Arnaldo, Jr., looks into the everyday practices of Filipina/o Americans and their consumption and understanding of Philippine pugilist Manny "Pac-Man" Pacquiao as a (inter/national) sporting body. Through ethnographic research and critical readings of receptive practices (Mankekar 1999), Arnaldo, Jr., provides a refreshing window into the ways in which the borders between the Philippines and the United States are blurred, recreated, and challenged through viewing practices of sport. Pacquiao's global fame provokes very real localized pleasures, desires, and affective connections that help participants invert dominant U.S. racializations of Filipina/os while also reimagining how Pacquiao's victories produce alternative narratives of nationalism.

Part III. Complicating "Model Minority" Myths, Orientalism, and Gendered Stereotypes

Moving from iconicity and community formation, the chapters in this section examine how Asian Americans and South Asian Americans perform, contest, and affirm their racialized status as "model minorities" and intersecting gendered stereotypes (Prashad 2000; Gopinath 2005; Bascara 2006). In the process, the chapters by Pawan Dhingra, Jessica W. Chin and David Andrews, and Christina Chin destabilize the category of "model minority" and related racialized stereotypes through the frames of gender and sexuality. Highlighting the intersectional nature of identities, South Asian American spelling bee participants, Asian American mixed martial arts (MMA) female fighters, and Japanese American youth basketball players trouble the norms of both Asian American identity and sporting masculinity.

Pawan Dhingra explores the overlooked but fascinating site of spelling bees. Through his ethnographic investigation of spelling bees and other academic contests, Dhingra forces us to rethink sport concurrently with a questioning of how sporting participation in spelling bees challenges mainstream racializations of the participants as "nerds." Instead of dismissing the pleasures and nonnormative potentials within this sporting culture and reaffirming a strong, tough, aggressive, heterosexual sporting masculinity, he centers the pleasures derived for the participants (Rand 2012), new forms of hero-making, and the possibilities for a new forum of sport that is equitable for all.

Jessica W. Chin and David L. Andrews look at how gender and sexuality play a critical role in the racialization and "Orientalism" (Said 1979) evident in the violent contact sport of mixed martial arts. In particular, they examine the stories of Asian American female fighters, the hypersexualization (Shimizu 2007) of Asian American bodies, and how the violence of MMA demands a reimagining of mainstream stereotypes of Asian American women. As sport is generally thought of as masculine and male bodies are normalized in performing acts of aggression (Halberstam 1998), the case of female Asian American mixed martial artists demands a reconfiguration of that hegemonic discourse.

Christina B. Chin surveys participation in Japanese American youth leagues in Southern California. Instead of locating the prevalence of these leagues only in the Jeremy Lin moment, she takes a much deeper historical, generational, and transnational view of how Japanese American identity making and community building takes place through sport. As Japanese Americans are racialized as "forever foreign" and "model minorities" in the game of basketball, intraethnic relations in these leagues become a way to center a performance of Japanese American identity that challenges these mainstream racializations. In doing so, Japanese American youth and their families invoke and maintain a counter-space to preserve a legacy of sports participation that directly challenges microaggressions and reimagines their bodies, ability, and place on the court as Asian athletes.

Part IV. Refugees, Pacific Islanders, and Sport

The last section takes a very important turn to underscore the lives of certain Asian American communities that are not easily allowed into the fold of "Asian America" or its "model minority" moniker, categories that are politicized and policed. Membership in the pan-ethnic category of Asian America is not so easily claimed for all groups. For example, Hmong Americans and Pacific Islanders are racialized as "thugs" and "barbaric" in ways that dislocate them from the middle-class, professional respectability associated with the "model minority." In this volume, the cases of Hmong American and Pacific Islander communities provide spaces that refuse an essentialized, singularly classed, and predominantly East Asian (Chinese, Japanese, and Korean American) hegemony of Asian America (Diaz 2002; Võ 2004). Sport becomes a site where members of these communities can be racialized, gendered, and sexualized in multiple ways.

Chia Youyee Vang examines the lives of Hmong Americans and their sporting cultures. Whereas Hmong Americans are frequently racialized as "gangsters" (Schein et al. 2012; Schein and Thoj 2009), as emasculated welfare-dependent refugees (Ong 2003), and as petite, nonnormative bodies, Vang demonstrates their active involvement and success in a variety of sports including American football, volleyball, and specifically Hmong games. Participation in a variety of sporting cultures showcases gendered realms of participation while highlighting the relation that working-class Hmong American communities have to sport. Their sporting participation provides an important window into conceptualizing the impacts of late capitalism and neoliberalism.

David Leonard gives us a nuanced comparative examination of Taiwanese American star Jeremy Lin and Pacific Islander American Manti Te'o. Whereas Jeremy Lin's body and iconicity give us a way to read through the category of Asian America, his Asian American–ness is refracted through the presence of other Asian Americans and Pacific Islanders. Pacific Islanders have a historical relationship to U.S. colonialism, imperialism, and capitalism in U.S. sport unlike that of Taiwanese Americans and Chinese Americans. Their lands have been colonized by the U.S. nation-state and their landscapes are places of various types of American military testing (Smith 2005). Within this problematic connection, Pacific Islanders, including Samoans and Tongans, are racialized as "excessive bodies" yet seen as fit for some U.S. sports. Accordingly, Manti Te'o is racialized differently but in ways that normalize the presence of Pacific Islanders, especially Samoans, in the National Football League. Not content to rest on this theoretical point, Leonard illustrates how Asian American and Pacific Islander American subjectivity is always in flux, fragile, and queered in multiple ways. He offers a queer reading of the hoax against Te'o to showcase how Asian American racial formations are always gendered and sexualized.

Through engagement with this volume, readers can comprehend how Asian American sporting cultures are not sites where identity is already consolidated prior to social interaction. Rather, racial meanings, racial subjectivities, gendered affects, and sexualized meanings are expressed, transformed, challenged, managed, and negotiated through sport.[27] Sport thus provides one key site through which to understand Asian American lives. The critically attuned exploration of Asian American sporting cultures in this volume explicates how identity, nation, and diaspora are always fluid sites. Varying affective and material attachments to sport illuminate how Asian American identity in the U.S. sporting field is always performed in relation to larger racializations of Asian

Americans, in relation to whiteness and normative gendered identities, and in relation to other communities of color. A thorough analysis of Asian American sporting cultures provides an important counterpoint to the hegemonic discourse of sport as only a site of meritocracy. This volume highlights both the political nature of sport and the political realm of belonging in Asian American communities. As the chapters unfold, the field of Asian American sporting cultures provides a provocative space in which to tease out micro-level practices of identity and macro-level social phenomena in the United States.

NOTES

1 This is what Audre Lorde (1984) defines as the "mythical norm."
2 See Ferguson (2004) and Roediger (2014, 2008).
3 See Thangaraj, Burdsey, and Dudrah (2014); Carter (2008); Burdsey (2007a); and Fausto-Sterling (2000).
4 See Farred (2006); Dyreson, Mangan, and Park (2012); Tyrrell (2013); and MacAloon (2013).
5 See King (2014) and Regalado (2012).
6 See Yep (2009) and Thangaraj (2015).
7 See Yep (2009); España-Maram (2006); Thangaraj (2013); and Regalado (2012).
8 See Thangaraj (2015).
9 See Yep (2009); Christgau (2009); and España-Maram (2006). See also Thangaraj and Arnaldo, Jr. (2014) and Arnaldo, Jr., and Thangaraj (2014).
10 See Vescey (2009) and Thangaraj (2015).
11 See Nguyen and Tu (2007); Davé, Nishime, and Oren (2005); Thangaraj, Burdsey, and Dudrah (2014); España-Maram (2006); Regalado (2012); and King (2014).
12 See Andrews (2000); Carter (2008); Carrington (2010); Burdsey (2006, 2007a, 2007b); Rand (2012).
13 See Võ (2004).
14 See Kwon (2013).
15 See Võ (2004).
16 See Lowe (1996); Manalansan (2003); and Cruz-Malavé and Manalansan (2002).
17 See Smith (2005); Vang (2010); Ong (2003); Schein and Thoj (2009); and Diaz (2002).
18 See Puar and Rai (2004, 2002); Maira (2009); Rana (2011); Afzal (2014); and Thangaraj (2015).
19 See Abelmann (2009) and Joo (2012).
20 See Nguyen and Tu (2007).
21 For discussions of the relationship of sex to gender and the regulatory schemes at work, see Fausto-Sterling (2000) and Butler (1993).
22 See Fausto-Sterling (2000); Halberstam (2005); and Rubin (2012).

23 See Shimizu (2012).
24 See Thangaraj (2015).
25 For more discussion of sport as voluntary organization, see the seminal work of C.L.R. James (2003) and Ben Carrington (2010).
26 See Eng (2001); Chan (1991); Shimizu (2012, 2007); Vang (2010); and Afzal (2014).
27 See Hylton (2008); Carrington (2010, 2012); and Hartmann (2003, 2012).

REFERENCES

Abelmann, Nancy. 2009. *The Intimate University: Korean American Students and the Problems of Segregation.* Durham, NC: Duke University Press.

Afzal, Ahmed. 2014. *Lone Star Muslims.* New York: New York University Press.

Alsultany, Evelyn. 2012. *Arabs and Muslims in the Media: Race and Representation after 9/11.* New York: New York University Press.

Andrews, David. 2000. "Excavating Michael Jordan's Blackness." In *Reading Sport*, ed. Susan Birrell and Mary MacDonald. Boston: Northeastern University Press.

Arnaldo, Constancio, Jr., and Stanley I. Thangaraj. 2014. "Asian American Athletes." In *Asian American Society: An Encyclopedia*, ed. Mary Danico. New York: Sage Publications

Bachin, Andrea. 2005. *Building the South Side.* Chicago: University of Chicago Press.

Bald, Vivek. 2013. *Bengali Harlem.* Cambridge, MA: Harvard University Press.

Bascara, Victor. 2006. *Model-Minority Imperialism.* Minneapolis: University of Minnesota Press.

Bow, Leslie. 2010. *Partly Colored: Asian American and Racial Anomaly in the Segregated South.* New York: New York University Press.

Brooks, Scott. 2009. *Black Men Can't Shoot.* Chicago: University of Chicago Press.

Burdsey, Daniel. 2006. "'If I Ever Play Football, Dad, Can I Play for England or India?' British Asians, Sport and Diasporic National Identities." *Sociology* 40(1), 11–28.

———. 2007a. *British Asians and Football: Culture, Identity, Exclusion.* Abingdon: Routledge.

———. 2007b. "Role with the Punches: The Construction and Representation of Amir Khan as a Role Model for Multiethnic Britain." *Sociological Review* 55(3), 611–631.

Burgos, Adrian. 2007. *Playing America's Game.* Berkeley: University of California Press.

Burns, Lucy. 2012. *Puro Arte: Filipinos on the Stages of Empire.* New York: New York University Press.

Butler, Judith. 1993. *Bodies That Matter: On the Discursive Limits of Sex.* New York: Routledge.

Carrington, Ben. 2010. *Race, Sport, and Politics: The Black Sporting Diaspora.* London: Sage.

———. 2012. "Introduction: Sport Matters." *Ethnic and Racial Studies* 35(6), 961–970.

Carter, Thomas. 2008. *The Quality of the Homerun.* Durham, NC: Duke University Press.

Chan, Sucheng. 1991. *Asian America.* New York: Twayne Publishers.

Christgau, John. 2009. *Kokomo Joe: The Story of the First Japanese American Jockey in the United States.* Lincoln: Bison Books (University of Nebraska Press).

Cruz-Malavé, Arnaldo, and Martin Manalansan (eds.). 2002. *Queer Globalizations: Citizenship and the Afterlife of Colonialism.* New York: New York University Press.

Davé, Shilpa, Leilani Nishime, and Tasha G. Oren (eds.). 2005. *East Main Street: Asian American Popular Culture.* New York: New York University Press.

Davis, Angela. 1985. *Women, Culture, and Politics.* New York: Vintage Press.

Desai, Jigna. 2004. *Beyond Bollywood: The Cultural Politics of South Asian Diasporic Film.* New York: Routledge.

Diaz, Vicente M. 2002. "'Fight Boys till the Last': Football and the Remasculinization of Indigeneity in Guam." In *Pacific Diaspora: Island Peoples in the United States and the Pacific*, ed. Paul Spickard, Joanne Rondilla, and Deborah Hippolite-Wright. Manoa: University of Hawai'i Press.

Dyreson, Mark, J. A. Mangan, and Roberta J. Park (eds.). 2012. *Mapping an Empire of American Sport: Expansion, Assimilation, Adaptation and Resistance.* Abingdon: Routledge.

Eng, David. 2001. *Racial Castration: Managing Masculinity in Asian America.* Durham, NC: Duke University Press.

España-Maram, Linda. 2006. *Creating Masculinity in Los Angeles's Little Manila.* New York: Columbia University Press.

Farred, Grant. 2006 *Phantom Calls.* Chicago: Prickly Paradigm Press.

Fausto-Sterling, Anne. 2000. *Sexing the Body.* New York: Basic Books.

Ferguson, Roderick. 2004. *Aberrations in Black: Toward a Queer of Color Critique.* Minneapolis: University of Minnesota Press.

Gilbert, Matthew S. 2010. "Hopi Footraces and American Marathons, 1912–1930." *American Quarterly* 62(1), 77–101.

Gopinath, Gayatri. 2005. *Impossible Desires: Queer Diasporas and South Asian Public Cultures.* Durham, NC: Duke University Press

Gurn, Alexander M. 2014. *Courting Corporate Sports Partners in Education: Ethnographic Case Study of Corporate Philanthropy in Urban Public Schools* (PhD thesis). Chestnut Hill, MA: Boston College.

Halberstam, Judith. 1998. *Female Masculinity.* Durham, NC: Duke University Press.

———. 2005. *In a Queer Time and Place.* New York: New York University Press.

Hall, Stuart. 2003. "Cultural Identity and Diaspora." In *Theorizing Diaspora*, ed. Jana Braziel and Anita Mannur. Boston: Blackwell.

Hartmann, Douglass. 2003. *Race, Culture, and the Revolt of the Black Athlete: The 1968 Olympic Protests and Their Aftermath.* Chicago: University of Chicago Press.

———. 2012. "Beyond the Sporting Boundary: The Racial Significance of Sport through Midnight Basketball." *Ethnic and Racial Studies* 35(6), 1007–1022.

hooks, bell. 1999. *Ain't I a Woman.* Boston: South End Press.

Hong, Grace. 2006. *The Ruptures of American Capital.* Minneapolis: University of Minnesota Press.

Hong, Grace Kyungwon, and Roderick Ferguson (eds.). 2011. *Strange Affinities: The Gender and Sexual Politics of Comparative Racializations*. Durham, NC: Duke University Press.
Hylton, Kevin. 2008. *"Race" and Sport: Critical Race Theory*. Abingdon: Routledge.
James, C.L.R. 2003 [1963]. *Beyond a Boundary*. Durham, NC: Duke University Press.
Joo, Rachael. 2012. *Transnational Sport*. Durham, NC: Duke University Press.
King, C. Richard (ed.). 2014. *Asian Americans in Sport and Society*. Abingdon: Routledge.
King, C. Richard, and Charles Springwood (eds.). 2001. *Beyond the Cheers*. Albany: SUNY Press.
Kwon, Soo Ah. 2013. *Uncivil Youth*. Durham, NC: Duke University Press.
Lloyd, Earl. 2011. *Moonfixer: The Basketball Journey of Earl Lloyd*. Syracuse, NY: Syracuse University Press.
Lorde, Audre. 1984. *Sister Outsider*. Berkeley, CA: Crossing Press.
Lowe, Lisa. 1996. *Immigrant Acts*. Durham, NC: Duke University Press.
MacAloon, John. 2013. *Muscular Christianity and the Colonial and Post-Colonial Worlds*. Abingdon: Routledge.
Maira, Sunaina. 2009. *Missing*. Durham, NC: Duke University Press.
Manalansan, Martin. 2003. *Global Divas: Filipino Gay Men in the Diaspora*. Durham, NC: Duke University Press.
Manalansan, Martin, and Arnaldo Cruz-Malavé (eds.). 2002. *Queer Globalizations: Citizenship and the Afterlife of Colonialism*. New York: New York University Press.
Mankekar, Purnima. 1999. *Screening Culture, Viewing Politics: An Ethnography of Television, Womanhood, and Nation in Postcolonial India*. Durham, NC: Duke University Press.
May, Reuben. 2007. *Living through the Hoop: High School Basketball, Race, and the American Dream*. New York: New York University Press.
Naber, Nadine. 2012. *Arab America: Gender, Cultural Politics, and Activism*. New York: New York University Press.
Nguyen, Mimi, and Thuy Linh Nguyen Tu (eds.). 2007. *Alien Encounters: Popular Culture in Asian America*. Durham, NC: Duke University Press.
Omi, Michael, and Howard Winant. 1994. *Racial Formation in the United States*. New York: Routledge.
Ong, Aihwa. 2003. *Buddha Is Hiding*. Berkeley: University of California Press.
Prashad, Vijay. 2000. *The Karma of Brown Folk*. Minneapolis: University of Minnesota Press.
———. 2001. *Everybody Was Kung Fu Fighting*. Boston: Beacon Press.
Puar, Jasbir, and Amit Rai. 2002. "Monster, Terrorist, Fag: The War on Terrorism and the Production of Docile Patriots." *Social Text* 20(3), 117–148.
———. 2004. "The Remaking of a Model Minority: Perverse Projectiles under the Specter of (Counter) Terrorism." *Social Text* 22(3), 75–104.
Rana, Junaid. 2011. *Terrifying Muslims*. Durham, NC: Duke University Press.

Rand, Erica. 2012. *Red Nails, Black Skates*. Durham, NC: Duke University Press.
Regalado, Samuel. 2012. *Nikkei Baseball: Japanese American Players from Immigration and Internment to the Major Leagues*. Urbana: University of Illinois Press.
Roediger, David. 2008. *How Race Survived U.S. History*. New York: Verso.
———. 2014. *Seizing Freedom*. New York: Verso.
Rubin, David. 2012. "'An Unnamed Blank That Craved a Name': A Genealogy of Intersex as Gender." *Signs* 37(4), 883–908.
Said, Edward. 1979. *Orientalism*. New York: Vintage Books.
Schein, Louisa, and V. M. Thog. 2009. "Gran Torino's Boys and Men with Guns: Hmong Perspectives." *Hmong Studies Journal* 10.
Schein, Louisa, V. M. Thoj, Bee Vang, and Ly Chong Thong Jalao. 2012. "Beyond *Gran Torino*'s Guns: Hmong Cultural Warriors Performing Genders." *positions* 20(3), 763–792.
Shimizu, Celine. 2007. *The Hypersexuality of Race*. Durham, NC: Duke University Press.
———. 2012. *Straitjacket Sexualities: Unbinding Asian American Manhoods in the Movies*. Palo Alto, CA: Stanford University Press.
Smith, Andrea. 2005. *Conquest: Sexual Violence and American Indian Genocide*. Boston: South End Press.
Thangaraj, Stanley I. 2013. "Competing Masculinities: South Asian American Identity Formation in Asian American Basketball Leagues." *South Asian Popular Culture* 11(3).
———. 2015. *Desi Hoop Dreams: Pickup Basketball and the Making of Asian American Masculinity*. New York: New York University Press.
Thangaraj, Stanley I., and Constancio Arnaldo, Jr. 2014. "Asian American Sporting Cultures." In *Asian American Society: An Encyclopedia*, ed. Mary Danico. New York: Sage Publications.
Thangaraj, Stanley I., Daniel Burdsey, and Rajinder Dudrah. 2014. *Sport and South Asian Diasporas: Playing through Space and Time*. Abingdon: Routledge.
Thomas, Damien. 2012. *Globetrotting: African Americans and Cold War Politics*. Urbana: University of Illinois Press.
Tyrrell, Ian. 2013. *Reforming the World: The Creation of America's Moral Empire*. Princeton, NJ: Princeton University Press.
Vang, Chia Youyee. 2010. *Hmong America: Reconstructing Community in Diaspora*. Urbana-Champaign: University of Illinois Press.
Vecsey, George. 2009. "Pioneering Knick Returns to Garden." *New York Times*, August 11, B-9.
Võ, Linda Trinh. 2004. *Mobilizing Asian America*. Philadelphia: Temple University Press.
Yep, Kathleen. 2009. *Outside the Paint*. Philadelphia: Temple University Press.
Zirin, David. 2008. *A People's History of Sports in the United States: 250 Years of Politics, Protest, People, and Play*. New York: New Press.
———. 2014. *Brazil's Dance with the Devil*. Chicago: Haymarket Books.

PART I

Asian American Sports in Historical Context

1

From Perpetual Foreigner to Pacific Rim Entrepreneur

The U.S. Military, Asian Americans, and the Circuitous Path of Sport

RYAN REFT

"In these 'tense and tender ties' of empire," Ann Laura Stoler writes, "relations of power were knotted and tightened, loosened and cut, tangled and undone. These ties are not microcosms of empire but its marrow."[1] Stoler's anthology *Haunted by Empire* mapped the "geographies of intimacies" between colonizers and colonized. Indeed, beginning in the late nineteenth century, American imperial relations with the Pacific Rim rested on notions of intimacy in practice and in rhetoric. American officials in the Philippines depended on what Paul Kramer (2006) calls "the politics of recognition."[2] U.S. officials used the language of family, in particular racially heteronormative conceptions of domesticity, to invoke feelings of unity, though relations did not unfold on an equal playing field. American officials spoke of their "little brown brothers" and the United States' role in tutoring their (nonnormative) sibling in the ways of democracy and self-governance. "Benevolent assimilation," as some Americans called it, not only acknowledged U.S. superiority but also co-opted Filipino elites, known as *Ilustrados*, by acknowledging them as the class that would lead their countrymen to eventual independence, thereby securing their support in the pursuit of U.S. interests.[3]

For the average Filipino however, he or she encountered U.S. officials and Christian missionaries who enacted a physical education program that heavily emphasized sports like baseball.[4] Missionaries believed that "muscular Christianity" warded off sin and guaranteed piousness, while American military officials thought it a civilizing force for Filipinos and a clean, safe outlet for U.S. servicemen. The commander of the Philippines Department, General James Franklin Bell (1911–1914), "boasted that baseball had 'done more to 'civilize' Filipinos than anything else'" and shielded American soldiers from "tropical degeneracy."[5] Colonial governors sponsored nationwide baseball tournaments, and by the 1920s more than 1,500 schools fielded teams across the archipelago. Baseball brought with it middle-class respectabilities and appropriate racial sensibilities that local sports, like cockfighting, could not promise within U.S. imperialism.[6] Ultimately, basketball would win the hearts of Filipinos, but from 1910 to 1930, the U.S. heavily promoted its national pastime of baseball among its colonial subjects.[7] As most sports historians will tell you, few activities facilitate camaraderie, fraternity, and friendship like athletics.

While baseball served to inculcate American ideals among Filipino subjects, it also functioned to assert equality and independence.[8] Filipinos embraced the sport for different reasons than their occupiers. "The Philippines' shift from traditional folk games to modern organized athletics was no doubt facilitated by the fact that sports stimulate equality," notes historian Sayuri Guthrie-Shimizu. On baseball fields and later basketball courts, "the application of uniform rules and regulations to all participants, both the colonizer and the colonized," guaranteed a certain level of egalitarianism, even if briefly.[9]

Throughout the twentieth century, U.S. militarization has heavily influenced the migration of certain Asian communities and the respective diasporic formations in the United States. Though the 1934 immigration legislation, the Tydings–McDuffie Act, virtually halted Filipino immigration to the U.S. for much of the early twentieth century residents of the Philippines enjoyed the ability to migrate to American shores despite prohibitions on Asian American citizenship. By the 1930s, 45,000 Filipinos lived in the U.S. with nearly 70 percent living in California and 80 percent working as migratory laborers.[10] The U.S. occupation of the Philippines enabled this pattern of migration even as other Asian peoples found America off limits.

In retrospect, U.S. occupation of the Philippines would serve as the knife's edge of both U.S. intervention in Asia and the Pacific and the proliferation of various Asian American communities in the U.S. In addition, intimacies, whether formulated around male camaraderie or heterosexual love affairs and marriages as illustrated by the 1945 War Brides Act and subsequent revisions to the law, facilitated the growth of these immigration flows.[11] World War II, the postwar occupation of Japan, and the Korean and Vietnam wars would contribute to the growth of Japanese, Vietnamese, and Chinese diasporas while the 1965 Hart–Celler Immigration Act would pry open the gates of immigration further for Asians previously denied entrance.

Post-1965 military interventions continued to build intimacies and encourage Asian immigration to the U.S., thereby further diversifying Asian American demographics. Relationships established through masculine camaraderie helped Vietnamese refugees to settle in the suburbs of Northern Virginia. "Identification by empire," writes Friedman, "may have voided the landscape of South Vietnam as their homeland, but it allowed them to settle and claim the CIA and Pentagon's suburban landscape as their own."[12] Likewise, the combination of U.S. Pacific imperialism and sport created relationships that could be utilized by Asian immigrants in similar fashion. Therefore, from the United States' first imperial steps into the Pacific, Asian immigration to America interacted closely with militarization and the bonds of intimacy that such intervention facilitated. In this way, Filipinos' embrace of baseball in the 1920s embodies the winding road of sport and the means by which Asian immigration and Asian American sporting culture have been heavily influenced by militarization. U.S intervention abroad helped to create diasporas, while pre–and post–World War II sport enabled Japanese, Chinese, Filipino, and Vietnamese Americans to bond not only intra- and interethnically, but also interracially to their fellow American citizens.

In her landmark work *Immigrant Acts*, Lisa Lowe provocatively argues that Asian American history did not rest on European immigrant tropes about plucky ancestors who left the indulgent and corrupted old world for the meritocracy of America. Instead, on the trail of U.S. imperialism and Cold War military engagements and occupations, Asians found entry into American culture and eventually claims to citizenship. Using Asian American sport as a lens, one can better determine the influence of U.S. militarization on athletics and Asian American citizenship, while also broadening understandings of interracial relations, transnational connections, and racial binaries that have often limited discussions of race in America to a white-black paradigm. Importantly, as noted, Asian American citizenship hinged to a large extent on the

United States' military engagement and foreign policy prerogatives. Pre-1945 policies regarding Asian Americans limited citizenship to those born on U.S. soil but granted Filipinos national status. However, in the wake of World War II and the initiation of the Cold War, Asian Americans emerged as a valued example of U.S. inclusiveness, a symbol of America's benevolence and a signpost for Asian observers. As a means to undercut Soviet efforts in Asia, U.S. officials scrambled to incorporate Asian Americans, in theory at least, as welcomed members of the nation's body politic.

Through an examination of twentieth-century baseball and basketball in Asian American history, three themes emerge: the influence of the American military in Asian American sport, the changing meanings of Asian American citizenship, and the ways in which sport has helped create bonds of intimacy between Asian, Mexican, and African Americans in an era largely defined by segregation.[13] Moreover, tracing the divergent meanings of sport for different Asian American ethnicities reveals the differences that exist at the heart of the Asian American moniker, a categorization that though useful for political mobilization, obscures a great deal in terms of culture, relations to sport, placement within global capitalism, and racial location.

1900–1945: Transnational Baseball and a Segregated U.S.

From the late nineteenth century beginning with the Chinese and expanding with stricter immigration laws through the 1920s and 1930s, Asians were largely banned from immigration.[14] Government prohibitions prevented those Asians not born on U.S. soil from naturalization and in the 1910s several Western states passed Alien Land Laws that banned noncitizens, primarily Asians, from property ownership. Chinese women, public discourse alleged, were seductive prostitutes, licentious, and disease ridden, while men were "coolies" living in "bachelor societies" corrupted, effeminate, and exploitative in their "queer domesticity."[15] "Neither was considered capable of the free consent and voluntarism requisite for American political allegiance," points out Nancy F. Cott. This perception that Asians were incapable of being assimilated had already resulted in the passage of the Page Act of 1875 and the Chinese Exclusion Act of 1882, which greatly restricted immigration.[16] As Erika Lee has demonstrated, these acts, the latter especially, shaped not only Asian immigration but also established ethnically and racially biased precedents for immigration restrictions that were later applied to Eastern and Southern Europeans.[17]

Japanese and Filipino Americans endured their own set of racializations foisted upon them by whites, but restrictions on their immigration came later than those aimed at the Chinese. Japanese immigration slowed after the Gentlemen's Agreement of 1908, yet from 1900 to 1910, 130,000 Japanese nationals immigrated to the U.S., many to California, where by the early 1900s public opinion and state legislation had turned discriminatory.[18]

In regard to immigration, Filipinos occupied a unique position. Living under imperial rule, they enjoyed the status of U.S. nationals, enabling their immigration to American shores despite prohibitions against other Asian ethnicities. However, fears over Filipino sexuality, particularly in reference to the seduction of white women, made many whites uneasy.[19] While members of the predominantly male Filipino diaspora in California sought out taxi dance halls as a means of physical and emotional release and defiance of emasculating racist stereotypes, many white observers reacted negatively to the intermixing of race and gender. "[T]he worst part of his [the Filipino] being here is his mixing with you white girls from 13 to 17," argued the nativist Judge D. W. Roherback of Watsonville, "keeping them out till all hours of the night. And some of these girls are carrying a Filipino baby inside of them."[20] When American leaders signed the agreement granting Filipino independence in 1932, they did so due to the accumulation of racial nativism, heterosexual fears, and agribusiness/labor protectionism.

American imperialism complicated the nation's relationship to Asia and its peoples. As a result, U.S. attitudes toward Asians developed much as American military expansion increased. For example, in the wake of World War II, intimate relations between U.S. servicemen and Japanese and Chinese women forced changes in immigration laws, enabling the first trickles of post-1945 Asian immigration to the United States.[21] From a foreign policy perspective, the rise of the Cold War and the related occupation of Japan by American forces encouraged U.S. officials to emphasize the importance of U.S.-Asian relations transforming the once duplicitous Japanese into a symbol of democracy and capitalism.[22]

While heterosexual romantic intimacies undoubtedly influenced bonds between Asians and Americans, sport too, also promoted by military engagement, helped to consolidate relationships between U.S. occupiers and indigenous peoples. If American expansionism into Asia largely began with the Spanish-American War in 1898, so too did the use of sport, particularly baseball, as a means to control the behavior of soldiers. Teddy Roosevelt worried about Rough Riders idling away, so the Army instituted organized sports in occupied Cuba to serve as a recreational outlet for service personnel. Though the Army had suggested weekly intercompany baseball games in the 1880s to ensure physical health and "combat readiness," not until 1898 did officials consolidate these ideas into set practice. [23]

In the U.S., the invention of baseball was often credited to Abner Doubleday, but contrary to this mythology, the sport developed in several places independently as a derivation of "various bat and ball folk games" and sometimes in relation to the British game rounders.[24] That said, the American military contributed greatly to baseball's popularization. The intersection of transoceanic travel, spreading industrialization, and U.S. imperialism combined to further popularize the sport. Visiting Navy vessels were filled with energetic sailors who organized teams that would square off in competitions against squads in Japan, Hawai'i, and the Philippines. The game's popularity took off with American expatriates in Japan.[25] By the 1880s, foreign settlements in Yokohama had established their own teams. Initially, they competed only against each other; U.S. policy prevented Japanese from playing on the athletic fields in the Yokohama foreign settlements. However, baseball's popularity eroded such racial boundaries.[26]

In the early twentieth century, American professional baseball remained limited racially and geographically. Competitions were segregated and no professional teams existed west of the Mississippi River. Military teams often contained players worthy of the pros. Elite Navy and Army teams thus had as much to do with popularizing the sport as professionals of the era.[27] After all, it was not until the 1930s that major league baseball officials made a concerted effort to tap into Asian markets.

While America's promotion of the sport carried colonial attitudes, Japan believed the sport could play an integral role in exerting its new international image. Baseball promoted the kind of values central to an industrializing and urbanizing nation and also facilitated transnational connections to imperial powers like the United States. Japan too would use baseball as a tool of imperialism as it expanded into East Asia in the early twentieth century.[28] As industrialism and Japan's global standing expanded between 1880 and 1910, so too did baseball's popularity among the nation's citizens.[29] Unlike the Philippines, where the sport first gained popularity among the laboring classes, in Japan, students from well-off and elite families attending universities first popularized it. This would later encourage transpacific competitions between collegiate sides in Japan, the U.S., and elsewhere.[30]

Much like their American counterparts, Japanese imperialists also embraced the sport. As a means to inculcate Japanese values and secure the support of younger Taiwanese, Japanese occupiers instituted Western athletics as part of the public school curriculum. Governor General Sakata Sakuma believed the sport would prepare Taiwanese youth for the Japanese military while simultaneously serving as a "penetrating device" that would create a level of "comity" between Japanese occupiers and resentful Taiwanese. In later decades, it would take on a third level of importance: a means to maintain Japanese cultural practices for those children born abroad in colonies like Taiwan, Korea, and Manchuria.[31]

Undoubtedly, baseball enabled Asians to push back against the damaging portrayals of Eastern culture. In the context of gender relations of the nineteenth and twentieth centuries, the West's tendency to portray Eastern nations as feminine, sensual, and erotic assigned Asia and its residents to a secondary status when compared to the rational, masculine, and scientific West. Now referred to as Orientalism, this theoretical formation justified European imperialism, leaving Filipinos, Japanese, Chinese, and other Asians at an economic, political, and social disadvantage.[32] Baseball, with its inherent masculinity, pushed back against such negative idealizations, or to paraphrase historian Akira Iriye, via baseball Japan went from sensual exoticism to masculine competitiveness.[33] Japanese leaders interpreted and implemented the sport as "'Ichiko Baseball' or '*Bushido* (the way of the Samurai) Baseball,'" a nationalistic reaction to twenty years of "westernization." Officials argued the game "fostered 'traditional Japanese virtues of loyalty, honor, and manly courage.'"[34]

Whatever meaning one assigned to the government's baseball policy, its economic strategy boosted industrialization and urbanization but extracted a toll on Japan's small farmers. For many Japanese, modernization efforts meant the loss of whatever lands they had for cultivation. Industrialization resulted in higher property taxes, which forced 300,000 farmers from the fields.[35] Widespread unemployment and currency deflation also plagued Japan to the extent that leaders accepted a request from Hawai'i's King Kalakuau to allow Japanese nationals to emigrate to Hawai'i for work.[36]

From 1885 to 1907, 155,000 Japanese traveled east to Hawai'i and the American West Coast. Hawai'i provided the first stop for many of these migrants, with nearly 25,000 settling there by 1896. By 1902, the Japanese accounted for almost three fourths of the islands' population.[37] These settlers brought their love of baseball with them and found that much of the archipelago's multiracial inhabitants, having adopted the sport in the mid- to late 1800s, felt the same. While many would remain in Hawai'i, thousands of others would uproot themselves to the continental United States, and in particular, California. As more Japanese immigrated to California, Washington, and Oregon, leagues formed. In 1900, over 24,000 resided in mainland America, with just over 10,000 in California alone. San Francisco fielded the first U.S. mainland team comprised of Japanese American players in 1903, with the creation of the Fuji Athletic Club.[38]

Baseball's popularity in the U.S. had been growing and in California this proved no less true. The California League emerged in the 1880s and eventually morphed into the Pacific Coast League (PCL) in 1903.[39] The PCL produced Hall of Famers like Joe DiMaggio of the San Francisco Seals and Ted Williams of the San Diego Padres. Segregation prevented Japanese Americans from playing for PCL teams. As a result, Japanese American leagues developed alongside the PCL and by the end of the first decade of the twentieth century, the California Winter League (CWL) emerged as the "first modern, integrated professional circuit" in the U.S.[40]

While the first Japanese American clubs formed in Northern California, by the 1920s and 1930s the best team, the L.A. Nippons, could be found in Los Angeles. By the mid-1930s worthy competitors like the San Pedro Skippers emerged from Japanese American enclaves around Los

Angeles. Southern California's weather enabled year-round play, which helped to give coherence to the Japanese American community across the broad L.A. region.[41] Clubs soon emerged in Fresno, San Jose, Stockton, and elsewhere, including Portland, Seattle, and their hinterlands, where many Japanese and Filipino laborers had settled to work in agriculture, domestic service, and canning industries.[42]

As the Japanese and Japanese American population grew, generational differences emerged. For example, in four years between 1926 and 1930, the percentage of Nisei households, second-generation Japanese Americans born in the United States, among the larger Japanese population increased from 26.7 percent to nearly 50 percent. As a result, by the 1930s, with a rising Nisei population, the Japanese American newspaper *Rafu Shimpo* began to print a daily English-language section and openly endorsed baseball to its Japanese American readers. The Nisei showed little interest in traditional sports like kendo or judo, the paper reflected: "Rather we should prompt them to take up whatever sports they like. Baseball it is!"[43]

Part of the game's utility lay in its appeal across generations. Issei—Japanese immigrants—saw it as a means to connect their American-born children with Japanese culture, and believed it emphasized Japanese values of loyalty, honor, and courage. In contrast, Nisei saw the game as more modern; it also provided an expression of their patriotism to the United States. Both believed the sport would serve as testament to their dedication to American ideals. In this context, baseball became a "safety net from the outside and allowed [Japanese Americans] to demonstrate their cultural traits before an audience of their own," argues historian Samuel Regalado.[44]

While Negro League teams came west to compete in the CWL and Japanese teams formed up and down the West Coast, in Central and Southern California, Mexican American squads also established themselves. In Hawai'i, sugar magnates saw baseball as a tool for placating organized labor and radicalism. American companies south of the Mexican-U.S. border viewed baseball as a means to spread industrialization and capitalism, particularly regarding the work habits of laborers. Southern California business structures like the California Fruit Growers Exchange (CFGE, aka Sunkist) incorporated baseball through its "corporate welfare system" of the 1920s. "In order to produce the desired workers, they have to become a member of a local society or baseball team," Sunkist industrial relations director G. B. Hodgkin told his fellow growers in 1921. Baseball, he argued, would "increase their physical and mental capacity for work." Ironically, Mexican American players used their baseball networks as conduit for a larger labor movement. Fields, teams, and individual players became sites of labor militancy.[45]

Many of these athletes did not necessarily replicate American play but rather imbued it with a sense of their own culture. In the Dominican Republic, "natives favored flair, grace, speed, and hustle," describing their version of the sport as "*beisbol romantic*," notes historian Gerald Gems. In Hawai'i, native athletes altered sports like volleyball and football to their own cultural interests.[46] Similar developments occurred with the spread of baseball in the Japanese American and Mexican American communities.

California proved a particularly compelling mix of race, ethnicity, and baseball. The sport created ties, sometimes competitive, sometimes business oriented, and promoted intimate relations between African, Japanese, and Mexican Americans. In 1927, on the heels of their 1926–1927 CWL championship, the Negro Leagues' Philadelphia Royal Giants arranged for a barnstorming tour of Asia including stops in Japan and Hawai'i. Led by black baseball promoter Lonnie Goodwin, the Royal Giants arranged for a tour of the Pacific Rim. Demonstrating the kind of interracial relationships baseball facilitated, George Irie, a prominent Nisei baseball promoter based in Seattle, arranged all of the Royal Giants' games abroad. The Royal Giants' play and decorum impressed their Japanese observers. This encounter with an accomplished African American baseball team revealed to Japanese observers that baseball was not the domain of whites alone and established some sense of solidarity.[47]

In 1929, the all-Mexican El Paso Shoe Store Zapatores took the field against the most prominent Japanese team in California, the Nippons. The game was played at Anderson Park, better known as White Sox Park, located in Boyle Heights; the stadium drew white professional and semi-pro teams along with squads from the interracial CWL.[48] Both the Nippons and Zapatores had been besting municipal white teams in Pasadena, Torrance, and elsewhere in the region. In a three-game series for the title of best foreign team, the Zapatores emerged victorious. Soon after, the Zapatores with the help of Japanese promoters departed for a barnstorming tour of Japan. Japanese observers experienced an intimate sense of connection with other nonwhite players, suggests historian Michael Willard.[49] Having experienced the condescension of numerous white opponents, Japanese promoters in particular shared a kinship with other nonwhites beyond nationality facilitated through baseball.[50] The Tokyo Giants' 1935 tour of California and the Western U.S. furthered such connections as the team competed against African American semipros in Imperial Valley, a team of Mexican all-stars just south of the U.S. border, Japanese Americans in what was dubbed the "Japanese World Series"—a three-game series with the Nippons.[51] Japanese American lives were connected intimately through sport with local politics and transnational networks that constantly challenged the contours of diasporic identity.

Eventually, Japanese and American imperialism collided. U.S. occupation of Hawai'i and the Philippines stood in direct conflict with Japan's own imperial ambitions as the newly industrialized nation expanded into China, Taiwan, Korea, and Southeast Asia. However, despite political tensions arising from competing imperial visions, during the 1930s baseball tours between the U.S., Japan, Hawai'i, and the Philippines persisted until the dissolution of diplomatic relations between America and Japan in 1940. In the wake of Pearl Harbor and amid the simmering racism of World War II California, the full weight of the U.S. government came to bear against Japanese Americans. Unlike Americans of European ancestry, notes Regalado, Japanese American guilt for the war was viewed as collective, as evidenced by Executive Order 9066, which pushed for Japanese American internment.[52] Only Nisei old enough for military service escaped internment.

In the internment camps, baseball provided an outlet for the trauma of incarceration.[53] White War Relocation Authority (WRA) administrators provided very little for internees; with a dearth of recreational facilities and equipment, Issei and Nisei created their own. Baseball once again took center stage. "Without baseball," former Japanese American ballplayer, manager, and eventual Houston Astros scout George Omachi noted, "camp life would have been miserable . . . it was humiliating, demeaning, being incarcerated in our own country."[54] Camp newspapers devoted nearly as much coverage to baseball as to those Nisei serving on the front. Far from inconsequential or frivolous, baseball occupied an essential place in internee life.[55] WRA administrators even occasionally allowed teams to play away games against other camps, which ironically, connected Japanese American residents from the far corners of the Western United States. Still, internment undoubtedly squashed the hopes and dreams of many Japanese American players. "If it wasn't for the war, I think we could have had a Japanese American major leaguer even before Jackie Robinson," former Gila River Eagles pitcher Tets Furukawa said years later.[56] While Robinson himself would later reminisce about his days playing baseball in Pasadena with Japanese Americans and others, none cracked the "big show" until the 1970s, though over the last twenty years Japanese players have proliferated at the professional level.[57]

Post–World War II: Baseball's Decline, Basketball's Rise, and Pacific Rim Opportunity

In the aftermath of World War II and internment and the onset of the Cold War, the place of Asian Americans in U.S. society changed radically. Again, California provides a unique window into these developments. As the United States entered the postwar era, the place of Asian Americans within U.S. culture took on geopolitical importance as Americans worried about the nation's interests in Asia, particularly in relation to its occupation of Japan and the Korean and Vietnam wars. Though still occupying the place of "perpetual foreigners" and subject to discrimination, Asian Americans found new economic and political opportunities previously denied to them.

"It was a grave and terrible injustice perpetrated on the Japanese in our midst," noted former Los Angeles mayor and one-time internment proponent Fletcher Bowron in 1956. "Those in who we lost faith, never lost faith in us," he acknowledged.[58] Reflecting wider shifts in public opinion, former supporters of internment, like Bowron, now expressed regret over their lapse in judgment. White Americans worried about the nation's image abroad, particularly among potential allies in Asia; the nation needed to incorporate Asian Americans, and to a lesser extent other minority groups, into white communities to demonstrate democracy and capitalism's benevolence.[59]

Sport also helped to secure these bonds. In the 1950s, California-born Korean American diver Sammy Lee, a two-time Olympic gold medalist, traveled across Asia performing in exhibitions as a means to demonstrate America's more open-minded racial policies. When Lee encountered white resistance to his family's settlement in Garden Grove, California, even conservative newspapers like the *Santa Ana Register* and *Long Beach Press* promoted his integration of the Southern California community. "If he went public with his story of discrimination, he might embarrass America and perhaps create propaganda fodder for the Soviets and Chinese Communists," writes historian Charlotte Brooks.[60]

In similar fashion, baseball once again also demonstrates this turn. If perpetual foreigner tropes now helped Asian Americans suburbanize, it also helped many to pursue economic benefit through their Pacific Rim connections. The postwar career of native Central Californian Tsuneo "Cappy" Harada encapsulates this shift. Born in Santa Maria in 1921, Harada worked alongside his father while playing semi-pro ball for the Santa Maria Indians. In 1936, the Indians played the famed Japanese Tokyo Giants, who had swung through the Central Valley on a barnstorming tour of the states. Noting Harada's dexterity and talent, the team pursued the native Californian but the teenager declined, deciding to remain with his father in the fields. By the late 1930s, however, Harada had established himself in Canada with a semi-pro team in Edmonton while working full time in a local lumberyard. With an invitation to the St. Louis Cardinals spring training on the horizon, Harada's athletic career seemed to be on the ascendency until December 7, 1941. While his Issei father and sister were sent to a concentration camp in Bismarck, North Dakota, Harada enlisted in the military.

Due to his proficiency in Japanese, U.S. officials placed Harada in the Military Intelligence Service's linguistic training program. He joined two thousand other Nisei language specialists and by summer 1942 had been stationed in Australia.[61] After the war, Major William Marquat, the director of the Supreme Command for the Allied Powers' Economic and Scientific Section (ESS) tapped Harada as his right hand in U.S. reconstruction efforts in Japan. Together, the two men would champion baseball as a means to impart democratic values to the Japanese people while also consolidating the sport as a commercial enterprise in the archipelago.[62] While Marquat remained the key decision maker,

Harada was involved in every policy enacted by the ESS commander and throughout served as a "forceful advocate for Japanese supplicants," notes Guthrie-Shimizu.[63]

Working with prominent figures from Japanese baseball, Marquat and Harada hoped to use athletics more broadly to bring a sense of normalcy to Japan while also using sports as the nation's first steps toward reconciliation with the U.S. and the world. For example, working with Los Angeles–based Japanese American businessman Fred Wada, Harada, Marquat, and Matsumoto arranged for Japan's best six swimmers to compete in Los Angeles at the U.S. National Championships in 1949, making it the first overseas tour of Japanese athletes since World War II. The event proved wildly successful as Furuhashi Hironoshin, the nation's most accomplished swimmer, broke records in three freestyle events (400, 800, and 1,500 meters). Observers hailed him as the "Flying Fish of Fujiyama" and the competition made Furuhashi a national hero in Japan while also providing Los Angeles Japanese Americans with a brief moment of pride and satisfaction as they adjusted to resettlement.[64]

In Japan, Harada helped to solidify American interests and baseball once again provided the opportunity. Mizuhara Shigeru had been a star third baseman for the Japanese team Tokyo Big Six and a member of the Tokyo Giants when they toured the U.S. in 1935 and 1936. Drafted in 1942 for service, Mizuhara had been captured in Manchuria by the Soviet Union's Red Army and placed in a forced labor camp. Upon hearing of his fate, Harada flew to the Soviet-controlled Far East to facilitate his repatriation. Harada ferried Mizuhara to a Tokyo Giants game where, in a teary-eyed speech, he told the crowd, "I, Mizuhara, have finally come home." The moment remained "etched into the minds" of Japanese baseball aficionados and provided them with a stark Cold War image: "the benevolent American occupier and protector and the ruthless Soviets who were still keeping Japanese nationals in captivity in Siberia's frozen wasteland."[65]

Along with former San Francisco Seals manager Lefty O'Doul, who had long been a presence in Japanese baseball, Harada pioneered postwar transnational connections. In 1953, *Yomiuri*, a Japanese newspaper, agreed to a Tokyo Giants tour of spring training as a nod to the hundredth anniversary of Admiral Mathew Perry's arrival in Japan.[66] Harada's travel agency booked the tour and made his own Santa Maria part of the arrangement, using the town's Elks Field as a central venue. The Giants earned victories against the 1952 Pacific Coast League's champions, but more importantly Harada had opened international eyes to the economic potential in transpacific cultural exchange. "The commercial success of pro baseball in postwar Japan, the Japanese adoration of things American and the permanent U.S. military presence in the postwar Far East," reflects Guthrie-Shimizu, "combined to create new markets for American led transnational sports and entertainment businesses."[67]

For Asian Americans in metropolitan Los Angeles and the surrounding region, whites' softening attitudes toward them and the promise of new markets for American industries enabled Japanese and Chinese Americans to capitalize on new economic and housing opportunities, thereby reshaping suburban Southern California. In Gardena, Asian Americans, particularly those of Japanese descent, settled in the once declining suburb and through transnational connections to Japan buoyed local fortunes. Gardena elected the nation's first Japanese American mayor in 1972 and whites embraced the new transnational orientation as they witnessed the town's fortunes rise. Japanese Americans poured into Gardena, earning it the title of the "ultimate Japanese American suburb." In San Gabriel Valley (SGV), Monterey Park followed a similar trajectory and emerged as a nexus of Asian American settlement. By the 1980s, observers designated Monterey Park as the "first suburban Chinatown," while the broader SGV region featured predominantly Asian American and Latino faces and culture.[68]

Baseball's fortunes among Asian Americans also changed. While it was undoubtedly still popular, a new sport drew the attention of Japanese Americans and Asian Americans of all ethnicities: basketball. Christina B. Chin examines this contemporary sports culture in a later chapter. Moreover, if baseball had been primarily the purview of men, with some notable exceptions, basketball would prove more gender inclusive, a reflection of women's growing rights.

Though Asian American basketball leagues proliferated in the 1960s, 1970s, and 1980s, they have roots in earlier decades and a California city long connected to Asian immigration: San Francisco. In the 1930s and 1940s, local teams like Nam Kus and the Boy Scout Troop Three competed in leagues like Wah Yin and Chi Hi. A team of working-class Chinese Americans, the Hong Wah Kues, barnstormed North America, even playing the Harlem Globetrotters. William Woo Wong became the first Asian American to grace Madison Square Garden's court as a member of the 1949–1950 University of San Francisco N.I.T. squad.[69] For men, the ability to compete pushed back against stereotypes of Chinese masculinity. With the Chinese Playground in the city's Chinatown as the setting, San Francisco's Chinese basketball leagues enabled athletes to reject these stereotypes through firm and aggressive play. At the same time, in places like Stockton, California, Filipinos and Filipinas competed against other Asian Americans, further testifying to the sport's popularity with Asian Americans and, in terms of gender, its more inclusive nature.[70]

While baseball and softball did provide some opportunities for women, particularly during internment, to a far greater extent, basketball enabled women to push back against not only American racial and gender prejudices but also those of their own immigrant peers. The Mei Wahs, a Chinese American female basketball team of the era, used their aggressive, physical play "to develop and articulate a sense of self respect as a member of a group marginalized by both the mainstream and Chinese communities," notes Kathleen Yep.[71] Sporting manuals of the day advised women to avoid extreme athletic exertion or physical play. The Mei Wahs dismissed such ideas, instead playing a fast, elbow-driven style. Drawn from the largely working-class Chinese American community, the Mei Wahs remade ideals regarding femininity and crafted their own identities through the sport. Likewise, nearly a decade later, midcentury San Francisco sports icon Helen Wong led the St. Mary Saints to championships in 1947 and 1949 in the city's predominantly white Catholic Youth Organization league. Sister to the aforementioned Woo Wong, Helen drew effusive comments from the *San Francisco Chronicle*: "We know now why the kids in Chinatown were telling us, 'Wait until you see Willie "Woo Woo" Wong's sister, Helen,'" exclaimed the paper.[72]

For Japanese Americans, the sport held great importance as well. If baseball had been the sport of choice in internment camps across the West, some internees preferred basketball. Jamie Hagiya, a former University of Southern California star and professional player, related her parents' story to a journalist in 2012. Moved to Wyoming and Arkansas, her mother and father developed a love for the sport amid the tragedy of internment. "Even though they had everything taken away from them, they always kept a positive attitude, and sports was a huge way for them to get through those days," she told *Colorlines* in 2012.[73]

Returning from internment proved a harrowing experience. Athletics provided many youth and adults with a means to regain a sense of normalcy. The famed Holiday Bowl in Crenshaw, funded by Japanese American businessmen, served as a critical space for not only this sense of normalcy but also a vibrant arena for interracial solidarities as Asian, Latino, and black bowlers competed and socialized.[74] In Southern California especially, Japanese American (JA) basketball leagues began to form in 1959, first with a youth service organization known as Friends of Richard (FOR) and later expanding to places like Santa Ana and across SGV and Orange County. Northern California experienced similar developments. These leagues boomed in the late twentieth century in California, especially between 1990 and 2000 when the state's Asian American population expanded by 38 percent. Asian American basketball leagues tended to be organized along lines of ethnicity, particularly among Japanese Americans. However, with the influx of Vietnamese, Filipinos, and others they expanded to include numerous ethnicities, even if at moments the celebration of one's ethnicity led to exclusion. "Today, we also have Chinese, Koreans, [Filipino], and more," noted Russ Hiroto, commissioner of San Jose's Japanese Community Youth Services (CYS) and former SoCal basketball participant himself. "In fact, it's more realistic to describe the JB (Japanese Basketball) program today as AB, 'Asian Basketball.'"[75]

In the early 2000s, the issue came to a head when Los Angeles's Community Youth Council (CYC) league expelled a Mexican American player because he lacked any Asian ancestry. While some observers believed such leagues to be "reservoirs of culture" in the context of out-marriage, geographic dispersal, and declining immigration rates of Japanese Americans, others saw only racism. "We live out in Santa Clarita," father and former league participant Bobby Uchiomo told the *Los Angeles Times* during the controversy. "We tell [our son] to watch out for skinheads and stuff . . . but he really learned a lot about racial prejudice from the CYC." At the time, CYC board member Yoshi Haria admitted that they encouraged teams to "keep it Japanese American" or, at the very least, "Asian American," but also acknowledged the tenuous legal ground upon which such positions rested. "If we were sued [successfully], we would fold."[76]

Despite such controversies, the leagues undoubtedly suture an Asian American identity, particularly for Japanese Americans. Documentarian Tadashi Nakamura conveyed this point in 2012: "I actually knew almost every Japanese American guy at UCLA my freshman year because we'd played against each other in the basketball leagues." In this context, Japanese American basketball leagues functioned as institutions equal to those associated with religion and language. "For people my age, fourth generation Japanese Americans, [basketball] is, in a weird way, the main cultural hub and the one commonality that most Japanese Americans have with each other."[77]

If the sport enabled Chinese and Chinese American women of the 1930s to redefine femininity, Japanese American leagues performed a similar function in the late twentieth century. "I think a lot of people underestimate Asian basketball players," one twelfth-grade girl told sociologist Christina B. Chin, "because when you look at them, and especially women, they're shorter, skinny, a lot of people don't really think they could muscle up anyone." Another young woman attending a private California University admitted she and her friend enjoyed playing pickup ball against "tall white guys" because "it's fun when we go there and we're dribbling around them and scoring all the time."[78] Parents too saw value in basketball. Nadia, a third-generation Japanese American, preferred her daughter play basketball instead of taking dance lessons. "I want her to be scrappy—not just a pretty dancer."[79] The results speak for themselves, as Asian American leagues produce far more high school, college, and professional female professionals than men. Hagiya, the former USC star, competed in the leagues from age five and by the time she graduated from college she was among the university's all-time top ten in assists, games played, and three-point field goals made.

Some former female JA stars have set their sights higher than women's professional leagues. Former JA star, three-time UCLA captain, and Orange County native Natalie Nakase became the first Asian American to play in the WNBA and later coach in Japan's top men's professional league for the Saitama Broncos. "My goal is to coach in the NBA," she asserted in 2012. In 2014, she nearly made the leap when the L.A. Clippers gave her a two-week position in the NBA's summer league as their centers coach. Though Nakase's primary job for the Clippers remains as a video intern, respected head coaches like Indiana's Frank Vogel and Miami's Filipino American Erik Spoelstra started their careers in the same position and her performance during the summer league bolstered her prospects.[80]

Basketball also serves as a window into the multiple meanings that sport holds for different ethnicities under the Asian American umbrella. As colonial subjects under U.S. authority and classified as U.S. nationals, Filipinos could travel freely between the U.S. and Philippines, while immigration law, particularly between 1917 and 1924, more or less prohibited other Asians from doing the same. Filipino immigration declined from 1934 to 1944, since U.S. officials, having put the territory on the path to independence, placed limits on new arrivals. The Tydings–McDuffie Act of 1934 established a quota of fifty Filipino immigrants a year. In addition, the Filipino Repatriation Act of 1935 promised to pay Filipinos' travel back to the Philippines with the expectation that they would not return to the United States.[81] World War II, the Hart–Celler Immigration Act of 1965, and increased U.S. military engagements in Southeast and East Asia sparked new waves of immigration from the two regions.

While Filipinos appear far less often in American popular culture than their Chinese, Japanese, and Vietnamese American counterparts, Filipino Americans constitute nearly 20 percent of the nation's Asian American population, with two thirds of the total of 2.8 million living in the American West. After Japanese Americans, whose rates of out-marriage reached 65 percent between 2008 and 2010, Filipino Americans exhibit the second highest rate of out-marriage among Asian Americans at 48 percent.[82]

Basketball began in the Philippines almost as an afterthought of U.S. imperial policy. As with other colonial projects, U.S. officials saw athletics as a tool for bringing U.S. ideals and democracy to the Philippines. Indeed, U.S. policies radically altered Filipino conceptions of physical exertion. Filipinos viewed hard physical activity as part of labor with no connection to recreation, leisure, or consumption. Attitudes changed as baseball proliferated and the sight of U.S. soldiers and sailors engaging in team sports reformulated ideas regarding exercise. In the early twentieth century, baseball received greater support and promotion than basketball and indeed it proved popular. However, basketball had begun to work its way into the Filipino body politic.[83]

Initially introduced as a sport for girls deemed unfit for track and field, basketball would ironically become a marker of masculinity in the post-1945 Philippines. Even in its nascent all-female form it drew spectators. In a 1911 photo of girls playing on a grass field with wood backboards and actual wooden baskets, a thick crowd can be seen gathered to watch the competition.[84] In fact, as early as 1910 at least one girls' team had been organized in Zambales. An American teacher had introduced the sport to encourage physical fitness among Filipinas who had been resistant to previous forms of systematic exercise. "[T]he girls took a great interest in the game from the first and soon became enthusiastic, insisting upon practicing every evening until a late hour," noted one report. "Their grades are higher, both in industrial and academic subjects, while in all tests requiring self control, skill or ability, they greatly outclass the non-athletic girls." One year later, five teams had organized in Manila and competed in the annual Athletic Carnival. Unfortunately, American notions of gender propriety resulted in girls' exclusion from the sport. "But by 1914, the American school superintendents in the Philippines were recommending dropping basketball for girls on the grounds that it was too rough and too manly," writes historian Janice Beran.[85] Later the establishment of the YWCA would encourage women's participation in sports like badminton, volleyball, tennis bowling, and even basketball. For all its proselytizing and efforts at social control, the YWCA did greatly expand recreation and sporting opportunities for Filipinas of all classes.[86] Evidence of similar efforts in other U.S. occupied territories and protectorates support this view. In Puerto Rico, the YMCA successfully organized women's basketball teams and competitions until "men commandeered the gym space," notes Gems.[87]

While one might have expected Catholic Filipinos to resist the Protestant YMCA and YWCA, many Filipinos instead had associated the church with Spanish rule. While the education system had become synonymous with American occupiers, many Filipinos had longed for secularized schools, having lived under Catholic Spain's institutions. Moreover, unlike their Spanish predecessors, who had remained somewhat distant and aloof from Filipino students, American teachers and missionaries directly engaged the Filipinos through sport. As one long-time American educator told observers, "No phase of education in the American model met with more enthusiasm than organized sport."[88]

Whatever the implications of the YMCA and YWCA's Protestantism, Manila's Catholic colleges soon embraced the sport, which led to its growth from "a curiosity to a national pastime," notes writer Rafe Bartholomew. The formation of the Philippine NCAA in 1924 furthered its popularity as officials constructed gyms and brought in American coaches. Weather in the Philippines also encouraged basketball's popularity as the stifling humidity, heat, and rain made nine-inning baseball games a slog for spectators and players alike. Manila's college-educated, economically prosperous elite preferred it to baseball. Basketball's resulting social cachet led to newspaper headlines and popular attention, which in turn drew more athletes to the sport until it encompassed all of Filipino society.[89]

The passion for basketball intersected with international competition and a burgeoning Filipino nationalism that sought independence from American imperialists. In the 1936 Berlin Olympics, the Philippines defeated every team except the U.S. and won nine of the first ten basketball titles at the Far Eastern Games, a precursor to the Asian Games. American imperialism had delivered the game to Filipinos earlier than other Asian nations such that "[t]he Philippine national team was fine tuning its game while players in other counties were still studying the rule book," notes Bartholomew.[90]

In 1975, the Philippines Basketball Association was launched, making it today the second-oldest professional basketball league in the world. By this time, baseball's popularity had long faded and Filipinos declared undying love to basketball. The game served as a rite of passage for young men. "That's the male entry into a larger sphere," Filipino academic Michael Tan notes. "And it's part of Filipino masculinity. The wider your sphere of influences, the better so basketball is there to make friends, build alliances. It even crosses class barriers."[91] For players in the PBA, it also promises post-PBA wealth and notoriety; former PBA standouts occupy political positions ranging from city councilman to senator to governor, and many of the nation's movie and television stars began their careers playing pro ball.

For Filipino Americans, basketball supplies a transnational connection to their ancestral home while also providing a talented percentage a nice paycheck. Filipino Americans (Fil-Ams) make up a solid proportion of the league, even if some Filipinos doubt their commitment to the Filipino identity and nation. Hailing from Fil-Am enclaves in California, Hawaii, and New Jersey, players like Mike Cortez (Carson, California), Jeff Cariaso (San Francisco), Nic Belasco (Stockton, California), Alvin Castro (Philippines born, Los Angeles raised), Ali Peek (Hawai'i), and John Arigo (Charleston, South Carolina) filled out rosters.[92] Championship teams like the 2006–2007 Alaskan Aces and their opponents Talk 'N Text all had prominent Fil-Ams contributing to their campaigns.

Mac Mac Cordona, a Talk 'N Text star, and Cortez reflect the varying routes Fil-Am players traveled to stardom. Cortez had starred on his local high school team in Carson, and like other Fil-Ams looked to the PBA for his basketball future. By the early 2000s, he had distinguished himself as one of the league's finest guards. Cardona took a much different route. Born in the Philippines, Mac Mac Cardona settled in California after a tough, transnational journey. First his mother escaped domestic service in Greece and settled in Los Angeles; soon after she married and sent for her son, who had been making ends meet shuttling between relatives and selling cigarettes on the Manila streets. Eventually finding his way to Carson, Cardona—unlike Cortez—took the "And1" street approach. The And1 basketball circuit celebrates basketball creativity, lower-class black aesthetics, organic forms of play, and rules that do not translate fully into professional leagues. Cardona worked at a local fast food restaurant while running in every pickup game around the neighborhood, before returning to the Philippines and eventually ascending to the professional level.

The use of American imports—each team is allowed one non-Filipino import, usually a former college standout, many of whom are black—highlights the transnational connections between the U.S., notably African American culture, and the massive archipelago.[93] White and black college standouts and NBA washouts regularly appear on PBA rosters, from current Harvard University basketball coach Tommy Amaker to ESPN NCAA expert Jay Bilas.[94] Furthermore, there are those Filipino players born from romantic couplings between U.S. servicemen and Filipinas. Willie Miller, star point guard for the 2006–2007 PBA champion Alaskan Aces, was born from one such relationship.[95]

Miller's personal history and antics underline the mixed nature of Filipinos and Filipino Americans culturally. While regaling his teammates, including African American player Rosell "Roe" Ellis with his version of "Ebonics," Miller demonstrated the unique place Asian Americans, notably Filipino Americans, occupy between racial binaries of black and white. "His imitation Ebonics had Roe and the team's four Fil-Ams howling," reflected Bartholomew. "His clowning created a tableau of the Philippines' unique and muddled cultural blend, a legacy of hundreds of years of Spanish and then American rule, followed by a contemporary society in which poverty drove a tenth of the population to work abroad as sailors, nurses, nannies, maids, and at countless other jobs.... Here was Willie, a half-African American, Zambales-reared Filipino regaling the team's black import from Seattle and their full blooded Filipino teammates with good renditions of American hip hop."[96]

Filipino culture absorbed such influences. The NBA enjoys unrivaled popularity; it gets more social media "likes" and "follows" from the Philippines than any other nation outside of the United States. More people in Manila have liked the Miami Heat Facebook page than in Miami.[97] The Tagalog rappers Legit Misfitz penned "Air Tsinelas" as an homage to the sport's centrality in Filipino culture, but did so through the most American and African American of modern musical forms.[98]

In America especially, notes anthropologist Constancio R. Arnaldo, Jr., Filipino basketball shapes masculinity, notably in the way it incorporates black culture. Filipino American team uniforms adopt the aesthetics of the NBA—a league clearly associated with blackness, more so than any of the other major American sports—but also with tattoos and team names that identify them as Filipino, he points out. Designed using NBA templates, many feature symbols of the Philippines stitched into the fabrics. Team names like the Funky Fresh Boys, Mermen, and Mambas abound. "Strategically placing the Philippine flag and sun on their uniforms demonstrates an identity rooted in the transnational flow of goods, commodities, currency and exchange," asserts Arnaldo. Family members traveling to and from the islands take requests for new uniforms to the archipelago for production. They then ferry the finished product to the United States, thus enabling teams to save money, but also simultaneously create physical and metaphorical connections to America and Southeast Asia.[99]

In this way, the intersection of black and Asian American culture should come as little surprise. Granted, model minority tropes imposed on Asian Americans and embraced by some in the community portrayed blacks and Chicanos as malcontents while privileging Asian Americans' alleged hard work and lack of political engagement. "Asian Americans are perpetuating white racism in the United States, as they allow white America to hold up the 'successful' Oriental image before other minority groups as the model to emulate," Asian American activist Amy Uyematsu told listeners in 1969 in her repudiation of model minority stereotypes.[100]

New Yorker columnist and novelist Jay Caspian Kang made a similar point regarding Taiwanese American Jeremy Lin and broader Asian American culture in 2012. As a fifteen-year-old, Lin had opened a Xanga account under the handle "chinkballa," an appropriation of an ethnic slur aimed at Asians and slang often associated with African American culture. For Asian Americans, U.S. culture placed them between the white-black binary that still largely defines conversations about race.[101] "Like many of the Asian American kids of my generation stuck somewhere between white and black," reflected Kang, "I filled the vacant parts of my identity with basketball and hip-hop." Even if Asian Americans experience racial discrimination less harshly than their African American counterparts, as scholars like Mark Brilliant have argued, few spaces reveal a linked sense of identity like basketball.[102]

SoCal Filipino American basketball players, and one could certainly argue some of their Chinese, Japanese, and Vietnamese counterparts, deploy "basketball cool" as a connection to "urban blackness." Uniforms, as argued by Arnaldo, provide a level of "Filipino street credibility" not dissimilar from Stanley Thangaraj's idea of "basketball cool."[103]

In 2012, Asians surpassed Latinos as the largest wave of immigrants to the U.S. and became the fastest-growing racial group in the nation.[104] As American demographics move toward majority-minority status, the place of Asian Americans in mainstream daily life will only expand. In this context, sport continues to provide a critical lens for evaluating their role and that of other Americans in the nation's culture. Today, former NBA stars like Tracy McGrady and Stephon Marbury ply their trade in China. Jeremy Lin might not be an all-star, but his more quotidian accomplishment of becoming a reliable everyday player, "the achievement of the unremarkable," wrote one journalist, makes him equally important. His reliability can only open more doors and change more attitudes for future Asian American athletes, while providing a symbol of a burgeoning Asian American culture.[105] Moreover, particularly in regard to basketball, sport enables historians, sociologists, and others a window into not only race relations and citizenship, but also changes in gender roles and sexuality. Both the NBA and WNBA have embraced openly homosexual athletes.[106] Considering the frequently conservative nature of Asian American domesticity, basketball provides a window into the dynamics of gender roles and sexuality in the Asian American community. More generally, it enables Asian American men and women to reject sexual stereotypes, thereby reshaping perceptions of Asians in new ways and pressing outward against long-established Orientalist boundaries. With American presidents from Bill Clinton to Barack Obama heralding the importance of America's relationship with Asia in the twenty-first century and the country's growing Asian American demographics, the importance of sport as a window into these issues will only deepen.

NOTES

1 Ann Laura Stoler, "Intimidations of Empire: Predicaments of the Tactile and Unseen," in *Haunted by Empire: Geographies of Intimacy in North America*, ed. Ann Laura Stoler (Durham, NC: Duke University Press, 2006), 1–3.

2 Paul Kramer, *The Blood of Government: Race, Empire, and the United States and the Philippines* (Chapel Hill: University of North Carolina Press, 2006).

3 Ibid.

4 Janice A. Beran, "Americans in the Philippines: Imperialism or Progress through Sport?," *International Journal of the History of Sport* 6.1 (1989): 62–87.

5 Sayuri Guthrie-Shimizu, *Transpacific Field of Dreams: How Baseball Linked the United States and Japan in Peace and War* (Chapel Hill: University of North Carolina Press, 2012), 54.

6 Janet M. Davis, "Cockfight Nationalism: Blood Sport and the Moral Politics of American Empire and National Building," *American Quarterly* 65.3 (September 2013): 549–574.

7 Rafe Bartholomew, *Pacific Rims: Beermen Ballin' in Flip-Flops and the Philippines' Unlikely Love Affair with Basketball* (New York: New American Library, 2010).

8 Samuel A. Regalado, *Nikkei Baseball: Japanese American Baseball from Immigration to Internment to the Major Leagues*, Kindle edition (Chicago: University of Illinois Press, 2013); Linda España-Maram, *Creating Masculinity in Los Angeles's Little Manila: Working-Class Filipinos and Popular American Culture, 1920s–1950s* (New York: Columbia University Press, 2005).

9 Guthrie-Shimizu, *Transpacific Field of Dreams*, 52.

10 España-Maram, *Creating Masculinity*, 4.

11 Ji-Yeon Yuh, "Out of the Shadows: Camptown Women, Military Brides, and Korean (American) Communities," in *Asian American Studies Now*, ed. Jean Yu-wen Shen Wu and Thomas C. Chen (New Brunswick, NJ: Rutgers University Press), 239–255; Rhacel Salazar Parreñas, "Asian Immigrant Women and Global Restructuring, 1970s–1990s," in *Asian American Studies Now*, ed. Wu and Chen, 357; Andrew Friedman, *Covert Capital: Landscapes of Denial and the Making of the U.S. Empire in the Suburbs of Northern Virginia* (Los Angeles: University of California Press, 2013).

12 Friedman, *Covert Capital*, 181–182. Moreover, while numerous scholars and movies have demonstrated the power of heterosexual relationships in doing the same, the 2014 documentary *The Last Days in Vietnam* provided further evidence of the intersection of Asian American diasporas, U.S. military intervention, and the power of intimacies.

13 Kathleen Yep, "Peddling Sport: Liberal Multiculturalism and the Racial Triangulation of Blackness, Chineseness and Native American-ness in Professional Basketball," *Ethnic and Racial Studies* 35.6 (June 2012): 971–987; Stanley Thangaraj, "Competing Masculinities: South Asian American Identity Formation in Asian American Basketball Leagues," *Sport and South Asian Diasporas* 11.3 (2013): 243–255.

14 Mae Ngai, *Impossible Subjects: Illegal Aliens and the Making of Modern America*, (Princeton, NJ: Princeton University Press, 2005).

15 Nayan Shah, *Contagious Divides: Epidemics and Race in San Francisco's Chinatown*, (Los Angeles: University of California Press, 2001), 91.

16 Nancy F. Cott, *Public Vows: A History of Marriage and the Nation* (Cambridge, MA: Harvard University Press, 2000), 138–139.

17 Erika Lee, "The Chinese Exclusion Example: Race, Immigration, and American Gatekeeping, 1882–1924," *Journal of American Ethnic History* (Spring 2002): 36–62.

18 Cott, *Public Vows*, 148–149. By 1913, eight states had passed laws prohibiting whites from marrying Chinese of Japanese. Alien land laws also came into practice during this period.

19 España-Maram, *Creating Masculinity*, 105–133.

20 Ibid., 111, 120; Mai Ngai, *Impossible Subjects: Illegal Aliens and the Making of Modern America* (Princeton, NJ: Princeton University Press, 2003).

21 Yuh, "Out of the Shadows," 239–255; Rhacel Salazar Parreñas, "Asian Immigrant Women," 357.

22 Charlotte Brooks, *Alien Neighbors, Foreign Friends: Asian Americans, Housing, and the Transformation of Urban California* (Chicago: University of Chicago Press, 2009); Scott Kurashige, *The Shifting Grounds of Race: Black and Japanese Americans in the Making of Multicultural Los Angeles* (Princeton, NJ: Princeton University Press, 2010).

23 Guthrie-Shimizu, *Field of Transpacific Dreams*, 48–49; Wanda Ellen Wakefield, *Playing to Win: Sports and the American Military, 1898–1945* (Albany: State University

of New York Press, 1997); Gerald R. Gems, *The Athletic Crusade: Sport and American Cultural Imperialism* (Lincoln: University of Nebraska Press, 2006).

24 Guthrie-Shimizu, *Field of Transpacific Dreams*, 31–33. See also Thomas Carter, *The Quality of Home Runs: The Passion, Politics, and Language of Cuban Baseball* (Durham, NC: Duke University Press, 2008).

25 Wakefield, *Playing to Win*; España-Maram, *Creating Masculinity*; Vicente M. Diaz, "'Fight Boys till the Last': Football and the Remasculinization of Indigeneity in Guam," in *Pacific Diaspora: Island Peoples in the United States and the Pacific*, ed. Paul Spickard, Joanne Rondilla, and Deborah Hippolite-Wright (Manoa: University of Hawai'i Press, 2002), 167–194.

26 Guthrie-Shimizu, *Field of Transpacific Dreams*, 31–33.

27 Ibid., 110–112.

28 Ibid., 40–74.

29 Regalado, *Nikkei Baseball*.

30 Guthrie-Shimizu, *Field of Transpacific Dreams*, 95–97.

31 Ibid., 61–63.

32 Edward Said, *Orientalism* (New York: Vintage, 1979).

33 Regalado, *Nikkei Baseball*.

34 Guthrie-Shimizu, *Field of Transpacific Dreams*, 34.

35 Regalado, *Nikkei Baseball*.

36 Guthrie-Shimizu, *Field of Transpacific Dreams*, 56–57.

37 Ibid., 57.

38 Regalado, *Nikkei Baseball*; Joel Franks, *Asian Pacific Americans and Baseball: A History* (Jefferson, NC: McFarland, 2008).

39 Kevin Starr, *California: A History* (New York: Modern Library, 2005), 299–301.

40 Guthrie-Shimizu, *Field of Transpacific Dreams*, 80.

41 Starr, *California: A History*, 300–301.

42 Akira Iriye, *Pacific Estrangement: Japanese and American Expansion, 1897–1911* (Cambridge, MA: Harvard University Press, 1972); Laura R. Barraclough, *The Making of San Fernando Valley: Rural Landscapes, Urban Development, and White Privilege* (Athens: University of Georgia Press, 2011); Regalado, *Nikkei Baseball*; Guthrie-Shimizu, *Field of Transpacific Dreams*; España-Maram, *Creating Masculinity*.

43 Starr, *California: A History*.

44 Regalado, *Nikkei Baseball*.

45 Jose M. Alamillo, "Peloteros in Paradise: Mexican American Baseball and Oppositional Politics in Southern California, 1930–1950," *Western Historical Quarterly* 34 (Summer 2003), 193.

46 Gerald R. Gems, "Sport, Colonialism, and United States Imperialism," *Journal of Sports History* 33.1 (Spring 2006): 13–15.

47 Guthrie-Shimizu, *Field of Transpacific Dreams*, 129.

48 Geri Strucker, "Winter Baseball in California: Separate Opportunities, Equal Talent," in *The National Pastime: Endless Seasons, Baseball in Southern California*, ed. Jean

Hastings Ardell and Andy McClue (Society for American Baseball Research, 2011), http://sabr.org/research/winter-baseball-california-separate-opportunities-equal-talent.

49 See Michael Nevins roundtable discussion in "Sports and the Diaspora," presented at the Organization of American Historians Conference, Atlanta, GA, April 10–13, 2014.

50 Ibid.

51 Guthrie-Shimizu, *Field of Transpacific Dreams*, 161–163.

52 Regalado, *Nikkei Baseball*.

53 Brian Niiya et al., *More than a Game: Sport in the Japanese American Community* (Los Angeles: Japanese American National Museum, 2000).

54 Kerry Yo Nakagawa, "Manzanar: Family, Friends, and Desert Diamonds Behind Barbed Wire," in *The National Pastime: Endless Seasons, Baseball in Southern California*, ed. Jean Hastings Ardell and Andy McClue (Society for American Baseball Research, 2011), http://sabr.org/research/manzanar-family-friends-and-desert-diamonds-behind-barbed-wire. See also Kerry Yo Nakagawa, *Through a Diamond: 100 Years of Japanese American Baseball* (San Francisco: Rudi Publishing, 2001).

55 Regalado, *Nikkei Baseball*.

56 Nakagawa, "Manzanar."

57 Regalado, *Nikkei Baseball*.

58 Hillary Jenks, "Seasoned Long Enough in Concentration: Suburbanization and Transnational Citizenship in Southern California's South Bay," *Journal of Urban History* 40 (January 2014): 9.

59 Charlotte Brooks, *Alien Neighbors, Foreign Friends: Asian Americans, Housing, and the Transformation of Urban California* (Chicago: University of Chicago Press, 2009); Scott Kurashige, *The Shifting Grounds of Race: Black and Japanese Americans in the Making of Multicultural Los Angeles* (Princeton, NJ: Princeton University Press, 2010).

60 Brooks, *Alien Neighbors, Foreign Friends*, 218–221; Ryan Reft, "Diving into Integration: Sammy Lee, Historical Memory, and the Complexity of Housing Segregation in Cold War California," KCET, October 31, 2013, http://www.kcet.org/socal/departures/columns/intersections/diving-into-integration-sammy-lee-historical-memory-and-the-complexity-of-housing-segregation-in-col.html

61 Guthrie-Shimizu, *Transpacific Field of Dreams*, 205–206.

62 Ibid., 199.

63 Ibid., 206.

64 Ibid., 218.

65 Ibid.

66 Sucheng Chang, *Asian Americans: An Interpretive History* (Woodbridge, CT: Twayne, 1991).

67 Guthrie-Shimizu, *Transpacific Field of Dreams*, 228.

68 Jenks, "Seasoned Long Enough in Concentration"; Wendy Cheng, *The Changs next to the Diazes: Remapping Race in Suburban California* (Minneapolis: University of Minnesota Press, 2013).

69 Kathleen Yep, *Outside the Paint: When Basketball Ruled at the Chinese Playground*, (Philadelphia: Temple University Press, 2009), 5–6.

70 Dawn Bohulano Mabalon. "Beauty Queens, Bomber Pilots, and Basketball Players: Second-Generation Filipina Americans in Stockton, California, 1930s to 1950s," in *Pinay Power: Peminist Critical Theory—Theorizing the Filipina-American Experience*, ed. Melinda L. de Jesús (New York: Rutledge, 2005), 102–116.

71 Yep, *Outside the Paint*, 69–70, 75.

72 Ibid., 65, 102–103.

73 Jamilah King, "The Asian American Basketball Leagues That Created Jeremy Lin," *Colorlines*, February 21, 2012, http://colorlines.com/archives/2012/02/japanese_american_basketball_leagues.html.

74 Vijay Prashad, *Everybody Was Kung Fu Fighting: Afro Asian Connections and the Myth of Cultural Purity* (New York: Beacon Press, 2002), 119; Ryan Reft, "Not Bowling Alone: How the Holiday Bowl in Crenshaw Became an Integrated Leisure Space," KCET, August 22, 2013, http://www.kcet.org/socal/departures/columns/intersections/not-bowling-alone-crenshaw-community-and-the-history-of-the-holiday-bowl.html.

75 John Salmon, "JA Basketball Evolves, but Not Elitist Cult, Experts Say," *Nikkei West*, December 25, 2013, 5,12.

76 Solomon Moore, "The Courts of Ethnic Identity," *Los Angeles Times*, July 14, 2000.

77 King, "Asian American Basketball Leagues."

78 Christina Chin, "Gender Dynamics within Japanese American Basketball Leagues," *CSW Update*, October 2010, http://www.csw.ucla.edu/publications/newsletters/2010-2011/article-pdfs/CSW_OCT2010_Chin.pdf.

79 Ibid.

80 Billy Witz, "Aiming at Glass Ceiling but Not with Her Jumpshot," *New York Times*, July 20, 2014, http://www.nytimes.com/2014/07/21/sports/basketball/clippers8217-nakase-aspires-to-be-nba8217s-first-female-head-coach.html?_r=0.

81 Mai Ngai, *Impossible Subjects: Illegal Aliens and the Making of Modern America*, (Princeton, NJ: Princeton University Press, 2003), 96–126.

82 Pew Research Center, "The Rise of Asian Americans," updated edition, April 4, 2013, http://www.pewsocialtrends.org/files/2013/04/Asian-Americans-new-full-report-04-2013.pdf.

83 Guthrie-Shimizu, *Transpacific Field of Dreams*, 50; España-Maram, *Creating Masculinity*; Janice A. Beran, "Americans in the Philippines."

84 Bartholomew, *Pacific Rims*, 57–58.

85 Beran, "Americans in the Philippines," 75.

86 Ibid.

87 Gems, *Athletic Crusade*, 102.

88 Beran, "Americans in the Philippines," 67, 79, 81.

89 Bartholomew, *Pacific Rims*, 58–60.

90 Ibid., 63–64.

91 Ibid., 74.

92 Ibid., 156, 199.
93 Ibid., 368–369.
94 Ibid., 204.
95 Ibid., 198.
96 Ibid.
97 Rafe Bartholomew, "The NBA Arrives in Manila, 80 Years after the Love of the Game," *Grantland*, March 7, 2013, http://grantland.com/the-triangle/the-nba-arrives-in-manila-80-years-after-the-love-of-the-game/.
98 Bartholomew, *Pacific Rims*, 16.
99 Constancio Arnaldo, Jr., in discussion with the author, December 12, 2013.
100 Amy Uyematsu, "Activist Amy Uyematsu Proclaims the Emergence of 'Yellow Power,' 1969," in *Major Problems in Asian American History*, ed. Lon Kurashige and Alice Yang Murray (New York: Houghton Mifflin, 2003), 421.
101 Leslie Bow, *Partly Colored: Asian Americans Racial Anomaly in the Segregated South* (New York: New York University Press, 2010).
102 Jay Caspian Kang, "A Question of Identity," *Grantland*, March 20, 2012, http://grantland.com/features/the-headline-tweet-unfair-significance-jeremy-lin/; Mark Brilliant, *The Color of America Has Changed: How Racial Diversity Shaped Civil Rights Reform in California, 1941–1978* (New York: Oxford University Press, 2012).
103 Stanley I. Thangaraj, "Competing Masculinities: South Asian Identity Formation in Asian American Basketball Leagues," *South Asian Popular Culture* 11.3 (2013): 243–255.
104 Kirk Semple, "In a Shift, Biggest Wave of Immigrants Is Now Asian," *New York Times*, June 18, 2012, http://www.nytimes.com/2012/06/19/us/asians-surpass-hispanics-as-biggest-immigrant-wave.html.
105 Beckly Mason, "Lin Does a Lot by Not Doing Much," *New York Times*, February 23, 2013, http://www.nytimes.com/2013/02/24/sports/basketball/jeremy-lin-is-fitting-in-well-with-the-rockets.html; Jere Longman, "From Phenom to Everyday Player," *New York Times*, April 21, 2013, http://www.nytimes.com/2013/04/22/sports/basketball/rockets-jeremy-lin-has-focused-on-improving-his-game.html.
106 Andrew Keh, "Jason Collins, First Openly Gay NBA Player, Signs with Nets, Appears in Game," *New York Times*, February 23, 2014, http://www.nytimes.com/2014/02/24/sports/basketball/after-signing-with-nets-jason-collins-becomes-first-openly-gay-nba-player.html; Ryan Reft, "Sporting Golden State: Women and Athletics in Twentieth-Century California," KCET, March 20, 2014, http://www.kcet.org/socal/departures/columns/intersections/sporting-golden-state-women-and-athletics-in-20th-century-california.html.

2

Reflections on Sport Spectatorship and Immigrant Life

SHALINI SHANKAR

In 1970, two sisters moved from what was then Bombay, India, to Morningside Heights, New York. They came together; one sister a recently trained MD looking for a job, the other with a BA about to enroll for her master's. They brought with them a couple of suitcases with saris and small possessions, including a container of yogurt to use as culture for further batches. They also brought an avid love of sport—especially cricket, soccer, tennis, and wrestling. When their nephew arrived from Bombay in 1973, he, my father, came bearing an interest in a multitude of sports. He immediately took an interest in wrestling, which he had followed in India; cricket, which he watched with his uncle as a boy and listened to on the radio; baseball, which he played in middle school in Madras; and tennis, which he had watched and supported at his college. As a young girl, I spent countless weekend afternoons and evenings in the 1970s sprawled out on their carpeted Flushing, New York, apartment, mildly interested in the sporting events on the television but enthralled by the cheering, booing, and color commentary my relatives directed at the television. So began my immigrant family's passion for sport spectatorship, which spanned genders and generations and continues to thrive.

In this essay, I reflect on aspects of my family's relationship to sport as a way of addressing a gap in the literature about sport spectatorship and immigrant acculturation. While playing sports has been shown to be a significant aspect of the immigration acculturation process, as I discuss shortly, sports spectatorship can also do important socializing work. I suspect that the experiences I reflect upon might closely mirror those of others who immigrated at this time, as they bring to light aspects of the acculturation process that receive relatively little attention. I emphasize two aspects of this process: the first is the role sport knowledge and spectatorship play in mediating diaspora and creating cultural entrées into mainstream American society, especially workplaces. I elaborate here on the experiences of older members of my family who arrived in the 1960s and 1970s and used their existing and newly acquired sports knowledge to create connections with individuals and institutions in their workplaces and communities. The second is the role of sport as a mediator of gendered intergenerational relationships. While the literature has often overstated generational differences and made the first generation into inassimilable subjects, stories of desi sporting cultures provide an important window into understanding community and identity formation.[1]

My own experiences with older relatives, as well as with my father, are deeply inflected with these memories and shared experiences, as well as the ones we continue to build. Spectating in these contexts can range from diehard fandom to seeing sport as part of social life; viewing and talking about sport in everyday life can be an integral part of familial culture. Through these areas, I argue for a more thoughtful consideration of sport as part of migration and diasporic experiences.

Sport, Homeland, and Diaspora

Recent studies of immigrant groups show how sport participation and spectatorship enabled the construction of community and social networks. Wallace (2009) illustrates how Hispanic/Latino immigrants in North Carolina use soccer to develop a sense of comfort and belonging. Primarily this has been through league play, as Joseph (2012) similarly illustrates. In Wallace's study, as in Joseph's, spectators are generally family members and those in the community who come to see friends and neighbors, thus creating a social outlet. Similarly, Thangaraj (2015) explains how South Asian American institutions, like cultural centers and religious institutions, were deeply involved with American sport by offering spaces for basketball. However, these spaces, he contends, were not available equivalently across gender, sexual, and class divides. Moreover, they were certainly not as commonplace several decades ago as we find them today. Immigrants in the 1960s and early 1970s had but a handful of the social, retail, and other venues tailored to South Asian Americans. There were a handful of desi restaurants, grocery stores, and electronics and apparel stores, but nothing on the scale of today's Jackson Heights, New York, or parts of Silicon Valley, Chicago, or Edison, New Jersey. Nor were there the types of large, established South Asian American communities that have come to characterize these areas. In the late 1960s and early 1970s, many Indian immigrants had to find their own way. I was a year old when my parents settled into an apartment complex on Colden Street in Queens, one in which numerous desi families lived. Reconnecting with old family friends and quickly making new ones, they certainly had opportunities to socialize among themselves. As community members, family, we did our share of socializing, eating, gossiping, and catching up. Yet in the time we spent among ourselves, my parents, my aunts, uncles, relatives visiting from India, and children watched our fair share of sports on television, and occasionally live. In retrospect, I realize it was one of the more enjoyable ways my family made sense of their lives in the U.S. and how America worked. It is also an important window into early assimilation processes in a transforming ethnic landscape.

In the 1970s, cricket, a sport with great popularity worldwide, was virtually nonexistent in the United States. Appadurai (1995) contends that cricket is important in diasporas of former British colonies, and others have likewise explored how those in diasporas relate to teams from their homelands (Walle 2010). For instance, Fletcher explores how cricket is linked to British Asians' diasporic identities by discussing Conservative MP Norman Tebbit's controversial "cricket test"—the assessment of immigrants' loyalty to British society based on whether they supported England's cricket team or that of their native country—as "a superficial measurement of fidelity and assimilation of migrant groups in Britain" (2012:614; see also Burdsey 2010). Perhaps one way to understand these differences is to consider how my family came to experience what Joo calls "media sport," a term she uses for "competitive sports that are structured by commercial mass media and manufactured for mass consumption" (2012:3). This is a different way of experiencing sport than what was happening in India pre-immigration in the 1960s, and certainly was not at its current height even in the US in the 1970s. Approaching sporting events, their media coverage, and the personalities in ways that resonate with other dimensions of social life, Birrell and McDonald (2000) advocate for a reading of sport events and personalities as informed by a critical cultural studies approach that incorporates feminist, Marxist, and critical race approaches. I similarly consider how sport might allow us to better understand dynamics of gender, social mobility, and racial belonging, to the extent I can given that these are my subjective family memories, supplemented by interviews with my father, brother, and uncle.

Some American sports were not entirely unfamiliar. Even baseball had enough of a presence in India that it trickled down into the schools. My dad remembered playing baseball in Madras when he was in sixth and seventh standard (grade) as a child: "I had played baseball in Madras. I had also played in Bombay but in Madras too." Baseball was "assumed to be a form of Americanization" in Japanese internment camps and evidence of adaptation to life in the United States (Joo 2012:78). These and other pre-1965 sports experiences of prominent Asian American athletes are groundbreaking. These earlier experiences of Asian American sporting cultures took place before the substantial immigration from South Asia to the United States after the 1965 immigration act. Finding one's way into American sport spectatorship and developing fandom during these times involved crossing unchartered terrain. Sports were not likely to be at the top of new immigrants' agenda, but fortunately, they did not slip too far down among my family's priorities. Some of my relatives played sports in India before emigrating. My mother's brother Shekhar, who was educated in India, became interested in cricket in high school. Initially mastering popular games like *kitti-pullu* (called *gilli-danda* in Hindi) and *kabaddi* in the South Indian village of Senthangudy, he recalled, "These games were played right in the middle of the main street running through the village." Moving to the South Indian town of Kumbakonam, he began playing cricket "in an abandoned field in the back of a dilapidated old fort." Once he moved north to begin a degree at Delhi Polytechnic, he resumed playing cricket. A better bowler than batsman, he reflected to me in an email, "What I remember about those days is the time the Delhi Polytechnic cricket team (of which I was a member) played our arch rival team from Delhi University and we won. I bagged 4 wickets for my team as a leg-spin bowler! I sometimes wish I had saved the trophy I got as a member of this winning team."

Unlike Britain, where colonial pastimes have found a home in the diaspora, the United States was something of a blank slate. With a bachelor's degree in chemical engineering, Shekhar moved to the U.S. for graduate studies in 1962, before most of the new immigration. At that time, cricket was virtually unknown in the United States. There were few if any opportunities to support a homeland team, as India as a nation, and Indian Americans as a population, had no presence in baseball, football, basketball, or golf. The Amritraj brothers would shine on an international tennis stage in the early 1970s, which would offer Shekhar one sport to continuously follow. Yet, he, as well as my "chittis" (my father's kin term to refer to his aunts), father, and other relatives who arrived in the 1960s and early 1970s, found sports to be entertaining as well as important spaces of community building, especially when few other outlets for the latter were available.

My father came to New York in 1973 to visit his aunts in Morningside Heights en route to Chicago, where he had intended to settle near his brother-in-law. With a recently earned IIT Madras bachelor's degree and a few years of work experience in Bombay, my father had come to establish himself with a job and apartment here before bringing my mother and me. It was a hopeful time in which the professional immigration anticipated by the 1965 Hart–Celler Act had become a reality, and a new wave of immigrants were beginning to populate neighborhoods in America's cities. New York City's borough of Queens, with its Flushing and Jackson Heights neighborhoods, seemed to hold great pull with this group.[2] They worshiped at a newly constructed Hindu temple in Flushing, and soon established a gurdwara and masjid for Sikhs and Muslims, respectively. While not likely the primary draw for Indian immigrants, Flushing also housed the sprawling Flushing Meadows Park, the recently constructed Shea Stadium, in which the Mets baseball franchise and the Jets football franchise both played, and the USTA National Tennis Center, where the US Open grand slam tournament is held.

Seeing New York City for the first time was quite thrilling, my father recalled, even though he moved from the even louder and more crowded city of Bombay. For three weeks he stayed with his aunts, who then lived in a small dorm room at Columbia University. His aunt Ambuja was earning a master's in education from Teachers College, which she would apply to her years of dedicated service at United Cerebral Palsy on 23rd Street near 5th Avenue. Viji, already an MD by training in India, was becoming certified to practice medicine in the United States. She would soon work in a Veteran's Administration hospital, rehabilitating those wounded in military combat. During his three weeks in New York, my father squeezed into their tiny dorm room on the floor, and by day, saw sites in New York City that were perhaps lower down on the list of tourist attractions. In particular, he visited the New York Public Library and enrolled in a course on resume writing, sent his resume out in response to any ads in the paper from firms needing mechanical or electrical engineers, and was offered a position at a small company named Tork in Mt. Vernon, Westchester. The gentleman who hired him was the president of the company, one that his family had founded. The suggestion that my father Ratnaswamy Shankar go by the name of "Sam" in the workplace, seemed to not be a deal breaker, and so he stayed in New York. While some would view this act of renaming one of forced conformity, he shrugged it off and began his new life as Sam. Intentionally or inadvertently, Sam began to build a life at this new company that was an apt fit not only for his professional growth, but also with his excitement about sports.

Sport as an Entrée into American Society

Sport spectatorship is primarily about fandom and viewing, but also about becoming socialized into aspects of regional cultures. Indeed, sport can play an important role in acculturating to American society and joining conversations and social worlds that perhaps would not otherwise be easily entered. Understanding how and when to talk about certain sports, talking about players, knowing their nicknames, keeping up to date with standings and injuries, and the like, greatly enhances this performance. Growing up in a society allows children to develop these skills along the way, as they learn from peers, parents, and others. For immigrants however, such knowledge is generally outside of one's diasporic comfort zone and puts them at a marked disadvantage of having to build knowledge as adults to become skilled spectators. My father was fortunate that his first job as a mechanical and electrical engineer offered opportunities for socialization beyond those in the workplace through sport. The president of the company at that time, Dorset White, had inherited it from his father, taking over the family business despite not being an engineer or a businessman. Rather, this fair-minded, well-spoken Stanford grad was a sportscaster before running an electrical manufacturing company. It was a small company based near the border of Westchester and the Bronx, right on the edge of New York City. Due to Dorset's love of sports, spectatorship became an integral aspect of company recreation, beginning with the purchase of a field-level box at Shea Stadium, between third base and home plate, which would have been somewhere around the 20-yard line when the field was used for football. Yankee tickets would have made more geographic sense, what with the stadium being right in the Bronx and so close to the company, but Dorset was a Mets fan, and that worked fine for my family. By that time we had moved to Flushing, along with my great aunts Viji Chitti and Ambuja Chitti, and our building was a mere subway stop away from world-class sport being staged in our own corner of New York City.

It is quite commonplace for American men to strike up conversations about sport with one another, but it is much harder for women and new immigrants to enter this world. As a young child, it was clear to me that sports were not marketed toward my family. Suffice it to say, we did not find many Tamil-speaking vegetarian baseball fans in those days. Sports marketing today identifies Asian Americans as excellent consumers, but this population has never really struck sports marketers as comprising "typical" fans (Clarke and Mannion 2006:23; see also Shankar 2015). Normative fandom seemed to center on white or black men, with Latinos as a growing audience; other racial and ethnic groups required qualification, unless the athletes themselves were of Asian heritage. For instance, Joo (2012) notes the role of media in furthering the recent popularity of Korean athletes globally. Unlike fandom today, which is cultivated by the internet, social media, and global marketing, spectatorship in the 1970s had much more delimited audiences. Tennis and golf, sports that bridge the gap between spectatorship and participation and are especially favored for corporate socializing, seemed to draw whites as well as upwardly mobile minorities. When I went to baseball or football games with my father and brother, we were among a predominantly white, male audience. During this time before fantasy sports became widespread, the primary ways to learn about the NFL, MLB, and NBA—as well as entertainment-based spectacles like professional wrestling—were by reading the newspaper, watching events with commentary, and speaking to people about them.

My father became interested in football in the 1970s by going to Jets games at Shea Stadium. The Jets had won the Super Bowl at the end of the 1968 season, and people were talking about players with an excitement that seemed contagious. When I asked him how his co-workers regarded his sports knowledge, he remarked, "Actually, some of the serious fans, they were surprised initially. You know, that I'm into football, baseball, and I know the teams and the players. I didn't get the stats right, but yeah, they were quite surprised." Sports spectatorship as well as recreational play were part of my father's office culture. Over time, he slowly acquired the embodied dispositions required to manage talking about sport with co-workers and clients, while also learning new sports well enough to participate. Learning how to perform embodied ways of being a fan, and expressively exhibiting them, is a mark of knowledge and authenticity. The anthropologist Victor Turner (1982) discusses sports mimicry as part of play, and the embodied identification with which spectators watch a sport. This could include celebrations of points scored, gesturing, leaning, miming, and any number of other dispositions that offer a departure from simply sitting still and watching. At the annual softball game, where the company divided into teams of factory workers versus office staff, my father was able to draw on his background in India, where he was first exposed to baseball: "There was no T-Ball. Baseball was part of the sports activities of the school. We played with a regular baseball and bat, not a softball. The regular baseball is similar in . . . hardness to a cricket ball, a piece of sporting equipment I was used to."

Despite softball being read as a more feminine sport in the United States, the game promised greater inclusivity, but also proved difficult for my father to play. He remarked that the ball was much larger than a cricket ball, and pitching was so different from bowling: "I would never have the proper technique or softball throw. I found it difficult to hold the ball and throw the distance an average player in that league did." With batting as his strong suit, pitching and fielding remained a challenge and he limited his participation to the annual picnic. He did, however, have an avid interest in viewing baseball games. "Baseball was somewhat familiar to cricket," he recalled, when we spoke in February 2014. It was easy to follow and similarly paced, making it a natural game to follow. Totally unrelated to baseball, bowling was another popular sport in the 1970s, and my father's co-workers had formed a bowling league. "I had quite a bit of fun," my dad remarked about the season in which he accepted an invitation to participate. Ultimately the secondhand smoke and his busy work schedule kept him from playing in subsequent seasons.

Tennis is by far the most popular sport among desis, both for entering workplace or neighborhood leagues, or forming them from one's own social networks. My father recalls that tennis had been a popular sport in India, and that he watched his college team play and supported them. He described the sport as being "for the richer people" of India, emphasizing that tennis camps and coaches were pricey, and court access was quite difficult if one did not belong to a club. When he arrived in the US, he was excited to realize that access to tennis courts and tennis equipment was not as exclusive as it was in India, but hadn't thought to see a grand slam event until his brother-in-law suggested it and took my father to the US Open. My uncle himself only began what would be a lifetime love affair with the sport when he arrived in Brooklyn to pursue a PhD at Brooklyn Polytechnic. Since his cricket-playing college days in Delhi, he had not initially taken to tennis when his PhD advisor involved him in a doubles match with other academics. Swearing to never play again after what he recalled to be an abysmal performance, it would be nearly a decade until he picked up a racquet again.

When his colleague at Allied Chemical where he had then began working invited him to a 90-minute clinic for beginners in 1972, he found a great connection with the game. Practicing with other beginners for a year, it then took "three more years of constant playing (three to four times a week in the evening after work) for my game to be good enough to make me eligible to play in my company's B team (I still wasn't good enough to play in the A team)." Eventually he moved up to the A team in doubles and played until retirement. Closing in on his 80th birthday in 2015, he proudly recalled, "After my retirement in the mid-1990s, I have kept playing both singles and doubles regularly to this day, but as one would expect my game today is just a shadow of what it used to be up until 15 years ago." He did remark that he still plays with some of the original co-workers he began to play with in the 1970s. My father likewise noted, "Tennis also helped me in business. For many of them, the golf course was the number one business venue. But at conventions and meetings, tennis was a part of activities, and a lot of people participated. It gave me a chance to play with the president of some of the biggest companies who were represented there and get to know them. Sometimes their spouses participated too, as most of those companies were family owned. We used to have a good camaraderie." Tennis and golf were also more accessible to women and more readily adapted to co-ed participation.

An analogous camaraderie developed with his friends in Flushing. He began to play tennis with a group of South Asian American friends on local courts in Queens, occasionally traveling to Long Island to play in bubble courts during the winter. "We started to play more seriously, continuing in the winter months, on clay courts that were in a heated bubble," he explained, as they tried to keep the sport active year-round. Although their court time was for 7.30 a.m., they tipped the staff to begin playing at 6.45 when the staff arrived to heat up the courts. Playing on the cold, dim courts that had yet to be warmly lit was worth it to get the extra 45 minutes of play in, signaling their dedication to and enjoyment of the sport, as well as the company they shared. Though all of them, including my family, eventually moved out of Queens to different regions of New York and New Jersey, the group continues to play on local courts in the summer and indoor courts in the winter. His is the longest-running group of people to play together that he knows—they have been together for nearly 40 years. Of all the sports we followed or played, participation in tennis was the most constant and important for professional and social integration into US society.

One sporting activity inspired a keen interest among my family that seemed to not be shared with colleagues or other desi families: the World Wrestling Federation (now known as World Wrestling Entertainment). My father could not recall when our family became taken with what we called "WWF," but placed it some time in the late 1970s or early 1980s. In his essay "The World of Wrestling," Barthes calls wrestling's primary virtue "the spectacle of excess," and comments that it is a spectacle rather than a sport (1972:15). Barthes differentiates "true" or amateur wrestling from professional or "false wrestling," but nonetheless acknowledges the great potential for spectacle: "The public is completely uninterested in knowing whether the contest is rigged or not, and rightly so; it abandons itself to the primary virtue of the spectacle, which is to abolish all motives and all consequences: what matters is not what it thinks but what it sees" (1972:15). According to my father, he followed wrestling back in India, where it was very popular. It has been argued that the sport was a staging ground for colonial resistance in India (Alter 1992), not unlike Trobriand cricket (Leach and Kildea 1975). My father recalled that when he was around ten years old, in the early 1950s, there were popular Indian wrestlers with names like "Tiger Govinda" and "King Kong." Once his family took him to see a competition that he had read about in the newspaper, in which foreign wrestlers came to compete with Indian wrestlers. He commented on how impressed he was with the event, reflecting, "It was real wrestling," and that all the things that they do in America to "stage" competitions didn't happen in India.

Apparently, the spectacle of the WWF was no less riveting; as Barthes observes, suffering is meted out and attempts at justice are on display, and especially "in America, wrestling represents a sort of mythological fight between Good and Evil" (1972:23). Live WWF events were occasionally held in New York City, and my father, aunts, and uncles went to Madison Square Garden to watch a couple of times. Coincidentally, complementing my family's interest, Ambuja Chitti's workplace, United Cerebral Palsy, often received free tickets to WWF matches. She would accompany the children to whom the tickets were distributed in their ringside seats—a further opportunity to watch the spectacle live. When asked why he watched the WWF if he knew it was staged, my father responded that it was still "entertaining enough." To me it seemed to resemble the excess of Bollywood, with its choreographed moves, dramatic lighting, feuds that continued outside of the ring, and overly produced nature with loud music and bombastic commentary. The overall event offered excellent potential for outsider critique, much like American critics comment on the melodramatic spectacle of Bollywood.

Wrestling, baseball, football, tennis, and other sports were an integral part of my family's life, long after we had settled into the social worlds of the New York City area. While we never felt unwelcome, our presence at sporting events was never seamless either. In the early days, we seemed different from the other fans, and even today, still do. Being a fan of the home team certainly helped create camaraderie, but so too did the absence of overt tension between Indian Americans and other racial and ethnic groups in a pre-9/11 era. Scholars have debated whether sport can act as a unifier among conflicted societal groups, and act as a progressive force in helping individuals overcome prejudice and discrimination (Bairnar 2001; Burdsey 2010). Race has been carefully considered in sport participation, both from a media standpoint (Rowe 2003) and from an everyday participant perspective (Thangaraj 2010, 2015). Joseph illustrates the relevance of sport in diasporas and how cricket connects English-speaking Caribbean immigrants in Canada. She notes the sport is especially marketed to Indian and Pakistani immigrants in ways that unite them beyond their communal differences. In this regard, she identifies how homeland cultures that are "reproduced on the cricket ground are linguistic, culinary, musical, and kinesthetic" while they are also "exclusionary and racist" (2012:16). Such a divergent set of findings is a useful reminder of the myriad roles that sport can play in the lives of immigrants, and how they may ease some tensions while furthering others.

Overall, sport spectatorship and participation brought my family into the mainstream of American culture in the 1960s, 1970s, and into the 1980s. They offered avenues to enjoy and build upon familiar pastimes and build up new ones, and my family used sport to find a place for themselves in American workplaces, find avenues for socialization, and expand the range of their desi community activities to those beyond food and fine arts performances. Equally significant is the work that sport did in building familial relationships across continents, generations, and genders in my immediate and extended family.

Intergenerational Spectatorship

What is most striking about sport in my family is its potential to create intergenerational connections between people whose social knowledge and interests are so dramatically different from one another. A good portion of my childhood in Flushing in the 1970s that I didn't spend in the park, elementary school, or at desi events with my parents was spent sprawled out in Viji Chitti and Ambuja Chitti's carpeted apartment watched wrestling on television. Viji and Ambuja were born in the early 1930s, and vividly recall participating in India's freedom struggle. Viji spoke about "Gandhiji's mission" and participating in marches, rallies, and other forms of civil disobedience. Perhaps wrestling was part of this struggle for them, as Alter's (1992) work argues. I was not able to ask them about it specifically, as Viji passed in 2010 and Ambuja was never as intense a fan, but I gathered that the popularity of the sport pervaded my extended family. Treating me like the daughter they never had, Saturday nights were sleepover opportunities for me. Regaling me with details about wrestlers to which the average six-year-old was probably not privy, my chittis would watch while munching on a bowl of Hot Mix while I happily peered out of pillow forts built just for me. What captivated me more than the costumed men thrashing about was the sociability of watching with my chittis, and seeing that strange world through their lens. Of course we watched other programming as well, but this was what I remember as most distinctive of my viewing time with them.

Not until decades later did I understand that that such intergenerational sport spectatorship was a well-established, if seldom discussed, practice in my family. My father had experienced the same with the chittis' older brother in colonial and postcolonial India. In Bombay, Viji and Ambuja's older brother Chandru was an airline navigator by profession, but an umpire for league cricket matches by hobby. As a certified umpire, he refereed as many matches as his work schedule permitted, and was given season tickets that he distributed among my father, his brothers, and cousins. As a young boy, he took my father to test matches on Fridays, "a whole-day affair," as my father happily remembered. He recalled seeing India play visiting teams from Pakistan, England, and other nations. He described his aunt Viji as an avid cricket fan. He recalled, "She would be very critical and passionate of the teams and matches at times." Cricket constituted one way that my family found ways to offer their visions of India and the larger world.[3] The entire family listened to cricket matches on the radio. "We used to huddle around transistor radios, or the radio at the tea stall if we were out, with all the crowds." With more extensive cricket coverage in the United States still a few decades away when they settled into New York City in the early 1970s, their passion for cricket was redirected toward other sports.

In the late 1970s and throughout the 1980s, my father, his aunts, and other members of my extended family seemed to thoroughly enjoy watching wrestling. They seemed familiar with the sport, in a way that extended beyond the costumes and trash-talking that characterized the WWF in its day. Due to the early, ongoing exposure to sport, the younger generation of my family, those of us born in the US or who immigrated when very young, had something to talk about with our parents and older relatives that we truly shared. Outside the bounds of education, discipline, family, and heritage, sport was easy and pleasurable to discuss. Without the tension of politics and the disjuncture about tastes in film, art, and literature, sport conversations were accessible. It was easy to watch on television as a group, especially in the 1970s and 1980s, when sports broadcasting was simple and analog, and commercials were not as fixed on pharmaceuticals aimed at men's virility. Viji was open to watching any sports that her grandnieces and -nephews were excited about, including soccer, which was popular with younger members of our family in India and the United States.

In case it seems like my family never left the living room, we did have a robust period of attending live sporting events. We happily attended the company picnic, at which my father participated in the softball game while my younger brother and I did the sack races and tug of war for kids. Everyone in my father's company—both factory and management workers alike—were given a chance to take their families to Shea Stadium for baseball and football games. His company continued to buy Jets season tickets when the team moved to the Meadowlands. For my father and his co-workers, going to that box was "like a family tradition"—people brought their kids, and grandkids too. Employees would share extra tickets with others they didn't know as well within the company so that everyone had the chance to share in the experience of the game. "Baseball is like a family game—entertainment for the whole family. In those days you could go early during practice, and the players would sign autographs on the ball. Then it became big business and they stopped doing the signing." My father took me to Shea every year, at least once per season. I can't fully rely on the accuracy of those early memories, as I was only around six or seven years old, but I vividly remember the visceral sensation of going to the game: it was simultaneously incredibly thrilling and unimaginably boring. As a young girl, I had no first-hand experience of baseball, and my father's knowledge was quite limited as well. We seemed to figure it out together, especially because our seats were so amazing and my father prioritized taking me, even though he probably would have enjoyed the game more with his male colleagues or friends. Sitting about ten rows behind the third-base line, we could direct our gazes to the players' facial expressions, observe their slight hand twitches, and occasionally feel the grit of sand in our teeth generated by a player sliding into home.

Growing up, our most exciting outings were to sports events. My family didn't follow Hollywood movies, and the only English-language film I recall seeing with them in the theater was *Gandhi*. We went to Bollywood movies when theaters began to show them, but ours was not a family that frequented museums, galleries, ballet, or orchestral performances. Of course, we went to South Indian Karnatic dance performances and music concerts staged in local auditoriums or peoples' homes. As far as public spectator events went, sports was it. Over the years, as my brother and I grew up and moved out of the house, we still met our dad for various games. We were socialized to attend games a certain way. We had to show up before the national anthem and be in place for the first pitch. We were taught to be present for the entire game, unless it was a complete blowout. Exiting a crowded stadium was a precision act for my father, and my brother and I scrambled to keep up with him. Moving as if he had a stadium map for each venue etched in his brain, my father would weave through tipsy crowds of fans to make it out of the building and to his car in record time. He implied that parking nose first in a stadium lot was a sign of dangerously low intelligence and basically meant being among the last to leave. Backing in and noting the nearest exit (often different than the entrance) was the only way to properly navigate the experience.

Although his enthusiasm for American sports in general has endured, tennis and golf seem to be the ones he still shares with his Indian social networks. He seems comparatively alone in his American football fandom: "There are still people in our community who say, 'Look at football! I don't even know what they're doing, they're all falling on each other. They call it football and they touch it with their hands.'" His arguments that it is a game of "fine movements, finer aspects" fall on deaf ears, but he maintains, "I think it's amazing that someone who weighs 250 pounds can run a hundred yards in 12 seconds. Moreover, the bounce of the ball when fumbled is completely unpredictable—another element that makes it highly entertaining." In my family, however, he has little trouble gathering an audience for the game, and notably, one that is not entirely male.

As the years wore on, we tuned into live sporting events as they were happening, and discussed them in the hours following, creating something shared that would impact each of us differently. My brother would take his love of sports into all aspects of his play and social life, well into college and post-college life. He wrote a sports column for the *Columbia Daily Spectator* and considered a position at ESPN before deciding to keep sports a hobby and mild obsession rather than career as well. For me, these memories and current practices remain an anticipatory space that is unpredictable and exciting, allowing a convening of generations, genders, and otherwise divergent interests. Celebrating victories, "smack talking" about teams we dislike, and supporting one another during crushing defeats has only brought us closer—an unlikely family glue. Of course we share numerous other interests, but sport remains an interest and priority. We try to make it out to CitiField now that Shea Stadium is no longer, MetLife Stadium instead of the Meadowlands, and to the USTA Billy Jean King National Tennis Center at least once a year. We try to meet up with cousins and catch games in other cities as we travel. At the very least, we watch football during major holidays, try to coordinate our US Open ticket buying, and text each other during games.

Intergenerational relations among immigrant groups such as these bear noticing, especially because sport passing from men to boys is complicated by the strong presence of women, like my great aunts or the role I play in my son's life and hope to play in my daughter's as she finds her own relationship with our shared interests. With my chittis and elder relatives ready to tune into whatever game we wanted to watch, sports viewing was never a male-dominated activity in my family. This certainly differs from broader responses I have observed in the desi community and beyond being a sports fan. Especially as a female academic, I have seen that prioritizing watching tennis, football, basketball, and other competitions live or on television has not made as much sense to my colleagues, and this is the most I have ever discussed it. Spectating seriously has its own value in many social worlds, as it certainly did in my family. For generations, women have been considered serious spectators and knowledge was not passed just from men to women, but from aunts to nephews, from mothers to sons, and so on. While there is no dearth of sources for sports knowledge in my own household, my nine-year-old son has myriad sport questions on our daily walks to school. My brother generously took me on as a fantasy football protégé and proudly watched me win my first championship as the only woman in my league. Several years later, I established a family fantasy football league with aunts, cousins, parents, and family friends and am now my father's mentor—a first for me. Together we managed a team in which I made the lion's share of decisions as he watched and collaborated. We text each other about our team, about the Jets and NFL injury reports, as well as during the US Open. My brother and I do as well, and add new events as we go. This year we texted throughout the National Spelling Bee, which we started to watch in tandem from different locations.

Concluding Thoughts

"So sports kind of ran in the family, and it is one of our genes," my father laughed as we wrapped up our conversation. I had to laugh too, wondering if spectator skills, like athletic ability, could also be inherited. Perhaps the more important matter to consider is the often unnoticed ways that sport is integral to immigrant lives. Over the past decade, I have observed that my family of early adopters is no longer so unusual, as sport has become so much more prevalent among desis and Asian Americans more broadly. In an era of NBA star Jeremy Lin, golfer Vijay Singh, and numerous Pacific Islanders on NFL teams, our connections to sport are far less mediated through whiteness or born of marginality. They do, however, complicate the range of generational experiences and how each finds a place in America. There are so many small ways that sport spectatorship can be rewarding. My uncle Shekhar, who has been a loyal spectator at the US Open since the 1970s, was surprised to once find himself in the pages of *Tennis* magazine:

> The side courts at Flushing Meadows [now the USTA Billy Jean King Tennis Center] are generally packed with large crowds waiting forever outside to get a chance to go in. There are a few spectators who give up waiting in line to get in and instead get a glimpse of the game by peeking through the fence that surrounds the court. In 1985, TENNIS magazine was going to run a story on this and their field photographer was roaming the grounds looking for these folks peeking through the openings in the

fence. I happened to be one, squatting on the ground with a BOAC air bag over my shoulder and intensely observing the match inside!

Being on the outside looking in is often the overriding theme of the immigrant experience, at least for first-generation immigrants. Finding a way in is far more challenging, but ultimately can be so much more rewarding. Over the years, my relatives have moved to different regions of New York City and other parts of the state and the country, and developed a wide range of interests. Their love of sport, however, has remained unwavering, acting at once as entertainment, a social bond, and a way to find a place in American society at a time when far less was established for new immigrants. Embracing new sports, becoming more invested in familiar ones, and learning how to talk the talk about them, all played an important role in finding a way into pockets of American society.

It wasn't until my twenties that I realized that my experience was somewhat atypical, and that if sport was as avidly watched in other immigrant families, I had no way of knowing. "The cultural stakes surrounding sport are greater than they may at first appear," Birrell and McDonald contend, identifying areas of importance including "hegemonic masculinity, heteronormativity, economic power, and white privilege" (2000:13). But what if we consider the cultural stakes from a different perspective, from that of marginalized Americans trying to find a place in this country? Studies of migration and diaspora systematically come up short when considering sports as part of a gendered, immigrant experience, but such an inquiry can be a vital link to understanding dynamics of acculturation, gender, and sociability.

NOTES

1 See Shankar (2008) for a fuller discussion of intergenerational commonalties and differences among South Asian American communities in Silicon Valley.

2 See Shukla (2002).

3 For an examination of fandom and critique of the state and national identity, see Thomas Carter's (2007) exploration of Cuban baseball.

REFERENCES

Adair, Daryl, and David Rowe. 2010. "Beyond Boundaries." *International Review for the Sociology of Sport* 45(3): 251–257.

Alter, Joseph S. 1992. *The Wrestler's Body: Identity and Ideology in North India*. Berkeley: University of California Press.

Appadurai, Arjun. 1995. "Playing with Modernity: The Decolonization of Indian Cricket." In *Consuming Modernity: Public Culture in a South Asian World*, ed. C. A. Breckenridge, pp. 23–48. Minneapolis: University of Minnesota Press.

Barthes, Roland. 1972. *Mythologies*. New York: Macmillan.

Bairner, Alan. 2001. *Sport, Nationalism, and Globalization: European and North American Perspectives*. Albany: State University of New York.

Besnier, Niko, and Susan Brownwell. 2010. "Sport, Modernity, and the Body." *Annual Review of Anthropology* 41: 443–459.

Birrell, Susan, and Mary McDonald. 2000. "Reading Sport, Articulating Power Lines: An Introduction." In *Reading Sport: Critical Essays on Power and Representation*, ed. Susan Birrell and Mary G. McDonald, pp. 3–13. Lebanon, NH: University Press of New England.

Burdsey, Daniel. 2010. "British Muslim Experiences of English First-Class Cricket." *International Review for the Sociology of Sport* 45(3): 315–334.

Carter, Thomas F. 2007. "Family Networks, State Interventions and the Experience of Cuban Transnational Sport Migration." *International Review for the Sociology of Sport* 42(4): 371–389.

Clarke, Irvine, and Ryan Mannion. 2006. "Marketing Sport to Asian-American Consumers." *Sports Marketing Quarterly* 15: 20–28.

Dyck, Noel. 2004. "Getting into the Game: Anthropological Perspectives on Sport: Introduction." *Anthropologica* 46(1): 3–8.

Fletcher, Thomas. 2012. "Who Do 'They' Cheer For? Cricket, Diaspora, Hybridity and Divided Loyalties amongst British Asians." *International Review for the Sociology of Sport* 47(5): 612–631.

Joo, Rachel M. 2012. *Transnational Sport: Gender, Media, and Global Korea*. Durham, NC: Duke University Press.

Joseph, Janelle. 2012. "Culture, Community, Consciousness: The Caribbean Sporting Diaspora." *International Review for the Sociology of Sport* 49(6): 669–687.

Leach, Jerry, and Gary Kildea. 1975. *Trobriand Cricket: An Ingenious Response to Colonialism*. Video rec., produced by Office of Information.

Rowe, David. 2003. *Sport, Culture, and Media*. New York: McGraw-Hill.

Shankar, Shalini. 2008. *Desi Land: Teen Culture, Class, and Success in Silicon Valley*. Durham, NC: Duke University Press.

———. 2015. *Advertising Diversity: Ad Agencies and the Creation of Asian American Consumers*. Durham, NC: Duke University Press.

Shukla, Sandhya Rajendra. 2002. *India Abroad: Diasporic Cultures of Postwar America and England*. Princeton, NJ: Princeton University Press.

Thangaraj, Stanley I. 2010. "Ballin' Indo-Pak Style: Pleasures, Desires, and Expressive Practices of 'South Asian American' Masculinity." *International Review for the Sociology of Sport* 45(3): 372–389.

———. 2015. *Desi Hoop Dreams: Pickup Basketball and the Making of Asian American Masculinity*. New York: New York University Press.
Turner, Victor. 1982. *From Ritual to Theatre: The Human Seriousness of Play*. New York: Performing Arts Journal Publications.
Wallace, Tim. 2009. "The Soccer Wars: Hispanic Immigrants in Conflict and Adaptationat the Soccer Borderzone." *Napa Bulletin* 31: 64–77.
Walle, Thomas. 2010. *A Passion for Cricket: Masculinity, Ethnicity, and Diasporic Spaces in Oslo*. Unpublished PhD Thesis, University of Oslo, Norway.

PART II

Asian American Sporting Celebrities

3

Everybody Loves an Underdog

Learning from Linsanity

OLIVER WANG

It began, as things often do these days, with an item that popped into my Facebook newsfeed on Sunday, February 5, 2012. Several friends shared the same story of how the New York Knicks' fourth-string point guard, Jeremy Lin, had enjoyed a spectacular game the previous evening. A few posts linked back to the *New York Daily News*' recap of the game, which announced, "It's Lin-sanity! Knicks Score Win Over Nets."[1]

That headline may have helped popularize the pun but it hardly invented it.[2] Even during the game, a "#linsanity" hashtag began appearing on Twitter, mostly from Knicks' fans using it to punctuate their marvel at Lin's performance in real time.[3] After that first day, "Linsanity" had morphed into meme, becoming so ascendant that (1) Lin himself trademarked the term on February 13, (2) *Time* used it for the magazine's February 27 cover story, and (3) it eventually became the name of a hagiographic documentary dedicated to Lin's career from high school through his season with the Knicks.[4]

As far as puns go, Linsanity works at least two ways: it lends a pithy name to the phenomenon that surrounded Lin and serves as an apt description for the giddy illogic that accompanied it. People "went crazy" for Lin, expressing an exuberant irrationality for his playing ability and general character. But beyond that, the phenomenon itself felt maddeningly out of control, with a cacophony of voices continually trying to make sense of it all, my own included.

In early March, barely a month after that February 4 game, I had published 6,000 words on the topic for the *Los Angeles Review of Books*.[5] It was written as "retro-diary," an attempt to revisit some of the key narratives that erupted during just the first three weeks of the phenomenon.

At the time, I wrote, "How can anyone make sense of an experience when they're still in the midst of it?" Yet, even now, over three years later, I don't know if it's become any easier to parse the myriad ideas and issues that have bobbed up in the wake of Linsanity's initial splash. To be sure, this entire anthology could have been dedicated solely to analyzing Linsanity along any number of compelling vectors. My goal with this essay is to revisit/extend what I began in 2012, an attempt to—forgive the pun—advance the ball further down the court. For this iteration, I want to focus on the tangled threads involving Lin's racial difference as an Asian American, plucking out the competing, sometimes contradictory stock narratives that mainstream media writers spun about the importance of Lin, his racial background, and its relevance to sports and society.

* * *

To start, I find it useful to frame Linsanity as a time-delimited phenomenon, one that formally began on February 4, 2012, hit its peak over the next three weeks, and then quietly tapered off over the next month before all but officially ending on March 24, the day Lin sustained a torn meniscus in his knee, an injury that would end his season—and thus career—with the Knicks.[6] Given the incredible pace at which sports media creates, advances, and then abandons various storylines, Linsanity felt like it had ended weeks prior, especially after Lin's seemingly magic touch could no longer prop up a troubled Knicks team struggling through multigame losing and winning streaks *and* a head coaching switch, all of which happened over the first 50 days.[7] Those two months or so constitute a loose—but still discrete—unit for analysis, what writer Jay Caspian Kang calls "the original Jeremy Lin story," which is the story of Linsanity itself.

As I explore in the remainder of this essay, as rambunctious as Linsanity felt as a phenomenon, the various narrative threads around it quickly coalesced into familiar stock stories, that is, stories that explain, affirm, and justify "the world as it is."[8] Whether you describe them as parables, narratives, or otherwise, stories are a basic but fundamental way through which social groups establish and reinforce shared realities. As Richard Delgado puts it, "stories build consensus, a common culture of understandings, and deeper, more vital ethics."[9] Among the different narratives and counternarratives that may exist to frame a particular concept or phenomenon, the "stock story" is one that flattens the social reality of the dominant group, valorizing its values, celebrating its conventions.

Linsanity, in its earliest moments, felt like a rupture in those conventions, given how Lin challenged public expectations about Asian American athleticism, particularly in a professional league dominated by black and white bodies. However, over the ensuing days and weeks, reporters and pundits in mainstream publications quickly assimilated various angles to Lin's rise into familiar stock stories, not just about American sporting culture but of American society itself. In particular, the popular framing of Lin as an *underdog* became a way to reinforce traditional beliefs around the "American Dream" and Asian Americans as so-called model minority. For Delgado, underdog stories are supposed to offer counternarratives to confront or destabilize stock stories but, as I suggest here, the Lin-as-underdog theme allowed writers to wedge Linsanity back into a conservatively ideological framework lest his racial difference threaten to disturb dominant notions of race, opportunity, the NBA, and American society.

* * *

Almost from the very beginning of Linsanity, writers sought to describe Lin's rising notoriety via the popular sports cliché of being "more than just a game." This is hardly unusual in sports writing; as basketball analyst Zach Lowe puts it, "The need to turn games into something grander is natural. It can feel silly to invest so much anguish into a game that doesn't hold larger metaphysical importance."[10] With Lin, I suggested in March 2012 that "his story has become a loom for a skein of narratives through which myriad constituencies weave their needs and desires."[11] Of those "myriad constituencies," my primary interest has been in so-called "mainstream media" reporters, columnists, and pundits—i.e., people writing for newspapers, magazines, and high-traffic websites. Those outlets constituted a powerful, formative echo chamber that amplified numerous angles and story lines that have since become part of the story of Linsanity itself (however accurately or not).

As I return to at the end of the essay, these mainstream outlets were hardly the only ones shaping stories around Lin. In an insightful forum discussion on "Asian American Studies after Linsanity," in the *Amerasia Journal*, Konrad Ng convincingly argues that "Linsanity solidified the digital world as the preeminent site for Asian American cultural activism and scholarship."[12] In doing so, it also empowered Asian American writers to assert their voices just as they were also seeing themselves get constructed in those same spaces; it was the headiest of discursive times. For all this however, those countervoices were still often reacting to what was being said/written in the mainstream press. The latter's musings on Linsanity became its own cottage industry in a remarkably short period of time.

To offer some perspective on the pace/volume of the media's Linsanity industry, consider that when NBA superstar LeBron James televised his decision to leave the Cleveland Cavaliers for the Miami Heat in 2010, at least 1,500 news articles appeared about the event—dubbed "The Decision"—during the 30 days after. However, there were *over twice* as many news stories about Jeremy Lin in the 30 days after his February 4 game.[13] Even the term "linsanity" itself appeared in at least 1,278 stories during that same time frame. The interest in Lin/Linsanity grew at a seemingly exponential pace. The first week saw hundreds of stories appearing, but the second and third weeks saw *thousands*.[14] With that kind of volume of stories being generated, even reporting-on-the-reporting-of-Linsanity became a popular story. For two days, the most read story on the *Wall Street Journal*'s website, *WSJ.com*, wasn't even directly about Lin but rather was a profile of a part-time blogger and FedEx deliveryman who had predicted Lin's rise two years before.[15] Much like pop, news will eat itself too.

There were myriad factors behind how/why Linsanity became the media phenomenon it did. At the very least, the fact that it happened in the largest media market in the U.S. is surely relevant.[16] Moreover, as Kathleen Yep astutely asserts, "the rocket speed and broad scope of Linsanity" also reflects "the many dimensions of sport as a transnational corporate/entertainment complex."[17] But Linsanity couldn't have been manufactured purely through the will of news outlets. It seems unimaginable that media corporations would collude to push a story of a Taiwanese American basketball player unless there was already an initial story galvanizing public demand for more content. That particular hook, the *ur*-story at the core of Linsanity, was, of course, Lin-as-underdog.[18]

* * *

The appeal of the underdog has deep roots in American culture. It is carried in core Judeo-Christian parables—David and Goliath, for example. It's become part of the American mythos of competitive individualism, as enshrined in the rags-to-riches tales written by pulp novelist Horatio Alger, Jr. However, nowhere does the valorization of the underdog appear more frequently than in sporting culture. Examples abound in actual events, such as the U.S. hockey team's defeat of the U.S.S.R. at the 1980 Winter Olympics, but it's even more omnipresent in popular culture depictions of sports, from boxing (*Rocky*) to baseball (*Major League*) to football (*The Longest Yard, Rudy*) to basketball (*Hoosiers*). The specter of the underdog has become so embedded in American sporting culture that for any given game, spectators and commentators seem inevitably drawn to establishing one player/team as the underdog, regardless if the playing field is relatively even or not.[19]

Technically, the underdog simply refers to the player/team expected to lose a competition, but the appeal of the underdog goes beyond betting lines. Writing about the trope in 1954, historian David M. Potter asserted that "American fondness for the underdog is perhaps not so much a matter of sympathy for causes which are losing (America cares little for causes which are lost) as of desire to see the creed of equality proved by the success of those who appear less than equal."[20] In other words, we champion underdogs not just to see them beat the odds but to see them overcome some kind of injustice that explains those odds. The underdog is an implicitly aggrieved actor, someone who has been treated unfairly and, therefore, their struggle to succeed is inherently redemptive, rather than just statistically unlikely. To put it a different way, in the words of sports writer Brian Phillips, "you don't root for underdogs if, because of innocence or its opposite, you see the game as a metaphor for the world as it ought to be. You start rooting for underdogs when you see the game as a metaphor for the world as it is," which is to say, unfairly rigged for the benefit of the already privileged and powerful.[21]

In that regard, it's compelling to consider how one of the common framings of Linsanity was that Lin embodied something quintessentially "American." On February 13, the *New York Daily News* ran a Mike Lupica story titled "Jeremy's Tale All American"; the online version of the story included the swollen subhead "In the land of opportunity, Lin finally gets his chance and makes the most of it."[22] Not to be outdone, the next day, the *Wall Street Journal*'s syndicated columnist Mark Simon wrote an essay titled "Jeremy Lin Is All American" (subtitled, in case the headline was ambiguous, "Jeremy Lin is a great American story").[23] The fraternal twin to this theme was that Lin was "the American Dream given athletic form."[24] Some stories, such as Lupica's, used *both* loaded phrases and their invocation wasn't limited to just media personnel. In Connecticut, Democratic senate candidate William Tong invoked Lin—and himself—as American Dream success stories in a campaign email that, however self-serving for Tong, made plain how Lin was being celebrated: "[Lin's] the underdog who made it. He's living the American Dream. The dream I've lived, the dream Jeremy Lin is living, is the dream we can all live."[25]

As suggested, the Lin-as-underdog angle may be ostensibly framed as an "against all odds" parable but in the end, these stories merely reify a familiar, conservative worldview of American meritocracy and exceptionalism. The stock story of Lin's rise becomes a seductive affirmation of the American Dream's attainability (despite the fact that it's called "a dream"). However, as Lin is also Asian American, the framing of his accomplishments within the American Dream narrative aligns all too well with another deeply embedded stock story around American race relations: the model minority myth (MMM), that is, the belief that "through hard work and perseverance, Asian Americans supposedly show how any minority can overcome institutionalized inequality."[26] The MMM is, at its core, an underdog narrative as well, in which the immigrant minority stands up to the challenges of assimilation and upward mobility via stoic perseverance and the embrace of dominant/majority social values/norms.[27]

In that regard, Asian Americans who fall under the MMM—primarily well-educated, middle-class East Asians—are all constructed as underdogs, irrespective of their particular life details.[28] In Lin's case, his racial difference already colored him as an underdog before he ever laid a foot onto a gym floor. The remarkable details of his ascent into the NBA certainly burnished things further, but as Maxwell Leung pointed out, the constant discussion of "his hard work and focus—model behavior" made Lin a "poster child" for the MMM as well.[29] Linsanity provided a kind of vicarious experience of unexpected triumph, helping to, as author Eric Liu loftily put it, "[strum] anew those chords of narrative in which anyone with grit, talent and a little luck can make it in America."[30] However, there is an internalized set of contradictions at work here: to embrace Lin as an underdog means acknowledging that part of the unjust challenges he's faced exist because of his racial difference. The American Dream runs up against American race realities.

What accentuated the perceived unlikeliness of Lin's rise was not only his Asianness but that he is an Asian American playing in a league where almost no other Asians participate. As Jay Caspian Kang put it, "During the first few games of Lin's run, it was mentioned early and often that he was the 'first American-born player of Chinese or Taiwanese descent to play in the NBA.' Once the story got knocked off its hinges, that tedious mouthful got spat out for a good, generic 'underdog.'"[31] After all, part of what was inherently implied by constantly describing Lin an "underdog" was the idea that he "came out of nowhere," that is, he was overlooked by basketball personnel at every stage of his career: college recruiters, NBA scouts, coaching staffs on those teams, and so forth. However, while it was all but taken for granted that Lin was overlooked, *why* he was overlooked became a popular topic for discussion by the second week of Linsanity. By then, the Knicks had gone on a seven-game winning streak, with Lin leading the team in both points and assists in most of those. Because of those accomplishments, writers raised the question of how so many professionals, trained to identify NBA-caliber talent, managed to overlook or ignore a player who was—at the time—being compared to some of the all-time great guards in the NBA, including Steve Nash and Magic Johnson.[32] Not surprisingly, the answer that most pundits landed upon was Lin's racial difference.

On February 11, 2012, Barbara Barker, a *Newsday* reporter, dedicated an entire article to the topic ("How Did Jeremy Lin Get Overlooked?"), writing, "at almost every stage of his journey, he has been passed over by those who are paid to judge basketball talent. And those who have followed his career closely believe that his style of play, Ivy League roots and ethnicity all had something to do with that."[33] Similar arguments cropped up in other high-profile pieces from that second week, including on ESPN.com and in the *New York Times* and *USA Today*.[34] The last included several quotes from no less than the U.S. secretary of education, Arne Duncan (like Lin, a former Harvard basketball player, whom Lin had befriended), who forcefully argued that "this is classic low expectations and, frankly, stereotyping. [Lin] was under-appreciated and under-recognized. The fact that he's Asian American, those two things are absolutely linked."[35] Other commentators were far less political; Leland Stein, writing for the *Michigan Chronicle*, declared, "I think Lin is a victim of discrimination. He was overlooked by major collegiate programs and the NBA because he is Asian American. . . . If Lin were African-American he would have been drafted."[36]

As I discuss later, Stein was hardly the only commentator to attempt to explain Linsanity through a comparison to African American players, but for now, it's essential to highlight how the very construction of the model minority myth presumes that there are "model" minorities and therefore, "less than model" minorities, that is, African and Latino Americans. As the MMM came about as a counter to civil rights and nationalist movements of the 1960s and 1970s, Asian Americans framed by the MMM always exist in relation to other communities of color. That meant that Lin's entry into a predominantly African American league would almost certainly invite commentators to compare his rise with that of African American players. As Leung argued, Lin's educational background as a Harvard alum was an oft-cited part of the Linsanity narrative, thus reifying established binaries where Asians (and whites) receive praise for their mental gifts whereas African Americans are prized for their physical capabilities.[37] This idea that "if Lin had been Black, he wouldn't have been overlooked" was repeated by others, the suggestion being that Lin's racial difference lengthened his odds for success and thus, once again, establishes his underdog bona fides.

For his part, Lin largely avoided addressing this specific angle during the Linsanity period, but by 2013, he was affirming its basic tenets during an interview with *60 Minutes*.[38] It was also echoed, repeatedly, in the *Linsanity* documentary. For my part, I think one can have a healthy debate over whether Lin was (1) overlooked and, if so, (2) if that was due to racial stereotypes and/or "basketball reasons."[39] Either way, what's noteworthy is how the framing of Lin's underdog status was not merely linked to race; the two were treated as mutually constitutive. As I suggested earlier, underdogs earn our affections and passions partially because they serve as proxies for the *unjustly* underestimated and overlooked. During Linsanity, Lin's racial difference as an Asian American seemed sufficient to establish an a priori conclusion that he had been treated unfairly, thus enhancing his underdog aura.[40]

Especially by Linsanity's second and third weeks, race and ethnicity had practically become *de rigueur* themes within Lin's mainstream coverage and this represented an interesting moment of potential rupture, where an acknowledgement of racial hardship could have threatened to undermine the "feel good" dynamic of the early stock stories around Linsanity. Writers essentially created the conditions under which they were forced to address race, even if only then pivot to suggesting how Linsanity "transcended" or "went beyond" racial issues. Nonetheless, writers couldn't downplay race too heavily because they had already deployed Lin's racial difference as an integral part to the narrative around him to begin with, especially in framing Linsanity as an "all-American" or a fulfillment of the American Dream.[41]

To talk about Lin's appeal as being "all-American" may ostensibly seem like a move away from racial difference, to position him as a national figure, not just limited to an ethnic community. However, because pundits presumed that Lin had been overlooked *because* of his racial difference, two narratives merged: (1) Lin demonstrated all-American spirit by succeeding in an American society that (2) makes it hard for minorities to succeed. The first, as I've suggested, is a familiar enough stock story, but the latter is more destabilizing as it implies that racial difference is a hardship in a supposedly postracial society. Few (if any) commentators explicitly made this connection, but the insinuations were often there, intentional or not. In one of the more surreal moments during Linsanity, on Februrary 16, 2012, former Alaska governor-turned-conservative-media-celebrity Sarah Palin appeared on the Fox Business Network, brandishing a Knicks T-shirt and proclaiming her affection for Lin, saying, "I mean, talk about an all-American story where sort of the underdog, you know, but works so hard, just erased all the stuff out there on the periphery in his life."[42] Palin didn't specify the "stuff out there on the periphery in his life," but it's difficult to imagine that his racial difference wasn't being implicated. If so, Palin was implicitly suggesting that what it means to be "all-American" is to rise above the challenge of being Asian in America.

In another example, syndicated columnist Esther Cepeda expressed:

Watching Lin-sanity take root has been simultaneously uplifting and horrifying. Wonderful seeing a U.S.-born son or daughter of immigrants fulfill the promise of the American dream while being cheered on by basketball fans of every color and age. But a real drag to see racism against Asians and Asian-Americans.[43]

The anti-Asian racism Cepeda was referring to was the decision by Ben & Jerry's to create a "Taste the Lin-Sanity" ice cream flavor that included crumbled fortune cookie bits. Cepeda argued that these kinds of stereotype-driven jokes detracted from her enjoyment of Lin's fulfillment of "the promise of the American dream" as the "son . . . of immigrants." However, implicit in Cepeda's invocation of Lin's immigrant roots is that part of what Lin had to overcome was the challenge of having grown up Asian/minority/immigrant. In other words, if Lin hadn't faced barriers as the son of Asian immigrants, would his story be so "wonderful" or American Dream-y? Cepeda suggests that the "uplifting" and "horrifying" aspects to Linsanity contradict one another, but I would argue they actually complement one another. Without intending to, Cepeda describes the interplay of these two forces accurately when she says they coexist "simultaneously." One might also say, symbiotically.[44]

However, writers seemed to have difficulty in reconciling that duality. In a *New York Times* article specifically about how "Media Hype for Lin Stumbles on Race," the *Wall Street Journal*'s Jason Gay was quoted, "I think once you get past all of these interesting variables of race, it is the quintessential underdog story," while the article's author (Carr) himself writes, "The Lin story has broken out into the general culture because it is aspirational in the extreme, fulfilling notions that have nothing to do with basketball or race."[45] However, as I suggest, Lin became an aspirational figure and the embodiment of a "quintessential underdog story" precisely because of those "interesting variables of race." Remove Lin's racial difference and it irrevocably changes the Linsanity narrative.

Race also fueled one of the other narratives concerning Linsanity's spread: the novelty factor. Few writers articulated what this meant better than *Sports Illustrated*'s Pablo Torre, who told Carr:

I think there is every kind of demographic outlier in play with this story. The beating heart of the story, no matter what anybody says, is the fact that he is Asian-American. Yes, the N.B.A. has Yao Ming, but Jeremy is normal-size and from this country, so it creates this huge cognitive dissonance. There is a novelty factor to seeing someone who looks like Jeremy doing this.[46]

By using the phrase "no matter what anybody says," Torre was highlighting an implicit tension: people might have taken interest in Lin partially because of the novelty factor, but some wouldn't want to admit to it.[47]

To be sure, Torre's argument here feels rather strawman. Overwhelmingly, other commentators also recognized the "novelty factor" in Linsanity. Torre wasn't asserting a contrarian opinion; he was stating conventional wisdom. However, acknowledging that there was a racial novelty to Linsanity and attributing *all* of the phenomenon's power to race are entirely different arguments. Enter boxer Floyd Mayweather, Jr., who tweeted out on February 13: "Jeremy Lin is a good player but all the hype is because he's Asian. Black players do what he does every night and don't get the same praise."[48]

In one sense, Mayweather's sentiment wasn't wildly different from Torre's—albeit far more overstated and far less tactful—but by explicitly discussing Lin's racial difference in the manner it did, the Mayweather tweet helped fuel a paroxysm of outrage on Lin's behalf. There were other examples too, all within a week of one another. Fox Sports's Jason Whitlock sent out a crude, racist and sexist tweet on February 10, after the Knicks unexpectedly defeated the Los Angeles Lakers: "Some lucky lady in NYC is gonna feel a couple inches of pain tonight."[49] Then there was ESPN.com's controversial "Chink in the Armor" headline from the evening of February 17, after the Linsanity winning streak was broken by the New Orleans Hornets.[50] These three incidents, among others, helped to open the proverbial flood gates within the media to now tackle racial difference head on, rather than in more indirect ways such as referring to Lin as the "first American-born Chinese or Taiwanese player" or the like. Lin's underdog status wasn't simply being fueled by arguments of past discrimination, but pundits could now point to examples happening in real time.

One of the most ironic outcomes was how articles defending Lin from being singled out for his racial difference often times ended up emphasizing his racial difference, especially by placing him firmly within a model minority framework. The *Wall Street Journal*'s Asia correspondent Mark Simon wrote an online piece subtitled "Jeremy Lin is a great American story"; within it, he tried to situate Lin within a broader context of immigrant success: "Chinese-American success in the U.S. is no secret. Few immigrant groups have a more impressive economic, educational and civic record."[51] *Fox Sports* columnist Jen Floyd Engel took it one step further, drawing upon Amy Chua's "tiger mother" ideology to discuss how Lin's ethnic heritage helped explain his NBA success, all draped in neoliberalizing posturing:

> His being Asian-American is exactly why I am not surprised by Lin's success in the NBA. And I am predicting more and more kids like Lin, raised to emphasize academics, to dominate athletics as already has happened in mathematics and engineering, law schools and medical schools, and almost every inch of an ever-tightening global job market.[52]

Not to be outdone, New York University professor Jonathan Zimmerman penned an op-ed for the *Wall Street Journal*, invoking the model minority myth by suggesting:

> I'm troubled by the much-heard refrain that Lin—whose parents are Taiwanese immigrants—has "overcome the Asian stereotype." In the popular mind, this story goes, Asian Americans are quiet, studious and really good at math. By scoring 20 or more points in each of his first six NBA starts, including 38 against Kobe Bryant and the Los Angeles Lakers, Lin supposedly dealt a decisive blow against an insidious ethnic caricature. But isn't that stereotype—especially the part about studying hard—a very good model to follow? Why should anyone want or need to "overcome" it?[53]

Zimmerman then uses the remainder of his essay to somehow relate Lin's story to the history of anti-Asian admissions policies at Ivy League universities, using a logic that could be charitably described as "stretched." These too are all variations on the underdog theme, emphasizing Lin's "hard work" and "perseverance" as keys to his excellence; underdogs never randomly find success, they always have to earn or achieve it. As Zimmerman demonstrates, the MMM and underdog narratives align so well because both are premised around a stock-story valorization of meritocratic, competitive individualism.

However, it bears repeating that meritocracy for the "model" group—Asian Americans in this case—is always evaluated in comparison to "nonmodel" minorities, namely Latino and African Americans. The previous examples imply this by holding up Chinese/Taiwanese Americans as *exceptional* success stories, thus suggesting that there are nonexceptional groups by comparison. However, with the Mayweather tweet and other incidents of alleged anti-Asian sentiment directed toward Lin, other commentators rallied around Lin and explicitly drew on racial comparisons, arguing that Lin might actually face greater prejudice than other people of color.

In the aforementioned Cepeda op-ed, she argues, "let's face it, [anti-Asian racism] hasn't been as openly discussed as that against blacks and Hispanics."[54] Likewise, a *Washington Post* article following the Mayweather incident quotes media activist Guy Aoki claiming, "we're more sensitive to black history in this society," while the *Guardian's* Hadley Freeman responded to the ESPN headline specifically by arguing, "while no one would claim that racism against black people is no longer a problem in America, it is unthinkable that any news network or even half-brained TV presenter would use racial slurs against a black player equivalent to the Asian ones that have been used against Lin."[55]

In effect, Lin's stature—and body—became sites through which commentators sought to work through race, racializations, and racial stratification. These examples not only tried to make anti-Asian racism legible via comparisons to discrimination faced by other communities of color, but they asserted a kind of quantifiable hierarchy where one group's experiences with racism can be placed above or below another's. As David Leonard described in his own analysis of Linsanity, "'Asianness' has often located Asian Americans outside of African American blackness, which is to say, 'above' African Americans in the racial economy," adding later, "Lin's place in the media sporting culture, and society at large, cannot be understood outside its relationship to blackness."[56] Clearly, for some commentators, Linsanity became a way to process race in the NBA through a new lens, one where Linsanity could be celebrated as what Leonard called an "antidote to the NBA's ills—its blackness."[57] In other words, in a league where black bodies and the specter of blackness itself is under constant scrutiny and criticism, Linsanity provided a "feel good" story that allowed commentators to simultaneously address and dismiss blackness by positing that Lin's experiences in the NBA were "even worse" than that of other players of color.

In that respect, it can never be said that Linsanity somehow "transcended" race. Instead, to borrow from David Andrews, what happened with Linsanity was not a transcendence, but rather, a displacement.[58] In trying to articulate Lin's racial difference, pundits ended up also redirecting attention toward the black athlete as the dominant—and problematic—force in the NBA, enjoying privileges that Lin-the-underdog does not. Ironically, in trying to counter overstated racial comparisons, these responses ended up making their own overstated racial comparisons, especially in suggesting that Lin faced greater racial hardship as an Asian man in a black league.

In these ways, mainstream writers managed to quell potentially disruptive narratives around race by consistently assimilating Linsanity back into a variety of stock stories about Asian American perseverance, African American unruliness, and at the root, the power of the American Dream to reconcile this all. As the above examples suggest, Lin's racial difference continually perturbs the waters since to laud his underdog-ness is to acknowledge that "race matters," but in the end, his story is also used to reinforce a deeply conservative belief in American exceptionalism.

To accent that point, it's worth noting how often Linsanity-related headlines often used some variation on "lessons learned" or "what Linsanity teaches." Lin's story seemed to particularly inspire writers to discuss him within a "teachable moments" framing, least of all when it came to racial issues: "Jeremy Lin, race and lessons learned" (ESPN.com), "Hoopla over Lin a lesson for us all" (*South China Morning Post*), "Lin's lessons for African Americans" (*Philadelphia Inquirer*), et. al.[59] To be sure, many of these articles were well-intentioned and one could argue that any discourse on race in mainstream media is potentially productive, but what's significant here is that writers felt like they were meant to "learn something" from Linsanity to begin with. The idea that Linsanity should be "teachable" speaks to the frequent ways in which commentators sought to frame Lin's rise as a stock parable about humility, hard work, overcoming obstacles, and the like.[60]

* * *

In revisiting the Linsanity era, I kept thinking about something Jay Caspian Kang wrote in late March 2012: "This much is clear: We still haven't figured out how to talk about Asian Americans."[61] In particular, he stressed how the underdog narrative largely fixed Lin into a familiar set of Asian American archetypes, i.e., "the nerdy kid who, through hard work and natural intelligence, pulls himself into good standing."[62] However, Kang pushed back, arguing that this doesn't accurately describe Lin's personality as a player:

> Instead, we have a 23-year-old kid who dunks, keeps the ball for himself in pressure situations, preens, chest bumps, and gets caught up in Kim Kardashian rumors. The public record of Jeremy Lin might show a modest kid who praises Jesus, but that's not how he conducts himself on the court.[63]

In poring through Linsanity coverage from that era, it became clear that, to the extent that writers attempted to frame Lin through discussion of race/ethnicity, the vast majority suffered from being inaccurate/incomplete in the way Kang detailed. Lin's racial difference was oft-mentioned, but it was also wedged into time-worn, prefabricated narratives of Asian Americanhood rather than interrogated as part of an effort to understand Lin and Linsanity on their own, unique terms. Perhaps it's (ironically) cliché of me to describe this as a "missed opportunity," but given the general paucity of Asian American coverage within the mainstream media, it's easy to feel like Linsanity was, at times, (mis)appropriated by mainstream media writers who sought to capitalize on intense public interest. The Linsanity phenomenon's explosive growth was unique and unexpected, but for all its unruliness, mainstream coverage quickly managed to prune it back into more easily recognizable, stock forms, that is, Lin as the humble, plucky underdog, *ad nauseum*. Linsanity should have been a way to examine difference, but in the end, it felt like yet another way to affirm sameness.

The one exception to this—and a fruitful topic for future examination—would be the role that Asian American commentators and writers played in opening up broader/deeper examinations of Lin and Linsanity, both within mainstream media and "alternative" outlets (blogs, social media sites, etc.). Arnold Pan suggested that Linsanity arose at a time when "Asian American Studies was ready for its mainstream media close-up and the field made as much as it could with its time in the national conversation both about Jeremy Lin as well as race in general."[64] I concur but would expand that idea beyond just Asian American studies scholars to suggest that a generation of Asian Americans, capable of articulating nuances of race, identity, and community, were eager, insistent even, to make their proverbial voices heard during the Linsanity era. What's left uncertain is whether that moment was just that—an ephemeral moment—or whether Linsanity helped to alter the media landscape in such a way as to make it more inclusive of Asian American input. In that regard, two to three years isn't sufficient to evaluate the long-term affects of Linsanity; I suspect we'll still be debating these points long after his jersey is retired.

Postscript: Lingering Linsanities

I began writing this essay in May 2014, coincidentally at the time the Jeremy Lin was playing in the first round of the NBA playoffs. By this point in his mercurial career, Lin had gone from the Houston Rocket's starting point guard (PG) in the 2012–13 season to being relegated to the bench. His numbers during the 2013–14 season were, to put it politely, underwhelming: his efficiency rating was below average and he ranked among the worst PGs in terms of both turnover and assist ratios.[65] But then came Game 5, with the Rockets desperate to survive against the upstart Portland Trailblazers.

Lin was asked to start the game in place of an ailing Patrick Beverly, the team's normal starting PG.[66] The pressure on Lin and the entire team was enormous, given that a loss for Houston would have ended their season. Lin ended up having a spectacular game, especially in the second half where he kept Houston afloat through a dazzling bag of defensive plays and scoring tricks: running, teardrop floaters; pull-up jump shots from midrange; an off-balance rainbow with his foot (alas) on the three-point line. The Rockets ended up winning the game with Lin putting up a career playoff high of 21 points (plus four assists and two steals), serving as "a one-man roll of duct tape holding the Rockets together," according to *NBA.com*'s Fran Blinebury.[67] The reporter's post was entitled—what else?—"Linsanity Lets Rockets Keep Heads."

Blinebury was hardly alone in rolling out the pun again; I was following reactions to the game on Twitter and posters there wheeled Linsanity back out too (though many seemed to do so with a self-aware wink). It certainly says something about the enduring appeal of the pun itself, but it also has the inadvertent effect of saddling Lin's better performances as somehow beyond rational comprehension.[68]

That said, I recognize my own complicity in fanning the Linsanity flames over the years. I watched most of the games in that Houston–Portland series, partially because it featured two young, exciting teams, but mostly because I wanted to see Lin play . . . and play well. As this essay was always at the back of my mind, I was constantly interrogating my own impulses: Why was I—a loyal Los Angeles Lakers fan since childhood—invested in watching a playoff series between two of the Lakers' conference rivals?[69] Why did I care if and how Lin played? Why do I care about how he's framed in the media?

I do not buy into the idea—at this point—that Lin is undervalued. I never thought he was one of the best guards in the league (though I hoped he'd at least be above average). But for all that, I still want him to succeed, much as any fan might have for any player, but I recognize that my fandom is marked by factors that, as they say, go "beyond the game." I care because he is, like me, of Chinese/Taiwanese descent. Because I grew up with people like him, i.e., devout Taiwanese American Christians. Because he is the first and still only player of said heritage in the NBA. Because on some base level, I identify with him even if our personal differences far outstrip our similarities. My attachments—or, better said, projections—have not faded much over the intervening years since Linsanity first crested. I still view his performances through a lens that I surely do not apply to any other player for all the reasons I just listed. I recognize this is not reasonable or particularly rational, but that too has always been part of what Linsanity represents.

One of the people I spoke most to about Linsanity as it was happening was my friend/colleague Hua Hsu. He also penned his own analysis for Linsanity in *Amerasia* and his conclusion spoke directly to many of my own conflicted feelings: "Lin's rise has offered Asian American academics and writers an opportunity to rethink our horizons—our relationship to mass culture and pop, assimilation and acceptance, these moments that deliver us from the margins and challenge us to think about what it means to have won."[70] I think this is exactly right, that, at its core, Linsanity was never just a phenomenon about what we thought of or made of Jeremy Lin but also what his story made us think about ourselves.

NOTES

1 Isola, 2012a. Isola, who was one of the *New York Daily News*' main reporters assigned to the Knicks, wrote a number of stories during February 2012 for which the paper's headline writers found a way to work in Jeremy Lin puns, including "Knicks Adopt Lin-Now Look" (a less than intuitive spin on "win-now"), "That's Simply Lin-Credible," and, perhaps most painfully, "He's a Living LIN-Gend."

2 The groundwork for the "Linsanity" pun within the NBA had already been laid down in the late 1990s when writers used the term "Vinsanity" in reference to then Toronto Raptors star Vince Carter (Smith, 1999).

3 Based on Twitter's archives, the first to use the #linsanity hashtag was Alan Hahn. It began trending on the site soon thereafter (Hahn, 2012).

4 Yorkey and Florea, 2013; Gregory, Tso, and Ko, 2012; Leong, 2013.

5 In December 2012, I gave permission to have the *Los Angeles Review of Books* essay reprinted—with a new postscript—in an anthology on Asian Americans and sports (Wang, 2014).

6 Throughout the spring of 2012, sports writers expected that the Knicks would seek to offer Lin a longer-term contract to stay with the team; up until then, he was playing on short-term, provisional contracts. However, in July, the Houston Rockets offered Lin a three-year contract worth $25.1 million and, unexpectedly, the Knicks declined to match it and thus ended Lin's career with the New York team. See Kang, 2012b. Also, in a sad, personal irony, that March 24 game versus the Detroit Pistons was the first and last time I ever saw Lin, in person, playing for the Knicks.

7 Knicks head coach Mike D'Antoni abruptly resigned on March 14, 2012, after the Knicks had lost six straight games (Rymer, 2012). Stephen A. Smith (2012), one of ESPN's most prominent NBA analysts, suggested that D'Antoni's preference for playing Lin over the team's franchise players—Carmelo Anthony and Amar'e Stoudamire—created internal friction that quickly lead to D'Antoni's resignation. Whether Smith's assertions were correct or not is open to considerable debate, but it suggests the ways in which Linsanity all but overshadowed everything that happened in the back half of the Knicks' season. Also, once former assistant coach Mike Woodson took over the team on March 14, the Knicks went 9–2 for the reminder of March, including a five-game winning streak that inspired a string of "Woodsanity" stories (Begley, 2012). For a thorough (and entertaining) breakdown of that Knicks season, I recommend *We'll Always Have Linsanity* by Cavan, Kurylo, Rosenthal, and Silverman (2013).

8 Delgado, 1989: 2421.

9 Ibid.: 2415.

10 Lowe, 2014.

11 Wang, 2012. This certainly had extraspecial meaning for Asian Americans following Linsanity. As Hua Hsu wrote, "Lin became a surface upon which those of us most intrigued by his identity could project the anxieties, histories, and ideas associated with it" (2012: 128).

12 Ng, 2012: 130. I highly recommend the entire *Amerasia* forum of pieces as some of the best analysis of Linsanity from an Asian American studies perspective. My essay is focused elsewhere, but I'd like to think it's also in broad conversation with Hsu, Ng, and Yep (and to be sure, I was in actual, personal conversation with some of them during Linsanity).

13 In both cases, I used the Proquest Newsstand database to search for stories that mentioned both the player and their primary team, i.e., "LeBron James" AND "Cavaliers" and "Jeremy Lin" AND "Knicks" as a way to limit erroneous results (i.e., results about people named "Jeremy Lin" who were not the basketball player).

14 This basic methodology focused on mainstream news sources and didn't include the vast ways in which Linsanity also played out on social media: in posts, tweets, punny gifs, and other memes. Proquest was the most powerful search tool I had access to, but Proquest does not include social media outlets within its database. This is, of course, a major gap, since social media discussions far outnumber those in conventional, journalistic outlets. However, I did not have access to a proper search engine that could have yielded comparable results (for example, Twitter's internal search engine, which does not output aggregate results, only the unique tweets themselves). Therefore, as a compromise—and for the sake of methodological consistency—I used Proquest for all my queries, as its engine does yield aggregate results.

15 The WSJ.com story is Gay, 2012, and its popularity was mentioned in Carr, 2012. WSJ.com went a little "linsane" itself; a sidebar to Gay's story included links to no less than ten *other* stories on the site, all about Lin.

16 I generally avoid counterfactual scenarios, but it is intriguing to wonder how Lin's story might have played out in a smaller market, such as Sacramento, or in a non-U.S. city such as Toronto (would, for example, the latter have complicated the "All American" framings of Linsanity?).

17 Yep, 2012: 135.

18 Lin's teammate Amar'e Stoudamire was one of the first to invoke the u-word, telling reporters that, "I think fans love underdogs here in New York," referring to the crowd at Madison Square Garden chanting Lin's name during that breakout February 4 game (Isola, 2012b). During that first week, about 20 other stories referred to Lin as an "underdog," but by the end of the first month, that number would increase nearly tenfold.

19 For example, both teams that contested the 2014 NBA Finals, the Miami Heat and San Antonio Spurs, had been described as underdogs by different commentators despite the fact that Miami had been to the finals four seasons in a row while the Spurs had won four previous championships since 1999. Going into the finals, the consensus

was that the series would go at least six games, which suggests parity between the two teams rather than one being regarded as massively superior to the other.

20 As quoted in Sagarin, 1970: 427.

21 Phillips, 2014.

22 Lupica, 2012.

23 Simon, 2012.

24 Freeman, 2012.

25 Associated Press/Huffington Post, 2012. There is an odd irony that politicians, who should know something about the fickle, short-lived nature of "success," would be so quick to insist that Lin embodied the American Dream based on less than 14 days of evidence

26 Leung, 2013: 53.

27 After all, we generally treasure underdogs because they "win" while still "playing by the rules"; any other means would be considered deviant and thus undermine the underdog narrative.

28 It's crucial to note that the model minority myth, while typically presumed to apply to all Asian Americans, isn't nearly so inclusive. As other essays in this anthology discuss, certain Asian American groups, such as the Hmong and various Pacific Islander ethnicities, are viewed through framings that work against, or least apart, from the MMM.

29 Leung, 2013: 55.

30 Liu, 2012.

31 Kang, 2012a. In the same article, Kang wryly laid out the narrative arc that news outlets, including his own, developed to tell the Lin story: "In Act One, Jeremy faces down the doubters and all their doubts. In Act Two, he perseveres. In Act Three, perseverance pays off in the greatest city in the world. Along the way, he slays the Cyclops of Stereotypes and sails right on past the rock where the three Kardashian sirens sing their celebrity song."

32 I remember getting into an argument during week two or three of Linsanity with a few friends on Facebook, most of them insisting that Lin was an "elite" player because he was putting up remarkable numbers. While it's true that Lin was playing phenomenally in those first half-dozen games, I kept trying to point out that we were making pronouncements of Lin's long-term worth based on *half a dozen games* (insert obligatory "small sample size" retort). I don't take pleasure in the fact that over the two years since, Lin's performance hasn't just regressed to the mean, it's fallen considerably below it.

33 Barker, 2012.

34 Viera, 2012; Reilly, 2012; Zillgitt, 2012.

35 Zillgitt, 2012.

36 Stein, 2012.

37 Leung, 2013: 55. See also Brooks, 2009; Carrington, 2010.

38 Golgowski, 2013.

39 Because Linsanity happened while Lin was with the Knicks, his time with the Warriors—the first NBA team to sign him—has been less scrutinized. In a candid 2012 interview with then Warriors general manager Larry Riley, the *Mercury News*'s Marcus Thompson II quotes Riley making excuses for then coach Keith Smart, who opted to give journeyman free agent Acie Law more minutes than Lin during the latter's rookie season: "[Lin] should have played more, probably. But you understand where Keith was coming from. He was trying to win games, trying to save his job" (Thompson, 2012). Riley goes on to explain that Lin was eventually waived in December 2011 (which eventually made him available to sign with the Knicks) out of a strategic decision to use the saved contract money towards what would be a failed bid to lure center DeAndre Jordan from the Los Angeles Clippers (ibid.). My point here: without erasing the possibility that the team's expectations of Lin were lower because of his race, there were other, rational reasons the Warriors fell short in recognizing or developing his full potential.

40 This is purely anecdotal, but I recall several social media debates about whether an undrafted white or black player could ever have followed the same career trajectory as Lin and the consensus (largely among Asian American discussants) was that no white or black player would have gone overlooked for so long. Again, whether I agree with that assessment or not, its tenaciousness suggests the powerful ways in which Lin's Asianness was a key subnarrative to his celebration as an underdog.

41 Yep (2012) argues that Linsanity often centered around erasing Lin's race and racisms in society, often in the form of a "plea to see Lin as solely a basketball player [which] reinforced the mythology that race does not matter in sports and America," but I didn't find this to be true in the stories I surveyed. The closest example I found was an article by *San Jose Mercury News* writer Tim Kawakami (2012), who tried to insist that in watching Lin succeed on the court, "race didn't matter" to his greatness but a few sentences later acknowledged, "Lin's race is not incidental beyond the basketball floor, I know."

42 Labrecque, 2012.

43 Cepeda, 2012.

44 Ironically, the only way to avoid that contradiction would have been to claim that Lin was not overlooked because of race but, of course, that would have undermined the underdog angle. It's reasonable to suggest that the lack of NBA interest in him was because he came out of Harvard, not exactly a common feeder program to professional leagues, but "underdog from Harvard" itself feels like a contradiction in terms.

45 Carr, 2012.

46 Ibid. Yao Ming, who previously was a franchise center for the Houston Rockets (before Lin eventually signed there), makes for an interesting contrast as the first major NBA player of Chinese (but not American) descent. There's been insightful work written about Ming's own racial difference within the NBA, especially with a focus on his extraordinary physicality. See Farred, 2006; Yep, 2009: Conclusion.

47 One segment of the population seemed to have little self-consciousness over enjoying Lin's novelty factor: other Asian Americans. Many people who didn't normally follow the NBA—my Chinese immigrant parents for example—were suddenly taking massive interest in Lin's games, organizing viewing parties and group ticket buys.

48 Mayweather, 2012.

49 Dwyer, 2012.

50 Sandomir, 2012. Whitlock's tweet was indefensible, but the "Chink in the Armor" headline fiasco was complicated by the fact that the phrase is commonly used throughout sports discussions without any racial connotations. One can certainly question the appropriateness of using the term anywhere near a Chinese American athlete however, given "chink"'s double-meaning as a racial slur. Then again, it's also worth noting that Lin himself, as a teenager, once created an online handle "ChiNkBaLLa88" (Kang, 2012a).

51 Simon, 2012.

52 Engel, 2012.

53 Zimmerman, 2012.

54 Cepeda, 2012.

55 Aoki quoted in Wise, 2012. Freeman, 2012.

56 Leonard, 2014: 150 and 152.

57 Leonard, 2014: 152.

58 Andrews, 2001: 128. Andrews introduces this idea of racial displacement by discussing how the valorization of Michael Jordan created a "racially neutered image [that] displac[ed] racial codes onto other black bodies, be they Mars Blackmon, Charles Barkley, or the anonymous urban black male whom the popular media seems intent on criminalizing."

59 Adande, 2012; "Hoopla," 2012; Pitts, 2012.

60 On the lighter side, the desire to present Linsanity as some kind of "teachable moment" created instances of unintended levity given the lengths that some writers went to make those connections. Linsanity became a launching pad to discuss "5 tips for improving your entrepreneurial game," or social media strategies or pedagogical suggestions for primary school teachers (Sposato, 2012; Sreenivasan, 2012; Bochnak, 2012). Writing for the *Washington Post*'s "Ideas" webpage, Emi Kolawode (2012) awkwardly tried to use Linsanity as a way to push for pro-STEM (science, technology, engineering, math) access educational policies because Lin majored in economics—not a STEM discipline—and thus must have had some training in math. Meanwhile, General Electric CEO Jack Welch, alongside his wife, Suzy (2012), wrote an op-ed for the Reuters news service, suggesting that Lin's story contains important management lessons. His first takeaway was "give your bench a chance," which seems to miss the point that to be "on the bench" means that you're already expected to play and that any coach/manager who never uses his or her bench players is unlikely to remain employed for very long. At least other writers displayed a tongue-in-cheek sense of humor about their awkward hijackings. Sex columnist Dr. Ruth Westheimer (2012a, 201b) joined this parade in a more self-aware way by turning basketball puns into sex

advice, first in a series of tweets—"What might a good Lin position be? Pick and roll, where you turn over while together so he starts out on top and you switch places"—then in a February 24 column—"What Jeremy Lin, Basketball Teach Us about Sex"—where she doled out a series of sports-based puns, e.g., "Before the game begins, the teams go out onto the court and warm up. They shoot balls and run around to get the blood flowing. Such warm-up activities in sex fall into the realm of what we call foreplay."

61 Kang, 2012a.

62 Ibid. Also, as Pawan Dhingra describes in his examination of competitive spelling bees, mainstream sports coverage of Asian Americans often highlights the nerdy kid at the spelling bee.

63 Ibid.

64 Ng, 2012.

65 Player metrics taken from John Hollinger's database for ESPN.com: http://insider.espn.go.com/nba/hollinger/statistics/_/position/pg.

66 It's worth pointing out that Lin's standout game in Game 5 of the 2014 playoffs was partially made possible because Beverly was unable to start, thus thrusting Lin into a higher role. That parallels how Linsanity began when Lin took over PG duties for the Knicks on a night where the team's other guards were all unavailable due to injury. Though the similarity of the two cases may simply be accidental, it also speaks to the idea that an underdog narrative requires a moment where the underdog is finally given an opportunity to prove her/himself.

67 Blinebury, 2014.

68 When Russell Westbrook, star African American point guard for the NBA's Oklahoma Thunder, performs well, this is merely his "natural" state as a player, "Westbrook as Westbrook." When Lin performs well, it is coded as *super*natural. I don't want to make too much of this (though one could argue there are racial assumptions at play here too), except to say that over two years after the original Linsanity era, it still seems difficult for Lin to perform outside a binary of either being underwhelming or extraordinary. No one ever seems to say "let Lin be Lin."

69 The irony is that during the summer of 2014, Lin was traded to the Lakers by the Rockets so now I have two reasons to continue to follow his career.

70 Hsu, 2012: 129.

REFERENCES

Adande, J. J. "Jeremy Lin, Race and Lessons Learned." *ESPN.com* 22 Feb. 2012. http://espn.go.com/nba/story/_/id/7595841/nba-jeremy-lin-race-lessons-learned.

Ambinder, Marc. "What the GOP Can Learn from Jeremy Lin." *GQ.com* 14 Feb. 2012. http://www.gq.com/news-politics/blogs/death-race/2012/02/what-the-gop-can-learn-from-jeremy-lin.html.

Andrews, David. "The Fact(s) of Michael Jordan's Blackness: Excavating a Floating Racial Signifier." In *Michael Jordan, Inc.*, ed. David L. Andrews. State University of New York Press, 2001: 107–152.

Associated Press. "Heat Clamp Down on Jeremy Lin, Win 8th Straight." *ESPN.com* 23 Feb. 2012. http://scores.espn.go.com/nba/recap?gameId=320223014.

Associated Press/Huffington Post. "William Tong, Asian-American Connecticut Senate Candidate, Looks for Jeremy Lin Assist." *Huffington Post Politics* 16 Feb. 2012. http://www.huffingtonpost.com/2012/02/16/william-tong-connecticut-senate-asian-american_n_1282871.html.

Barker, Barbara. "Jeremy Lin: From Left Out to Legend." *Newsday* 11 Feb. 2012. http://www.newsday.com/sports/basketball/knicks/jeremy-lin-from-left-out-to-legend-1.3522817.

Begley, Ian. "Opening Tip: Can Woodsanity Last?" *ESPN.com* 20 Mar. 2012. http://espn.go.com/blog/new-york/knicks/post/_/id/14815/opening-tip-can-woodsanity-last.

Blinebury, Fran. "Linsanity Lets Rockets Keep Heads." *Sekou Smith's Hangtime Blog (NBA.com)* 1 May 2014. http://hangtime.blogs.nba.com/2014/05/01/linsanity-lets-rockets-keep-heads/.

Bochnak, Robert. "Learning from (Jeremy)Lin: What Teachers Can Take Away from the Rise of the NBA Star." *GradMatters: The Blog for Tufts' GSAS.* 22 Mar. 2012. http://sites.tufts.edu/gradmatters/2012/03/22/learning-from-jeremylin-what-teachers-can-take-away-from-the-rise-of-the-nba-star/.

Brooks, Scott. *Black Men Can't Shoot.* University of Chicago Press, 2009.

Carr, David. "Media Hype for Lin Stumbles on Race." *New York Times* 19 Feb. 2012. http://www.nytimes.com/2012/02/20/business/media/jeremy-lin-media-hype-stumbles-on-race.html?pagewanted=all&_r=0.

Carrington, Ben. *Race, Sport, and Politics.* Sage, 2010.

Cavan, Jim, Mike Kurylo, Seth Rosenthal, and Robert Silverman. *We'll Always Have Linsanity: Strange Tales on the Strangest Season in Knicks History.* 99: The Press, 2013.

Cepeda, Esther. "What We Can Learn from Jeremy Lin." *Lowell Sun* 4 Mar. 2012. http://www.lowellsun.com/newsletter/ci_20099670.

Conway, Tyler. "Jeremy Lin's Contract, Playoff Struggles Loom over Rockets' Off-season Plans." *Bleacherreport.com* 24 Apr. 2014. http://bleacherreport.com/articles/2041089-jeremy-lins-contract-playoff-struggles-loom-over-rockets-offseason-plans.

Delgado, Robert. "Storytelling for Oppositionists and Others: A Plea For Narrative." *Michigan Law Review* 87.8 (Aug. 1989): 2411–2441.

Dwyer, Kelly. "Jason Whitlock Apologizes for His Unfunny Jeremy Lin Comment on Twitter." *Yahoo! Sports* 13 Feb. 2012. http://sports.yahoo.com/blogs/nba-ball-dont-lie/jason-whitlock-apologizes-unfunny-jeremy-lin-twitter-145934497.html.

Engel, Jen Floyd. "Lin's Success Should Be No Surprise." *Fox Sports* 16 Feb. 2012. http://msn.foxsports.com/nba/story/Jeremy-Lin-New-York-Knicks-success-based-on-foundation-of-hard-work-021612.

Farred, Grant. *Phantom Calls: Race and the Globalization of the NBA.* Prickly Paradigm Press, 2006.

Freeman, Hadley. "Jeremy Lin Row Reveals Deep-Seated Racism against Asian Americans." *Guardian* 22 Feb. 2012: 5. http://www.theguardian.com/commentisfree/cifamerica/2012/feb/21/jeremy-lin-racism-asian-americans.

Gay, Jason. "The Delivery Guy Who Saw Jeremy Lin Coming." *WSJ.com* 16 Feb. 2012. http://online.wsj.com/news/articles/SB10001424052970204880404577225562995441868.

Golgowski, Nina. "Jeremy Lin Blames Asian Stereotypes for Why He Wasn't Offered a Basketball Scholarship or Early NBA pick." *Daily Mail Online* 6 Apr. 2013. http://www.dailymail.co.uk/news/article-2304879/Jeremy-Lin-says-race-wasnt-immediately-selected-NBA-awarded-scholarships.html.

Gregory, Sean, Natalie Tso, and Vanessa Ko. "Linsanity!." *Time* 27 Feb. 2012: 42–45.

Hahn, Alan. Twitter post, 4 Feb. 2012, 5:15 p.m. https://twitter.com/alanhahn/status/165967110533689344.

Hamill, Denis. "New Yorkers of All Stripes Feel Linsanity." *New York Daily News* 14 Feb. 2012: 32.

"Hoopla over Lin a Lesson for Us All." *South China Morning Post* 24 Feb. 2012. http://www.scmp.com/article/993532/hoopla-over-lin-lesson-us-all.

Hsu, Hua. "Everyone Else's Jeremy Lin." *Amerasia Journal* 38.3 (2012): 126–129.

Isola, Frank. "Jeremy Lin Runs Circles around Deron Williams to Score Career-High 25 Points in NY Knicks Victory over NJ Nets." *New York Daily News* 5 Feb. 2012a. http://www.nydailynews.com/sports/basketball/knicks/jeremy-lin-runs-circles-deron-williams-score-career-high-25-points-ny-knicks-victory-nj-nets-article-1.1017267.

———. "Jeremy Lin Could Get Start for NY Knicks against Jazz after Scoring 25 in Win over NJ Nets." *New York Daily News* 6 Feb. 2012b. http://www.nydailynews.com/sports/basketball/knicks/ny-knicks-adopt-jeremy-lin-article-1.1017523.

Kang, Jay Caspian. "The Lives of Others." *FreeDarko.com* 14 Jan. 2010. http://freedarko.blogspot.com/2010/01/lives-of-others.html.

———. "A Question of Identity." *Grantland.com* 20 Mar. 2012a. http://grantland.com/features/the-headline-tweet-unfair-significance-jeremy-lin/.

———. "Dumb Move, Dolan." *Grantland.com* 22 July 2012b. http://grantland.com/features/jeremy-lin-leaving-new-york-knicks-james-dolan-blundered-again.

———. "Jeremy Lin, Again." *Grantland.com* 21 Nov. 2013. http://grantland.com/features/the-rerise-jeremy-lin/.

Kawakami, Tim. "The Beauty of Jeremy Lin Isn't His Race; It's That He Looks as if He Belongs." *San Jose Mercury News* 15 Feb. 2012. http://www.mercurynews.com/ci_19973558.

Kolawode, Emi. "Jeremy Lin: Could STEM Advocates Catch 'Linmania'?" *Washington Post* 16 Feb. 2012. http://www.washingtonpost.com/blogs/innovations/post/jeremy-lin-could-stem-advocates-catch-linmania/2012/02/15/gIQA2jteGR_blog.html.

Labrecque, Jeff. "Sarah Palin Has Lin-sanity!" *EW.com* 17 Feb. 2012. http://popwatch.ew.com/2012/02/17/sarah-palin-has-lin-sanity/.

Leonard, David. "A Fantasy in the Garden, a Fantasy America Wants to Believe: Jeremy Lin, the NBA and Race Culture." In *Race in American Sports*, ed. James L. Conyers, Jr. McFarland & Company, 2014: 144–165.

Leong, Evan. *Linsanity*. Film. Ketchup Entertainment, 2013.

Leung, Maxwell. "Jeremy Lin's Model Minority Problem." *Contexts* 12.3 (Summer 2013): 52–56.

Liu, Eric. "Jeremy Lin Makes Us All American." *Time* 13 Feb. 2012. http://ideas.time.com/2012/02/13/jeremy-lin-makes-us-all-american/.

Liu, Ling Woo. "Why Jeremy Lin's Race Matters." *CNN.com* 14 Feb. 2012. http://www.cnn.com/2012/02/13/opinion/jeremy-lin-race/.

Lowe, Zach. "Death to Ringz: Chris Paul and the NBA's Broken Narrative of Success." *Grantland.com* 18 Nov. 2014. http://grantland.com/the-triangle/death-to-ringz-chris-paul-and-the-nbas-broken-narrative-of-success/.

Lupica, Mike. "Jeremy's Tale All American." *New York Daily News* 13 Feb. 2012: 49. http://www.nydailynews.com/sports/basketball/knicks/jeremy-lin-saga-true-american-classic-asian-american-kid-harvard-brought-life-back-ny-knicks-madison-square-garden-article-1.1021601.

Mayweather, Floyd. Twitter post, 13 Feb. 2012, 1:24 p.m. https://twitter.com/FloydMayweather/status/169170084739289089.

Moore, Matt. "Let Westbrook Be Westbrook." *Eye on Basketball (CBSSports.com)* 11 June 2012. http://www.cbssports.com/nba/eye-on-basketball/19331628/let-westbrook-be-westbrook.

Ng, Konrad. "#Linsanity." *Amerasia Journal* 38.3 (2012): 129–132.

Pan, Arnold. "Asian American Studies After Linsanity." *Amerasia Journal* 38.3 (2012): 125–126.

Phillips, Brian. "May the Best Team Win?" *Grantland.com* 21 Mar. 2014. http://grantland.com/features/2014-ncaa-tournament-underdogs-dayton/.

Pitts, Leonard, Jr. "Lin's Lessons for African Americans." *Philadelphia Inquirer* 25 Feb. 2012. http://articles.philly.com/2012-02-25/news/31098514_1_jeremy-lin-amar-e-stoudemire-people.

Reilly, Rick. "How Do You Like Me Now?" *ESPN.com* 14 Feb. 2012. http://espn.go.com/espn/story/_/id/7574087/overlooking-jeremy-lin.

Rymer, Zachary. "Mike D'Antoni Resigns as Coach of New York Knicks." *Bleacherreport.com* 14 Mar. 2012. http://bleacherreport.com/articles/1104677-mike-dantoni-resigns-as-coach-of-new-york-knicks.

Sagarin, Edward. "Who Roots for the Underdog?" *Journal of Popular Culture* IV.2 (Fall 1970): 425–431.

Sandomir, Richard. "When Brain, Fingers and Vocal Cords Drop the Connection." *New York Times* 21 Feb. 2012. http://www.nytimes.com/2012/02/22/sports/basketball/tv-sports-when-a-vile-ethnic-slur-goes-viral.html.

Simon, Mark. "Jeremy Lin Is All American; The Rise of the New York Knicks' Jeremy Lin Is a Great American Story." *Wall Street Journal* 14 Feb. 2012. http://online.wsj.com/news/articles/SB30001424052970204795304577220590992897070.

Smith, Doug. "Carter Legend Grows; Champion Spurs Fall Prey to Vinsanity as Raptors Come Up with Huge Win." *Toronto Star* 6 Dec. 1999.

Smith, Stephen. "D'Antoni Too Stubborn to Make It Work." *ESPN.com* 15 Mar. 2012. http://espn.go.com/new-york/nba/story/_/id/7688873/new-york-knicks-mike-dantoni-was-victim-own-stubbornness.

Sposato, Jonathan. "Startup Lessons from Jeremy Lin: 5 Tips for Improving Your Entrepreneurial Game." *Geekwire.com* 29 Feb. 2012. http://www.geekwire.com/2012/5-jeremy-lin-teach-startups/.

Sreenivasan, Sree. "Three Lessons from #Linsanity—So Far." *CNET.com* 24 Feb. 2012. http://www.cnet.com/news/three-lessons-from-linsanity-so-far/.

Stein, Leland. "Lin Takes NBA by Storm." *Michigan Chronicle* 15–21 Feb. 2012: C1.

Thompson, Marcus, II. "Warriors G.M. Larry Riley on Losing Jeremy Lin: 'We Have to Face Up to That.'" *Mercury News* 15 Feb. 2012. http://www.mercurynews.com/jeremy-lin/ci_19972040.

Viera, Mark. "For Lin, Erasing a History of Being Overlooked." *New York Times* 13 Feb. 2012. http://www.nytimes.com/2012/02/13/sports/basketball/for-knicks-lin-erasing-a-history-of-being-overlooked.html?_r=0.

Wang, Oliver. "Living with Linsanity." *Los Angeles Review of Books* 6 Mar. 2012. http://lareviewofbooks.org/essay/living-with-linsanity.

———. "Living with Linsanity." In *Asian Americans in Sport and Society*, ed. Richard King. Routledge, 2014: 172–188.

Welch, Jack, and Suzy Welch. "Jeremy Lin: Lessons from the Lin-sanity." *Reuters* 24 Feb. 2012. http://blogs.reuters.com/jack-and-suzy-welch/2012/02/24/jeremy-lin-lessons-from-the-lin-sanity/.

Wise, Mike. "Lin Challenges Defenses—and Stereotypes." *Washington Post* 19 Feb. 2012: D3.

Westheimer, Ruth. Twitter post, 16 Feb. 2012a, 8:55 a.m. https://twitter.com/AskDrRuth/status/170189588244074497.

———. "What Jeremy Lin, Basketball Teach Us about Sex." *Daily Beast* 24 Feb. 2012b. http://www.thedailybeast.com/articles/2012/02/24/dr-ruth-westheimer-what-jeremy-lin-basketball-teach-us-about-sex.html.

Yep, Kathleen. *Outside the Paint: When Basketball Ruled at the Chinese Playground.* Temple University Press, 2009.

———. "Linsanity and Centering Sport in Asian American Studies and Pacific Islander Studies." *Amerasia Journal* 38.3 (2012): 133–137.

Yorkey, Mike, and Jesse Florea. *Linspired*. Ebook. Zondervan, 2013.

Zillgitt, Jeff. "How Did Everyone Miss Jeremy Lin?" *USA Today* 17 Feb. 2012. http://usatoday30.usatoday.com/sports/basketball/nba/story/2012-02-15/how-did-everyone-miss-jeremy-lin/53124082/1.

Zimmer, Ben. "The Lin-guistics of Lin-sanity." *VisualThesarus.com* 17 Feb. 2012. https://www.visualthesaurus.com/cm/wordroutes/the-lin-guistics-of-lin-sanity/.

Zimmerman, Jonathan. "In Jeremy Lin, a Stereotype That Should Be Celebrated." *Washington Post* 16 Feb. 2012. http://www.washingtonpost.com/opinions/in-jeremy-lin-a-stereotype-that-should-be-celebrated/2012/02/15/gIQAEynYHR_story.html.

4

Manny "Pac-Man" Pacquiao, the Transnational Fist, and the Southern California Ringside Community

CONSTANCIO R. ARNALDO, JR.

Introduction

One night in December 2009, after taking a five-hour flight from Illinois to California, I had just walked into my brother and sister-in-law's house in Long Beach. My then two-year-old nephew, all thirty-six inches of him, enthusiastically ran up to me and started to twist his torso and swing his arms side to side. He was clearly emulating a boxer's movements. He then started to chant, "Pacquiao, Pacquiao, Pacquiao!" Not surprisingly, his energetic twisting and swinging elicited laughter from my family and me. This was an interesting encounter with my nephew, for he equated and replaced the verb "boxing" with the noun "Pacquiao." I asked my brother how he learned to chant Pacquiao's name and what spurred him to swing his torso while simultaneously flailing his arms. My brother replied that when they watch Manny "Pac-Man" Pacquiao fight, he tells his son that "that's Pacquiao" and that he wants him to recognize who he is. Since then, any time my nephew sees an image of Pacquiao, these movements soon follow.[1]

Literature on immigrant communities in the U.S. has often foreground a particular assimilationist narrative. This narrative emphasizes that, throughout time, immigrant groups gradually lose their ethnic characteristics, which ultimately results in their full incorporation into the fabric of American society. This narrative, however, has emphasized early European immigrants' experiences, often privileging the eventual assimilation of a homogenized white, middle-class group. However, even racialized white European immigration was never easy, continuous, or complete (Roediger 1991; Guglielmo 2005; Wray 2009). A far more appropriate approach to understanding immigrant experiences examines the differential experiences and outcomes for the aforementioned immigrants coming from Asia, in particular the Philippines. According to Claire Jean Kim's theoretical framework of racial triangulation, Asian Americans in general, and Filipina/o Americans in particular, manage race and assimilate into racial belonging in between whiteness and blackness (see also Bow 2010). Through what is termed "racial power," Asian Americans manage racializing ideas about African Americans and Latinos that inevitably place these groups in subordinate status. Asian Americans are thus "racially triangulated between Blacks and Whites" (Kim 2000: 16), maintaining an inferior position to whites while occupying a superior position to blacks. Asian Americans, in addition, continue to be held by the forever-foreigner status, unable to achieve full assimilation.

However, the vignette above tells us something far more is happening. Rather than identifying with African American or white sporting bodies, this third-generation Filipino American simultaneously connects to a sense of place and constructs a Filipino American ethnic identity through the figure of a Filipino boxer. Thus, rather than situating the immigrant experience only within U.S. national borders and within the black-and-white dichotomous terrain of racial citizenship, we see how global connections and transnational cultural productions contribute to a complicated understanding of belonging that does not solely take place within the United States. As critical sports studies scholars Toni Bruce and Belinda Wheaton put it, "The global sporting arena is a central site in which the 'struggle over nationhood, citizenship and the meaning, basis and authenticity of national identity' takes place" (Jackson 2004: 138). I argue that understanding the kind of resonance that Pacquiao has with the diasporic Filipina/o community must take into account globalization, transnational processes, and the postcolonial moment. My nephew and my brother, a third-generation Filipino American and a second-generation Filipino American, simultaneously embody and connect to this Philippine national icon in a way that expands practices of "cultural citizenship" (Maira 2009) in the U.S. while attaching meaning to a symbol of Filipino nationalism.

Method

This chapter draws upon a larger study that explores the experiences of Filipina/o Americans' participation in sports. The bulk of my research was based in Los Angeles and Orange counties in Southern California. I conducted twenty one-on-one structured and semistructured interviews with 1.5- and second-generation[2] Filipina/o Americans. They ranged in age from twenty-five to thirty-five years old, were college educated, and worked full-time jobs. Interviews took place in interviewees' homes, and coffee and tea shops. In addition to interviews, I also observed Pacquiao sporting spaces, which included his boxing gym in West Hollywood, fight-night spectatorship spaces,[3] and two of his boxing matches: one in Arlington, Texas, when he fought Ghanaian boxer Joshua Clottey on March 13, 2010, and the other in Las Vegas, Nevada, on November 12, 2011, when he fought Mexican fighter Juan Manuel Márquez. In addition to conducting interviews and observing sporting spaces, I also draw upon online media sources such as newspapers, YouTube videos, and blogs. I also provide a close textual analysis of a Nike video featuring Pacquiao.

In the pages that follow, we see how Pacquiao generates powerful affective responses to his rise and fall (or wins and losses) and the narratives that work in tandem with expressions of nationalism. Thus, narratives of Philippine loss and nostalgia are redeemed through Pacquiao's body, not only through mass mediated representations, but also by how the Filipina/o diasporic community reads him. Such longing, as I will show, further demonstrates the complexity of racialized experiences of Filipina/o Americans in the United States. In addition, I demonstrate the perils and possibilities of nationalism—as a site for the persistence of community and diasporic belonging and as a contradictory set of expressions and practices that privilege gender conventions in sport and in the Filipina/o American community. As a result, I argue that Philippine nationalism through Pacquiao's body is simultaneously empowering and excluding, uniting and troubling, and therefore produces outcomes that are critical and complicit in complex ways. In 2009, Pacquiao was sponsored by Nike, the preeminent global sporting apparel company. For the purposes of space, I focus on the content and analysis of the video while also acknowledging Nike's sordid past of sweatshop labor and its exploitive practices in the global south.

In this chapter, I examine how Pacquiao represents himself and how his representation is constructed by corporate media and consumed by Asian Americans (see Shankar 2013). In addition, I show how his body is negotiated and interpreted by Filipina/o Americans in ways that demonstrate how diasporic readings of nationalism, citizenship, and the nation-state are always in flux. In this way, we see how the idea of Americanness has particular racial, gendered, and sexualized contours that are imprinted on Pacquiao's body and are asked to be part of the diasporic imagination. Pacquiao thus becomes an ideal body of Asian Americanness that is not negotiated by Chinese, Japanese, or Korean Americans—who are seen as the quintessential Asian American figures—but rather by Filipinos.

Scholars focused on race and sports have made important contributions to our understanding of how race and racism are fundamentally tied to larger structures of power (Burdsey 2011; Carrington 1998, 2010; Carter 2006) while also acknowledging how sports cannot be removed from larger political and socioeconomic contexts that have shaped peoples' particular experiences of them (Burgos 2007; Yep 2009). Much of this literature has centered on African American male sporting bodies (Andrews 2000; Boyd 2003; Cole and King 1998; Majors 1998; May 2007; Brooks 2009). An emergent body of scholarship examines race and sport beyond black and white by examining how Asian Americans and Pacific Islanders negotiate the parameters of this binary in relation to black athletes (Chin 2012; Thangaraj 2015).

Much like the above-mentioned scholarship on black masculinity and sports, scholarship on race and boxing has examined race and the boxer's identity predominantly among African Americans (Jefferson 1998; Marqusee 1995; Wacquant 2008; Wynn 2003), Latinos (Delgado 2005; Rodriguez 2002), whites (Messner 1992; Rhodes 2011), and, to a lesser degree, South Asian and Filipino pugilists (Burdsey 2007; España-Maram 2006). My work adds to this body of literature by exploring how Pacquiao's global body shapes, and is shaped by, local readings of race, masculinity, and nationalism.

Manny "Pac-Man" Pacquiao: The Filipino Pugilist

Manny "Pac-Man" Pacquiao is an eight-time world boxing champion from the Philippines and is considered one of the best pound-for-pound fighters in the world.[4] As the Philippines' national hero, part of Pacquiao's lore stems from the fact that he has emerged out of the depths of poverty to achieve boxing success. Indeed, his life story reflects a kind of "rags-to-riches" narrative that boxing in particular, and sports in general, celebrates (see Carrington 2010). For example, Oliver Wang, in this volume, demonstrates how the "underdog" story embodied by NBA player Jeremy Lin becomes taken for granted with Asian and Asian American athletes, which also dovetails with the Horatio Alger storyline (see also Wang and Leonard herein). Pacquiao's life story is thus part of a larger immigrant narrative of achieving the American Dream. A narrative of this sort plays a key role in foregrounding him as a national and global hero who is celebrated by Filipinas/os throughout the diaspora.

One of the recurring themes attached to Pacquiao's image is his respectability, evidenced by his strong Catholic/Christian faith and the bodily rituals he performs before, during, and after his fights.[5] Before his fights, he kneels at the corner of the boxing ring and prays. In between rounds, and right before he meets his opponent at the start of each new round, he performs the sign of the cross. And throughout his interviews, he repeatedly thanks God. Informants, too, referenced his faith in God. Cynthia, a second-generation Filipina American from Los Angeles County, for example, shares, "In the last [24/7][6] documentary he shut down things that weren't more God centered, [he was] more into his religion and sharing the Bible." This quote demonstrates how Pacquiao's respectability is renewed by publicly sharing and disassociating himself from what is considered unvirtuous behavior. His fans acknowledge Pacquiao's recommitment to God and his Christians ways. Thus, through Catholic practices, Pacquiao is seen as a redemptive figure: Pacquiao himself publicly acknowledges his sins. As long as he is repentant and working toward correcting these sins, then Pacquiao's respectability is redeemed.

Indeed, such religious symbolism invites consumers to identify with its overtly religious meanings. Nike, for example, capitalizes on Pacquiao's muscular Christianity by selling him as a savior who sacrifices for the nation. In one T-shirt design, "Give Us This Day," Pacquiao is kneeling in the corner of a boxing ring, his back turned to the viewer with his arms extending outward and his head bowed. He is wearing Nike boxing shorts, shoes, and gloves.[7] The image shows him in a position similar to Jesus Christ on the cross, with a spotlight emphasizing his posture. These kinds of religious imagery are even more significant when placed in the context of the sociopolitical climate of the "war on terror" in which Arab, Muslim, and Sikh communities have been subjected to increased state surveillance in the aftermath of 9/11 (Rana 2011; Thangaraj 2012). Whereas Pacquiao's Christian respectability is celebrated, these communities are far more frequently disciplined by the state and are discouraged from displaying their spiritual practices. Constructing Pacquiao as a respectable figure works in tandem with the neoliberal moment and aligns with the celebration of sport as a system of meritocracy. Thus, as a "postracial" subject, Pacquiao's individual work ethic is celebrated—he has pulled himself out of poverty and "made it" despite the structural barriers that have shaped Filipina/o diasporic experiences as well as those of others from the global south. Pacquiao also works as a model minority figure, particularly in terms of how he is positioned in relation to African American and Latino boxers. This however, masks structural inequalities that are rooted in white privilege (Yep 2012).

Pacquiao's global appeal and popularity has led to endorsements from global corporations such as Nike, Hewlett-Packard, and Hennessy, as well as Philippine-based companies like San Miguel Brewery. His very Christianity is based on a tough masculinity that can sell alcohol in a way that is domesticated through both boxing and religion. Beyond Pacquiao's success in the ring, he represents Sarangani province in the Philippine House of Representatives and is celebrated for his philanthropic efforts on behalf of his country's people. He is represented in a positive light in the Philippine national media and within global media discourses as a respectable, just, muscular Christian hero.

Pacquiao has had a number of masculine-inflected boxing nicknames that incorporate but also stand in contradiction to his respectable, heterosexual, Christian masculinity. These nicknames include the racially charged "Mexecutioner," bestowed upon him when he was taking on and defeating Mexican fighters such as Marco Antonio Barrera,and Erik Morales;[8] "The Destroyer"; and, more recently, "Pac-Man,"[9] which stems from the video arcade game of that name produced by the Japanese company Namco. The game features a yellow ball that navigates a maze and eats dots and ghosts. The goal of the Pac-Man game is to dominate—to consume everything and anything and eventually be the sole occupier of the game space. Perhaps this is why—particularly between 2008 and 2010[10]—when Pacquiao was metaphorically and literally defeating boxers who stood in his way that he earned the "Pac-Man" moniker. Although Asians' and Asian Americans' eating behaviors are often configured as nonnormative, this type of physical domination metaphorically parlayed through eating up one's opponent is celebrated among sporting audiences. While the metaphor of Pacquiao as Pac-Man involves a gamelike feature, there is also a way in which the Yellow Peril trope is displaced through the nickname.

In the late nineteenth and early twentieth centuries, the Yellow Peril referred to perceptions of Chinese and Japanese bodies spilling over the U.S. borders, evoking anxiety, fear, and xenophobia, which in turn led to anti-Asian immigration laws (Chen 1991; Tchen and Yeats 2014). Filipinos were exempt from the Yellow Peril trope primarily because of the Philippines' colonial relationship to the United States. Whereas Yellow Peril fears were mapped onto Chinese and Japanese bodies, Filipinos were cast as "little brown brothers," an infantilizing term meant to subordinate Filipinos' status brought on by colonialism (Ignacio et. al 2004). For a brief period, Filipinos' brown masculinity was seen as less threatening than their Asian counterparts' yellow masculinity.[11] The Philippine-U.S. colonial relationship framed the status of Filipinos as U.S. nationals; they could move freely between U.S. borders and were not subject to deportation. However, they were still prohibited from owning land, and were also targets of antimiscegenation laws.

Pacquiao embodies the contemporary manifestations of race and masculinity in the postcolonial sporting moment. Much like his Filipino brethren, Pacquiao's consumption and domination of space neutralizes discourses of the threatening Yellow Peril. Whereas the Yellow Peril was feared, Pacquiao's brown masculinity is an "acceptable" one that literally and figuratively moves between transnational borders. And within the boxing ring, his presence is celebrated for consuming and dominating other bodies. He does not threaten U.S. national borders and, in the U.S.

imaginary, embodies a "childlike glow," reminiscent of the "little brown brother,"[12] reflecting residual U.S. colonial ideologies rooted in racializing and infantilizing discourses about Filipinos.

Moreover, Pacquiao's global popularity has transcended his performances in the ring. In fact, Pacquiao's promoter, Bob Arum, founder and CEO of Top Rank boxing promotions has on a number of occasions compared Pacquiao to Muhammad Ali (Davies 2010). While Pacquiao's Christian faith is part of the construction of a respectable boxing figure, the comparison to Ali invokes global iconicity while inserting his brown body within a Muslim blackness. In this way, Pacquiao's boxing exploits only partially explain his transformative power. While the mainstream media has focused on how Pacquiao has resonated with Filipinas/os in the Philippines, very little attention has been paid to how he resonates with Filipinas/os in the United States. By drawing upon Pacquiao's iconicity to generate meanings of nationalism, affirmations of ethnic identity, masculinity, and "oblique critiques" (Gonzalves 2010) of Filipina/o American (in)visibility, we can produce complex and contradictory meanings about Asian American lives. For many Filipinas/os in the Southern California diaspora, Pacquiao is a "transnational role model" (Barron 2013) because he enables them to craft meanings within and outside the boxing world while simultaneously moving across national borders.

Configuring Masculine Nationalist Sentiments

Sports are one of the primary institutions through which national affiliation, loyalty, and a shared identity emerges (Archetti 1999). Given the globality of mass media sport (Appadurai 1996; Joo 2012) and the fact that Pacquiao's identity carries the burden of representation for the Philippine nation, it comes as no surprise that nationalist sentiments are inscribed onto his body. Part of what makes nationalism appealing for Filipina/o American Pacquiao fans are the "myths" and stories that mobilize and sustain his narratives, which in turn, are interpreted and internalized by the diasporic community. In his seminal work, *Imagined Communities*, Benedict Anderson argues that nationalism is constructed, indeed, "imagined" because the members of even the smallest nation will never know most of their fellow members, meet them, or even hear of them, yet in the minds of each lives the image of their communion (1991: 6).

Thus, while, Filipinas/os in the diaspora will never truly know each other, their connection to an emblem of the Philippines vis-à-vis Pacquiao's body offers tangible proof of a national body, however imagined. Taken further, Pacquiao's *Filipinoness*—broadly understood as identifying with his brown body—is reiterated through familiar cultural practices (e.g., his Catholic religion, eating Filipino food, speaking Tagalog, and speaking English with a Filipino accent). Angelica, a second-generation Filipina American shared, "And then he embodies a lot of Filipino characteristics. He's always praying. I like that he has this thick accent, he sings karaoke on Jimmy Kimmel, it's fabulous!" Here, Angelica emphasizes how Pacquiao's performances of Filipinoness enable Angelica to identify with, and develop an affinity with the Filipino boxer. At the same time, because Pacquiao hails from the Philippines, one sees how space and place link Filipina/o Americans to the Philippines through Pacquiao's body (Gupta and Ferguson 1997). Yet the very same accent also plays a part in creating distance from Filipinoness and first-generation immigrants by which to emphasize Filipina/o American-ness. The contradictory registers of affinity through "Filipino characteristics" create distance through a "thick accent" and simultaneously perpetuate understandings of him as an unassimilable figure who cannot quite achieve full Americanness.

To make sense of how nationalism is worked out through Pacquiao's body, we must also contextualize how sentiments are linked to ideas of race and masculinity in the postcolonial moment. Indeed, boxing is a site where men of color excel and where they are pitted against each other. And sports in general are seen as systems of meritocracy and avenues for upward mobility. As a "manly art" (Gorn 2010), boxing requires masculine attributes of toughness, aggressiveness, and physicality not usually afforded to Asian or Asian American males (Burdsey 2007). These ideas of masculine characteristics, coupled with nationalism, enable Filipina/o Americans to draw upon conventional attributes of masculinity to counter unresolved issues of Philippine loss brought on by multiple legacies of colonialism. Thus, while attempting to rewrite narratives of Philippine nationalism through a masculine body, they also privilege men as the protectors of the feminized nation (Enloe 1990; Stoler 1991; Tengan 2008).

It is in this context where Pacquiao's material and symbolic global presence becomes a bearer of meanings for the diasporic Filipina/o American community and a pivot upon which expressions of Filipino nationalism and identity emerge. Pacquiao's success in the ring enables Filipina/o American nationalism and a sense of esteem and status not granted in other arenas of their everyday lives. For some, Pacquiao's larger-than-life persona serves as a critique of Filipina/o American invisibility. Carlos, a 1.5-generation Filipino American from Orange County echoes these sentiments: "It's really big for a Filipino American to be so successful in sports 'cause there's no other Filipino Americans that are successful in sports except Manny." Although Pacquiao is a Philippine citizen, Carlos's reflections demonstrate a perceived absence of successful Filipino sporting bodies in U.S. mainstream sporting cultures. Taken further, Pacquiao's success in the mainstream reflects what many diasporic Filipinas/os yearn for: a lifestyle of wealth, power, visibility, and achievement.

Critiques of mainstream visibility notwithstanding, Pacquiao as a mass-mediated representation is also read in much more complicated ways. These readings and interpretations simultaneously implicate issues of nationalism, race, and masculinity that traverse beyond the Filipina/o American community. In a contribution from Salon, a politically progressive news website, Thea Lim reflects on how Pacquiao's staying power resonates beyond the Filipina/o community and into the psyches of other people of color. One of Lim's informants, Kai, a black male, shared that while he is not Filipino, "Pacquiao's being nonwhite definitely was appealing for me. Not just that but being from a third-world country and the fact that he came from struggle. So I kind of supported him in solidarity" (Lim 2011). Here, Pacquiao provides a sense of cross-racial unity among people of color who understand the kinds of oppression other third world countries and racialized minority communities have experienced. Additionally, Ryan, another of Lim's informants, described Pacquiao's 2009 win over Ricky "The Hitman" Hatton as symbolically a duel between the colonizer and the colonized despite the fact that Spain and the United States, rather than England—Hatton's birthplace—had colonized the Philippines. It is clear that Hatton's white masculinity symbolically embodied the symbolic boundaries of the colonizer and Pacquiao's brown body, the colonized. The fight itself was promoted as "The Battle of East and West," an obvious title given the racial and nationalist undertones embodied by Hatton, as representative of the West, and Pacquiao, as representative of the East. One can also see how national markers of the Philippines and England were respectively worn by Pacquiao and Hatton on their boxing shorts—for Pacquiao, his Nike branded "MP" logo uses the Philippine sun emerging from the letters, while the Union Jack was featured prominently on the rear of Hatton's trunks. The "Battle of the East and West" theme indicates the link between nations and bodies.

More than simply a boxing match between two men, these fights are global contests of nations and their particular histories. Great Britain, along with the U.S., continues to confront its own legacies of racism, particularly in the realm of English football and cricket (Burdsey 2007, 2011). In this context, Pacquiao's body allows Filipinas/os to rewrite narratives of loss by positioning the Philippines as a challenger to colonial histories and colonialism's residual legacies. For my informants, this fight was consumed with a particular racial perspective, using nationalist vocabularies as proxies to think about race and racial subjectivity within the context of U.S. white supremacy. While Hatton embodies a nationalist English body, his white colonial body can also be read as a racialized whiteness that becomes visible as a result of its defeat at the hands of the formerly colonized, brown body. Indeed, a common theme among my informants was about the Pacquiao/Hatton fight and the dominance with which Pacquiao won. This is similar to the findings of España-Maram's (2006) study of Filipino boxers and the Filipino laborers who rooted for their countrymen in the early twentieth century, when the most popular fights were between white and Filipino boxers. Many of my informants indexed Pacquiao's victory over Hatton as one of Pacquiao's most memorable, indeed, remarkable fights:

CARLOS: I just mainly remember the knockout he gave to Ricky Hatton.
CYNTHIA: I think [the] Hatton [fight]. Just the way he knocked him and won and he wasn't expecting it.

EVELINA: When he knocked out that guy. [Hatton] was frozen stiff for five minutes? That one.

Filipina/o Americans symbolically insert Pacquiao's brown body as a dominant figure over a white, colonizing body. In this way, consumption of racial pugilism moves beyond the black/white racial paradigm and the fight between Pacquiao and Hatton thus symbolizes a duel between whiteness and brown masculinity.

Rewriting Dominant Narratives of Loss

Beyond reinscribing Pacquiao's national body as masculine, his remarkable success also pivots upon renarrating dominant narratives of Philippine loss, which are rooted in the material realities of Spanish and U.S. imperialisms and Japanese occupation. Yet it is important to note that Pacquiao's nationalist body is a collection of images and representations aimed at selling the heroic masculine body. Perhaps no other company conveys these messages more pervasively than Nike. I now turn to a Nike-sponsored Pacquiao video (drealkulit 2007) to analyze how the Philippine nation is mapped onto, and made meaningful to, Pacquiao's body. I came across the video by conducting a YouTube search for Manny Pacquiao Nike commercials and videos. Uploaded on September 27, 2007, by the user drealkulit, when I first encountered it in 2008, the video had been viewed 126,340 times from people throughout the world, though viewership is heavily concentrated in the Philippines and, to a lesser extent, the United States. I spoke to a second-generation Filipino American who grew up in Los Angeles County but now works for Nike in the company's Oregon headquarters. He shared that the video was created and disseminated by Nike Philippines. According to YouTube viewership numbers, the video is popular with a largely male audience in the age range of thirty-five to fifty-four. Online comments appear in English, Spanish, and Tagalog; many involve statements of national pride and debates about whether Mexicans or Filipinos produce superior boxers, as well as sexist, racist, and homophobic slurs targeting African American pugilist Floyd Mayweather, Jr., Pacquiao's biggest rival. One particular comment by user braindead piqued my interest in part because it questions the logic by which members of the Filipino diaspora uphold Pacquiao's status as the "national hero" of the Philippines. According to braındead,

> pac is not our national hero. heroes know to stand by the people, and clearly pac is standing with pgma [President Gloria Macapagal Arroyo]. He says he fights for the country, but it's really all about the money (mansions, cock derbys, etc.) what the hell happened to his Emmanuel Pacquiao Foundation? He used to be the people's champion, now he's the corporate champ—with the commercials and all. Although, I greatly admire him for his boxing skill, do not—please—do not say that he is our hero.[13]

While admitting to respecting Pacquiao's boxing skills, braındead forces the viewers to critique dominant assumptions of heroism because of the fighter's alignment with Gloria Magcapal Arroyo's politics, her neoliberal corporate policies, and his own corporate sponsorship by Nike. Thus, while the video aims to sell commodity images of Philippine nationalism, it is clear that not all members of the diasporic Filipino community agree on how to interpret it.[14]

The video looks to be a compilation of Pacquiao's two fights against Mexican fighters Marco Antonio Barerra and Erik Morales. It has a grainy look to it, appearing in vintage-style black and white, highlighting only the color red. Red appears on the headband of Freddie Roach, Pacquao's head trainer. It is also highlighted on Pacquiao's boxing gloves and shorts, and the boxing ring's top rope. The video opens with a close-up shot of Pacquiao's face. He is looking up, his body language speaking of exhaustion as if he is contemplating inevitable defeat. The clip then moves toward Pacquiao on the defensive, absorbing devastating right hooks to the head. Eventually Pacquiao gets knocked down, falling flat on his back. The next shot is similar to the first—Pacquiao is sitting on a stool in the corner, his right eye now bloodied. His trainer is placing a cotton swab inside the cut to prevent blood from dripping. Again, Pacquiao appears exhausted. He is looking down, signaling that his opponent has broken his will to fight. Then comes the final scene and the apex of the video. This time, it is Pacquiao throwing the punches despite his bloody eye. He throws and lands a right jab, followed by a left hook.

More punches ensue and his opponent falls to the canvas. The final shot from the boxing ring is of Pacquiao kissing his right glove, looking up, and raising both arms in triumph. He then looks down and back up, as if relieved that he won the fight. A concluding image shows the Manny Pacquiao logo in red followed by the patented Nike swoosh.

In the beginning, and throughout the video, we hear the voice of what I assume to be a child. It sounds as if he or she is singing a melodic hymn. The pitch wavers between high and low notes and the song fades in and out throughout the video until the very end, when Pacquiao raises his arms in triumph. The voice then utters the words, "Ang mamatay nang dahil sa 'yo," which translates "to die for you." The phrase is taken from the final lines of "Lupang Hinirang," the Philippine national anthem. As Christianity pivots upon Jesus Christ's life and death on behalf of humanity, and his resurrection, Pacquiao's victory parallels Christ's resurrection.

The video communicates a reversed narrative of sorts—it highlights themes of trials and tribulations, and of the struggle to continue in the face of overwhelming adversity. We are led to believe that Pacquiao is going to lose the fight, indicated by his mannerisms, the melodic tone of the music, and the clips of Pacquiao on the defensive. However, as the video unfolds, we see a counternarrative, one in which Pacquiao, for all of the adversity he previously encountered, is about to come back and claim victory not only for himself but, more importantly, for the Filipino nation. This video narrative thus attempts to reinsert Philippine nationalism through the use of Pacquiao's symbolic imagery—a narrative in which the Philippines, despite histories of colonialism has thus renarrated its emplotment to reverse the linear history of time. I am also thinking of the imagery of the color red. Red carries the symbolism of blood (Turner 1969). The image of Pacquiao's right eye dripping with blood suggests that this dripping is equated to a weakening state, a loss of energy and literally of blood. In fact, blood is accentuated on Pacquiao's face and animated on his shorts, the ropes, and the headband. The bleeding marks a liminal state, with possibilities of defeat or triumph.

The line "To die for you" is thus used to communicate Pacquiao's readiness to shed his blood for the Philippine nation, even if it comes at the cost of death. One can also think of references to sacrifice—though I do not wish to romanticize the use of religious imagery, one can see how Pacquiao embodies a kind of deified status, while still carrying with it the human element, as shown in the shedding of his own blood. The fall and rise of Pacquiao from the depths of despair follows the Catholic tradition of Jesus Christ's passion, or what historian Reynaldo Ileto terms the "pasyon." According to Ileto, pasyon is a Filipino idiom that follows Catholic traditions of suffering, sacrifice, and redemption during Holy Week, which was embodied, in particular by Filipino male revolutionary fighters to resist colonialism. Indeed, Spain colonized the Philippines for over 350 years, and with colonialism came the inculcation of Catholic beliefs, traditions, and values. This is evident in the fact that close to 90 percent of the Philippine population is Catholic (Gall 1998). In this video, I see metanarratives of Filipino passion referenced in the treatment of male heroism in Philippine culture like Jesus Christ, Bernardo Carpio, and José Rizal. Pacquiao follows the tradition of these male heroic figures precisely because the video transmits messages of suffering, sacrifice, and heroism—and perhaps of Pacquiao as masculinized savior of the nation.

This narrative concurrently parallels the contemporary experiences of Filipina/o global laborers, particularly seamen. According to anthropologist Kale Fajardo, "Although notions of sacrifice play a big part in the [Philippine] state's interpellation narrative, notions of Christian suffering and sacrifice also 'color' Filipino seamen's perceptions, experiences, and understandings of seafaring/maritime time-space in the global economy" (2011: 147). The narrative also suggests something of a twenty-first-century reclamation project for a national community of belonging and a renarration of victory and triumph as opposed to loss. But the narrative of winning comes at the expense of defeating other men of color, particularly Latino men—rather than Spanish or white American colonists. In this way, Pacquiao operates as a model minority figure upon whom tensions between former colonized, brown bodies are symbolically played out, and a clear-cut "winner" emerges.[15] Of course, such tensions are endemic to boxing, as ethnic identity and nationalism, paired with practices and performances of masculinity, frame the limits of cooperation between people of color (Rodriguez 2002).

Juxtaposing my description and interpretation of the video, I asked Roland, a second-generation Filipino American from San Diego, to view and discuss the video with me. When I asked what messages he thought the video conveyed, he suggested that it was "as if Pacquiao was a warrior or fighting for his people." He then referred to the phrase from the national anthem, "Ang mamatay nang dahil sa 'yo." He stated, "More wars and independence, but I guess it applies." The reference to "more wars and independence" is curious for it echoes a perpetual process of having to claim a Philippine nation marked by violence, occupation, and the struggle for national autonomy. "More wars and independence" means that the Philippines has never quite "won" and its status as an independent nation has never been on its own terms. At the same time, Roland genders the Philippine nation, linking notions of a heroic masculinity to "warriorhood." Ty Tengan and Jesse Markham (2009) note how ideas of "warriorhood" enable Polynesian football players to counter processes of emasculation brought on by legacies of colonialism. In the same way, Roland associates warriorhood to Pacquiao and thus to the Philippines, which enables Roland to reconstruct the Philippines as masculine. The act of shedding blood and subsequent violent practices in the boxing ring become taken-for-granted notions of national identity, be it in the U.S. or in the Philippines.

Beyond my and Roland's interpretations of the video, such perceptions of Pacquiao as an allegory of the Philippine nation have been articulated by other Filipina/o Americans. In an article featured in New America Media, for example, journalist Charisse Domingo reflects on how Pacquiao provides an alternative story of Philippine national narratives. This provides Filipinas/os throughout the world a sense of pride and esteem.

> You don't have to be a sports fan to love Manny Pacquiao. You just have to know the feeling of being fallen and fighting your way up. Many of us have felt that at one time or another, of course. But to the Philippines as a whole, this is more than a feeling—it's the entire story of our nation. We have a history of colonization by not just one but three colonizers—Spain, the United States and Japan. It's a little embarrassing sometimes to say you're Filipino because of our history of being the world's doormat. And Pacquiao's history is within the personal narrative of every Filipino in this world. (Domingo 2006)

Interestingly, Domingo deploys the "work of the imagination" (Appadurai 1996) by using the pronouns "us," "we," and "our" as a strategy of inclusion to recruit the presumably Filipina/o and/or Filipina/o American reader into a shared experience of "being the world's doormat." Indeed, according to Domingo, "[Pacquiao] is the physical expression of our psyche," precisely because he embodies the Filipina/o community's life stories and struggles. For Domingo and the rest of the Filipina/o diaspora, then, Pacquiao's life story, especially the fact that he figuratively and literally has fought his way out of poverty, serve as a symbol of ethnic and national pride and empowerment. At the same time, Domingo points to residual legacies of colonialism that have shaped her understanding of Philippine national history. In doing so, she is critical of how such legacies shape the contemporary experiences of Filipinas/os, many of whom serve as "migrants for export," (Rodriguez 2010) for the Philippine nation-state, and who constitute a "feminized" nation. According to anthropologist Kale Fajardo, "[T]he Philippines, its citizens, and its global migrant labor force (men and women) have been feminized through debt and dependency and gendered and sexualized through orientalism and colonialism by more powerful and wealthier nations such as the United States and Japan" (Fajardo 2011: 71). In this context, Pacquiao's boxing success and life narrative simultaneously provide a metaphorical voice for a national community burdened by both the legacies of colonialism and current socioeconomic conditions.

Conclusion

In this chapter, I have argued for taking stock of the mass-mediated sporting landscapes through the figure of the global boxing sensation Manny "Pac-Man" Pacquiao. Pacquiao's image and persona produce complicated identity formations brought on by globalizing process and transnational cultural practices that are mediated by and implicated with local identity formations, particularly in terms of race and gender. While Asian American studies' legacies are anchored to particular historical moments in the U.S., this chapter also looks beyond U.S. borders to understand how Filipina/o and Filipina/o Americans make sense of diaspora and nationalism that are complicated by global popular culture to demonstrate the heterogeneity and multiplicity of Asian American sporting audiences (Lowe 1996). As such, this chapter asks us to take seriously the multivocality and multilocality of bodies and communities (Gupta and Ferguson 1997) that are not accounted for in Asian American studies, ethnic studies, and sports studies. By emphasizing a transnational framework, we see that dominant representations are not simply mapped onto representations, but are constantly negotiated and struggled over. Finally, this chapter examines how the sport of boxing, and a boxing superstar of Filipino descent, generates scholarly discussions of sport that move beyond black-and-white-dominated discussions of sport. In this way, by considering how Pacquiao's respectable, racialized masculinity works in transnational relation to other communities, we see how racialization takes on different contours that are complicated by gender. As we've seen throughout this chapter, Filipina/o Americans' engagement with the spectacularity of Pacquiao and boxing reveal not only how globalizing forces are locally adapted, but also how their engagement with popular cultural forms allows for imagined communities within and outside of the U.S. borders.

NOTES

1 This chapter's title is inspired in part by that of Margaret Costello's MA thesis, "The Filipino Ringside Community: National Identity and the Heroic Myth of Manny Pacquiao." This chapter went through various iterations before submission and would not have been possible without feedback from a number of people. I want to thank Johanna Almiron and Lorenzo Perillo for providing comments and encouragement during the early stages of this chapter. At the University of Illinois, Urbana-Champaign, Ricky Rodriguez, Karoliina Engstrom, and Martin Manalansan helped refine my chapter. During the 2011 Association for Asian American Studies Conference, Kale Fajardo and Linda Maram posed probing questions to me and I have incorporated them here. A heartfelt thank you goes to Norma A. Marrun, Stanley Thangaraj, and the blind reviewer's feedback. This chapter is much better because of their critical and productive comments. Lastly, thank you to my brother, Chris, my sister-in-law, Orchid, and my nephew, Caleb, for inspiring this piece.

2 By first generation, I mean Filipinas/os born in the Philippines. By 1.5 generation, I mean Filipinas/os born in the Philippines who came to the U.S. as children. And by second generation, I mean US-born Filipinas/os

3 See Arnaldo (forthcoming), in *Global Asian America: Transnational Media and Migration*. Pacquiao fight-night spaces are spaces where predominantly Filipina/o and Filipina/o American friends and families gather to watch him fight.

4 Pound-for-pound is an unofficial term used in combat sports to measure the value of a boxer in relation to other boxers regardless of weight class. It is also used in

mixed martial arts. The term is often deployed by fans and boxing pundits in debates over who the best fighters are.

5   Lately, Pacquiao's religiosity has gone from practicing Catholic rituals, to more evangelical Christian practices.

6   24/7 is an HBO television series featuring the buildup to a fight.

7   "Customer Reviews for Nike Manny Pacquiao Give Us This Day Men's T-Shirt." *Nike.com*, n.d. http://reviews.nike.com/9191/415234/nike-manny-pacquiao-give-us-this-day-mens-t-shirt-reviews/reviews.htm.

8   Pacquiao, however, does not embrace the "Mexicutioner" nickname. See Satterfield (2011).

9   I emailed Pacquiao's publicist, Fred Sternburg, to find out when and how Pacquiao received the nickname "Pac-Man." Sternburg never responded to my emails.

10   I would argue that 2008–2010 were the years when Pacquiao was "destroying" his opponents in devastating fashion.

11   This does not mean that Filipinos were completely exempt from the anti-Asian sentiments and anti-Asian laws. Eventually, Filipinos became targets of white racial mobs and targets of exclusion.

12   While conducting fieldwork in Southern California, I was listening to ESPN radio. The hosts of one show, Scott Van Pelt and Ryen Russillo, were talking about Pacquiao. Van Pelt (2009), in an effort to describe Pacquiao stated that "Pacquiao has a 'childlike glow' about him.

13   braindead comment in thread accompanying drealkulit (2007).

14   See Nguyen and Tu (2007) for descriptions of popular culture and Asian American multiple, contradictory practices of consumption.

15   I thank David Coyoca for this important insight.

REFERENCES

Anderson, Benedict. 1991. *Imagined Communities: Reflections on the Origin and Spread of Nationalism*. New York: Verso.

Andrews, David L. 2000. "Excavating Michael Jordan's Blackness." In *Reading Sport: Critical Essays on Power and Representation*, ed. Susan Birrell and Mary G. McDonald. Boston: Northeastern University Press.

Appadurai, Arjun. 1996. *Modernity at Large: Cultural Dimensions of Globalization*. Minneapolis: University of Minnesota Press.

Archetti, Eduardo P. 1999. *Masculinities: Football, Polo and the Tango in Argentina*. Oxford and New York: Berg.

Arnaldo, Constancio, Jr. Forthcoming. "'I'm Thankful for Manny': Manny Pacquiao, Pugilistic Nationalism, and the Filipina/o Body." In *Global Asian America: Transnational Media and Migration*, ed. Shilpa Davé, Leilani Nishime, and Tasha Oren. New York: New York University Press.

Barron, Desiree. 2013. "Diasporic Pugilists and Fighting for National Belonging: Haroon Khan and the 2010 Commonwealth Games." *South Asian Popular Culture* 11(3): 313–324.

Bow, Leslie. 2010. *Partly Colored: Asian Americans and Racial Anomaly in the Segregated South*. New York: New York University Press.

Boyd, Todd. 2003. *Young Black Rich and Famous: The Rise of the NBA, the Hip Hop Invasion and the Transformation of American Culture*. New York: Doubleday.

Brooks, Scott. 2009. *Black Men Can't Shoot*. Chicago: University of Chicago Press.

Bruce, Toni, and Belinda Wheaton. 2009. "Rethinking Global Sports Migration and Forms of Transnational, Cosmopolitan and Diasporic Belonging: A Case Study of International Yachtsman Sir Peter Blake." *Social Identities* 15(5): 585–608.

Burdsey, Daniel. 2011. *Race, Ethnicity, and Football: Persisting Debates and Emergent Issues*. New York: Routledge.

———. 2007. *British Asians and Football: Culture, Identity, Exclusion*. New York: Routledge.

Burgos, Adrian. 2007. *Playing America's Game: Baseball, Latinos, and the Color Line*. Berkeley: University of California Press.

Carrington, Ben. 2010. *Race, Sport and Politics: The Sporting Black Diaspora*. London: Sage Publications.

———. 1998. "Sport, Masculinity and Black Cultural Resistance." *Journal of Sport and Social Issues* 22(3): 275–298.

Carter, Thomas. 2006. "Introduction: The Sport of Cities." *City and Society* XVIII(2): 151–158.

Chen, Sucheng. 1991. *Asian Americans: An Interpretive History*. London: Twayne Publishers.

Chin, Christina B. 2012. "Hoops, History, and Crossing Over: Boundary Making and Community Building in Japanese American Youth Basketball Leagues." PhD diss., University of California, Los Angeles.

Cole, Cheryl L., and Samantha King. 1998. "Representing Black Masculinity and Urban Possibilities: Racism, Realism, and Hoop Dreams." In *Sport and Postmodern Times*, ed. Geneviève Rail. Albany: State University of New York Press.

Costello, Margaret Louise, 2009. "The Filipino Ringside Community: National Identity and the Heroic Myth of Manny Pacquiao." MA thesis, Georgetown University.

Davies, Gareth. 2010. "Manny Pacquiao Transcending Boxing Like Muhammad Ali Says Bob Arum." *Telegraph*, July 13.http://blogs.telegraph.co.uk/sport/garethadavies/100010658/manny-pacquiao-transcending-boxing-like-muhammad-ali-says-bob-arum/.

Delgado, Fernando. 2005. "Golden but Not Brown: Oscar De La Hoya and the Complications of Culture, Manhood, and Boxing." *International Journal of the History of Sport* 22(2): 196–211.

Domingo, Charrisse. 2006. "Manny Pacquiao Is a Boxing Icon—Should He Be More?" *New America Media*, July 31.http://news.newamericamedia.org/news/view_article.html?article_id=bebf7eb040d855512c72c344385299ee.

drealkulit. 2007. "Manny Pacquiao Nike Video." *YouTube*. https://www.youtube.com/watch?v=n9y1Z6cO9q4.

Enloe, Cynthia. 1990. *Bananas, Beaches, & Bases: Making Feminist Sense of International Politics.* Berkeley: University of California Press.

España-Maram, Linda, 2006. *Creating Masculinity in Los Angeles's Little Manila: Working-Class Filipinos and Popular Culture, 1920s–1950s.* New York: Columbia University Press.

Fajardo, Kale B. 2011. *Filipino Crosscurrents: Oceanographies of Seafaring, Masculinities, and Globalization.* Minneapolis: University of Minnesota Press.

Gall, Timothy L. 1998. *Worldmark Encyclopedia of Cultures and Daily Life.* Detroit: Gale Press.

Gonzalves, Theodore S. 2010. *The Day the Dancers Stayed: Performing in the Filipino/American Diaspora.* Philadelphia: Temple University Press.

Gorn, Elliot. 2010. *The Manly Art: Bare-Knuckle Prize Fighting in America.* New York: New York University Press.

Guglielmo, Thomas. 2005. *White on Arrival: Italians, Race, Color, and Power in Chicago, 1890–1945.* New York: Oxford University Press.

Gupta, Akhil, and James Ferguson. 1997. *Culture, Power, Place: Explorations in Critical Anthropology.* Durham, NC: Duke University Press.

Ignacio, Abe, Enrique de la Cruz, Jorge Emmanuel, and Helen Toribio, eds. 2004. *The Forbidden Book: The Philippine American War in Political Cartoons.* San Francisco: T'Boli.

Jackson, Stephen J. 2004. "Exorcizing the Ghost: Donovan Bailey, Ben Johnson and the Politics of Canadian Identity." *Media, Culture & Society* 26(1).

Jefferson, Tony. 1998. "Muscle, 'Hard men' and 'Iron' Mike Tyson: Reflections on Desire, Anxiety, and the Embodiment of Masculinity." *Body and Society* 4(1): 77–98.

Joo, Rachael. 2012. *Transnational Media Sport: Gender, Media, and Global Korea.* Durham, NC: Duke University Press.

Kim, Claire Jean. 2000. *Bitter Fruit: The Politics of Black-Korean Conflict in New York City.* New Haven, CT: Yale University Press.

Lim, Thea. 2011. "Finally, an Asian Who Packs a Punch." *Salon*, November 12. http://www.salon.com/2011/11/12/finally_an_asian_who_packs_a_punch/.

Lowe, Lisa. 1996. *Immigrant Acts: On Asian American Cultural Politics.* Durham, NC: Duke University Press.

Maira, Sunaina. 2009. *Missing: Youth, Citizenship, and Empire after 9/11.* Durham, NC: Duke University Press.

Majors, Richard. 1998. "Cool Pose: Black Masculinity and Sports." In *African Americans in Sport*, ed. Gary Sailes. New Brunswick, NJ: Transaction.

Marqusee, Mike. 1995. "Sport and Stereotype: From Role Model to Muhammad Ali." *Race and Class* 36(4): 1–29.

May, Reuben. 2007. *Living through the Hoop: High School Basketball, Race, and the American Dream.* New York: New York University Press.

Messner, Michael. 1992. *Power at Play: Sports and the Problem of Masculinity.* Boston: Beacon Press.

Nguyen, Mimi, and Thuy Linh Nguyen Tu, eds. 2007. *Alien Encounters: Popular Culture in Asian America*. Durham, NC: Duke University Press.
Rana, Junaid. 2011. *Terrifying Muslims: Race and Labor in the South Asian Diaspora*. Durham, NC: Duke University Press.
Rhodes, James. 2011. "Fighting for 'Respectability': Media Representations of the White, 'Working-Class' Male Boxing 'Hero.'" *Journal of Sport & Social Issues* 35(4): 350–376.
Rodriguez, Gregory. 2002. "Saving Face, Place, and Race: Oscar de la Hoya and the 'All-American' Dreams of Boxing." In *Sports Matters: Race, Recreation, and Culture*, ed. John Bloom and Michael Nevin Willard. New York: New York University Press.
Rodriguez, Robyn. 2010. *Migrants for Export: How the Philippine State Brokers Labor to the World*. Minneapolis: Minnesota University Press.
Roediger, David. 1991. *Wages of Whiteness*. New York: Verso.
Satterfield, Lem. 2011. "Pacquiao Distances Himself from 'Mexicutioner' Nickname." *Ring*, October 20. http://ringtv.craveonline.com/news/169748-pacquiao-distances-himself-from-mexicutionerq-monicker.
Shankar, Shalini. 2013 "Affect and Sport in Asian American Advertising." *South Asian Popular Culture* 11(3): 231–242.
Stoler, Ann. 1991. "Carnal Knowledge and Imperial Power: Gender, Race, and Morality in Colonial Asia." In *Gender at the Crossroads of Knowledge*, ed. Micaela di Leonardo. Berkeley: University of California Press.
Tchen, John Kuo Wei, and Dylan Yeats. 2014. *Yellow Peril!: An Archive of Anti-Asian Fear*. London and New York: Verso.
Tengan, Ty P. Kāwika. 2008. *Native Men Remade: Gender and Nation in Contemporary Hawai'i*. Durham, NC, and London: Duke University Press.
Tengan, Ty P. Kāwika, and J. M. Markham. 2009. "Performing Polynesian Masculinities in American Football: From 'Rainbows' to 'Warriors.'" *International Journal of the History of Sport* 26(16): 2412–2431.
Thangaraj, Stanley I. 2015. *Desi Hoop Dreams. Pickup Basketball and the Making of Asian American Masculinity*. New York: New York University Press.
———. 2012. "Playing through Differences: Black-White Racial Logic and Interrogating South Asian American Identity." *Ethnic and Racial Studies* 35(6): 988–1006.
Turner, Victor. 1969. *The Forest of Symbols: Aspects of Ndembu Ritual*. Ithaca, NY: Cornell University Press.
Uperesa, Fa'anofo Lisaclaire. 2010. "Fabled Futures: Development, Gridiron Football, and Transnational Movements in American Samoa." PhD diss., Columbia University.
Van Pelt, Scott, and Ryen Russillo. 2009. *ESPN.com*, September 20.http://espn.go.com/espnradio/show/_/showId/scottvanpelt2009/postId/8402865/what-talking-about.
Wacquant, James Loic. 2008. *Body & Soul: Notebooks of an Apprentice Boxer*. New York: Oxford University Press.
Wray, Matt. 2009. *Not Quite White: White Trash and the Boundaries of Whiteness*. Durham, NC: Duke University Press.

Wynn, Neil A. 2003. "Deconstructing Tyson: The Black Boxer as American Icon." *International Journal of the History of Sport* 20(3): 99–114.

Yep, Kathleen. 2012. "Peddling Sport: Liberal Multiculturalism and the Racial Triangulation of Blackness, Chineseness and Native American-ness in Professional Basketball." *Ethnic and Racial Studies* 35(6): 971–987.

———. 2009. *Outside the Paint: When Basketball Ruled at the Chinese Playground*. Philadelphia: Temple University Press.

PART III

Complicating "Model Minority" Myths, Orientalism, and Gendered Stereotypes

5

Indian Americans and the "Brain Sport" of Spelling Bees

PAWAN DHINGRA

Sports for our community—we are not sporting people. . . . Everyone wants to be an athlete but you can't. You can practice hard, you can do what you want. But if you don't have the genes for it, you are not going to excel, no matter how hard. . . . African Americans have an advantage in sports, in the athletes. Because that's their gene. What it comes to studying or learning or knowledge, it is now almost, I don't want to say . . . I don't have a reference point, but it's clear that Asians and South Asians excel in that [sic].

This racialized belief held by an Indian American adult familiar with spelling bees is widely shared by those who participate in the bees, as well as by the general public. As the quote signals, Indian Americans may want to be athletes but believe that they cannot excel there. Genetics serves as a common, although problematic and scientifically disproven explanation for African Americans' participation in sports, a way to explain a perceived hypermasculinity and aggressiveness that is rewarded in most sports. As the assumed model minority, Asian Americans do not "belong" in sports. This is despite the growing number of Indian and other Asian American sports celebrities. Not fitting within the sports regiment signals an abnormal body, a possible queerness relative to strictly monitored gendered regimes in sports.

Partly in response to this separation from traditional sports, Asian American parents turn to educational competitions for their children. They come to dominate competitions read as the opposite of sports— ones of the mind, such as math, spelling, music, geography, and the like. For example, Indian Americans have dominated the annual Scripps National Spelling Bee for years. The past eight winners have been Indian American, as have thirteen of the past seventeen, dating back to

1999 (and with two Indian American champions in the 1980s). They are seen as the "hyper-model minority," as performing scholastically at high levels.

Yet as argued below, rather than being at odds with sports, educational competitions help solve the dilemma of Asian Americans who admire traditional sports but feel that they cannot compete in them. The competitions, in this case spelling bees, work as a liminal space. That is, they offer a nonnormative gender competition separate from traditional sports, one that does not endorse hypermasculinity. Contrary to popular assumption, Indian Americans' understandings of their bodies, not just their minds, motivate their participation in the bees. Yet these competitions are still embedded within sports logic and its neoliberal assumptions. As such the bees help connect families to sports while avoiding the racialized and gendered aspects of sports spaces. Outside of this liminal space, the hegemony of the sports logic that maligns yet entices Asian American families is affirmed. This is not to take away from Asian Americans' claim on traditional sports, but to offer an alternative model of competition.

While adored by many Indian American families, other Indian Americans (and non-Indian Americans) criticize the community's participation in bees as reinforcing negative stereotypes. The bees are read as unhealthy for the children, who instead should be engaged in a variety of extracurricular activities rather than one based on memorizing esoteric words. "Tiger moms and dads" presumably push their children too hard. Personally, I had shared some of these critiques before I investigated this topic. My goal in this paper is to help resuscitate the image of the bees in part as a nonnormative sports space for Indian American youth.

This chapter stems from fieldwork that I have conducted since 2011 on Indian Americans' participation in the bees. In that time I have attended two Scripps National Spelling Bees in Washington, DC, two finals of the North South Foundation (NSF), two finals of the South Asian Spelling Bee (SASB), a finals of the MastiSpell bee (in Washington, DC), four regional competitions of the NSF and SASB, and a networking event for SASB with a former Scripps champion. NSF and SASB are the United States' two largest sets of bee competitions designed primarily by and for Indian Americans. Each has regional competitions in a dozen or more metropolitan areas across the United States with substantial Indian

American populations. Winners from the various cities compete in a finals. I also have spent time with past Scripps champions and finalists, including in their homes. I also have observed families studying for competitions. On top of these observations I have interviewed a number of young people and adults affiliated with the bees, including organizers of the ethnic bees. The interviews involved a combination of one-on-one and group settings, resulting in over fifty interviewees.

The chapter proceeds in the following manner: Part 1 explains why Asian Americans and Indian Americans in particular have been separated from traditional sports in discursive and physical ways. Part 2 explains how bees, in particular spelling bees, serve as an alternative competitive space designed to solve this problem.

Part 1. Indian Americans and Sports

Indian Americans in Sports

Echoing the quotation at the top of the chapter, one father explained to me the shift from traditional sports to spelling as a competitive venue for Indian American children,

> Some of my [fellow Indian] friends with whom I spoke said, well, our kids cannot compete with the other kids in swimming, they get tired out very easily. . . . So those physical aspects and also other issues come into play. That's why you scale down at sports and look at other activities which bring you to the top.

Competition is a natural means to build up self-esteem (Findlay and Bowker 2009). The perceived inability to compete in sports creates a dilemma for certain youth, given the centrality of sports in American youth culture. Where does this notion of competitive disadvantage come from, and how does it lead to joining other competitive sites?

Jeremy Lin, Yao Ming, Vijay Singh, Michelle Wie, and the like are Asian American sports celebrities, belying the genetic argument against Asian Americans. Yet these stars are treated as exceptions and oddities as Asian Americans, ironically making Asian Americans' sports contributions even more unconceivable (and multiracial Asian Americans such as Tiger Woods often have their Asian ancestry ignored). Instead, popular notions of Asians and Asian Americans in sports involve peripheral activities such as cricket, along with Olympic sports such as diving, gymnastics, figure skating, and table tennis.

Indian Americans have their own sports interests beyond cricket that are not widely known, even among other South Asian Americans (Thangaraj 2010); Indian wrestlers toured the United States in the middle of the twentieth century.[1] There is not a single sport today that South Asian Americans frequently participate in at the professional level. Yet they, in particular men, have made their mark across a variety of sports. Since March 2006, Sunil Gulati has served as the president of the United States Soccer Federation, the sport's national governing body. He has been called "the single most important person in the development of soccer in this country."[2] In regards to playing sports, one of the most surprising venues has been the National Football League (NFL), which is synonymous with violent American sports. Four Indian Americans have played in the NFL. What is more, three of these have been to the Super Bowl, and two have earned rings. Most recently, Brandon Chillar was part of sports' biggest game. Of mixed Indian and white ancestry, he was a linebacker with the Green Bay Packers when they won the 2010 Super Bowl. Although on injured reserve for the game, he played a role in the team's winning season. Yet his achievements did not mean that Indian Americans gained a reputation within football, not even among his own teammates.

> I remember, and this happened on many occasions, when I come out of my locker room, I have my Indian family there and they are dressed in Indian clothes. Everybody else's family is white or black, and my family looks different. People didn't know I was Indian.

He would like his achievements to influence not only average Americans' perceptions of Indians but also Indians' perceptions of themselves.

> This has kind of been my stance the whole time, I like showing Indians it can be done. I want to represent, you know what I mean. Showing that Indians can do this too. . . . Let the world know it's not just all education and engineering. *We have some big dudes.*

Sports is not just the interest of a few stars. It is a pastime for many able-bodied persons who do not compete professionally. Grassroots cricket and basketball leagues are popular in major cities across the country. Cricket (most commonly Twenty20 and limited overs cricket) is enjoyed mainly by immigrants who grew up playing the game. Basketball is played by those who grew up in South Asia and in the diaspora (Thangaraj 2012). The turn to basketball is not despite young participants' parents but sometimes because of them. First-generation parents occasionally set up basketball courts at temples, mosques, churches, and gurdwaras so that their boys (and usually only boys) would be able to adjust to American culture through this popular medium (Thangaraj 2010). According to a founder of an Indian-Pakistani American basketball league, "Most parents are first generation: a lot of nurses, engineers, doctors. There also are folks who own 7/11s." These examples illustrate the ability of Indian American men to participate within the sports world.

The Model Minority Body

Despite these accomplishments and sports venues, popular ideas of Indian Americans as incapable of successfully participating in sports continues, perpetuated by both Indian Americans and others. This disconnect from demonstrated reality stems in part from the particular conditions of the diaspora. Indian Americans are a heterogeneous population in terms of occupation, education, language, generations, sexuality, and more. Yet within this diversity some trends exist. A startling 70 percent of Indian Americans (age twenty-five and above) have a college education or more, compared to 28 percent of Americans as a whole.[3] Almost three quarters are immigrants, born outside of the United States. Excelling in scholastic exams within India, in order to attend extremely competitive universities in India and eventually come to the United States, requires significant time and dedication. While this is not the only way to migrate to the United States, it is standard for the families whose children participate in the bees. This practice left these immigrants with little opportunity for other time-consuming pursuits. The limited infrastructure for sports within India also lessens immigrants' development of a sports ethos when younger, even as they might have enjoyed playing cricket or other games.

Those who immigrate within this profile typically have spent less time developing a body for and commitment to sports, even if they enjoy sports as a hobby. Building on the work of Bourdieu, Washington and Karen argue that parents have a particular body schema, which is a group's "relation to the body at its deepest and most unconscious level," shaped sharply by one's social class (2001: 191). The body schema gets passed down to children, since parents do not train their kids in sports (beyond occasionally enrolling them in youth leagues). Much of the South Asian diaspora in the United States occupies a peculiar position: immigrant parents were alright not being competitive in sports because of class aspirations in India, which was not affiliated with sports for most of them. Now that they are raising their own children, they do not have the sports body schema to pass down like stereotypical middle- and upper-class white Americans do (or have access to through relatives).

This perceived disassociation of the community from sports, despite ample evidence to the contrary, is due not simply to the upbringings of many Indian Americans but also to the controlling images, of groups in sports. The contemporary gendered and sexualized racialization of Asian Americans has established them in the popular imagination as antithetical to not only traditional American sports but also to athleticism. When Asian American men were primarily laborers, from the mid-1800s until the mid-1900s, they were characterized as having animalistic bodies fit for their manual labor jobs, such as in railroads, gold mines, and mills. The same presumed body type made them sought-after workers yet also threatening to "civilized persons" (Okihiro 1994). Women's bodies were framed as sexually deviant and nimble, making them either prostitutes or fit for sewing and other intensive tasks. This "yellow peril" threatened the economic security and heteronormative morality of white America.

In response to the U.S. Civil Rights Movement of the 1950s and 1960s, the racialization of Asian Americans transformed them into the neoliberal model minority, who do not rely on government but instead on a culture of hard work. This image gained currency as Asian Americans became better known for their educational and professional accomplishments. The apparent praise of Asian Americans was actually a celebration of a certain image of the United States and a critique of African Americans and other minorities resisting internal colonial oppression. If a minority can succeed in the United States as Asian Americans appeared to do, then racism supposedly is a minor force or practically nonexistent. Within the false binary of mind and body, Asian Americans became read as all "mind." They remain in subservient, technical positions supportive of white-led capitalism.

While the model minority is characterized as the "mind" relative to the yellow peril "body," the model minority stereotype carries a racialized body as well. The supposed model minority is not simply an economic and racial notion; it also is a deformed body. As argued below, spelling bees serve as a nonnormative space in regard to gender and the body that allows the model minority body to flourish within a competitive environment.

Gendered Constructions

The model minority body for Asian American men is imagined as unmuscular, bent over, and ready to serve—in other words, they are seen as not "real men." Even in an age of growing respect for homosexuality, hegemonic masculinity remains narrowly defined as physically commanding and overpowering of others (Pascoe 2011). In contrast, Asian American men have been characterized as sexually deviant, reserved, quiet, diligent, and studious. They can become hypercompetitive and unstable, but this is read as a failed attempt to compensate for their real, effeminate nature (Brandzel and Desai 2008; Chan 2001; Sue and Kitano 1973; Thangaraj 2013).[4] Such notions limit not only the wage power but also the credibility of Asian American men as heterosexual bodies (Mok 1998). If Asian American men are not represented in this fashion, they typically are not represented at all, which further defines the Asian American male body as illegitimate. Asian Americans made up only 2 percent of the characters of television commercials during the 1990s, and were the least likely compared to other minorities or whites to be portrayed prominently and in positions of authority (Coltrane and Messineo 2000; Shankar 2013). They are similarly absent from advertisements in print media, even compared to Asian American women (Kim and Chung 2005). These images shape how people treat Asian American men as passive and able to be controlled (Manalansan 2003). Not surprisingly, experiments have found that Asian American men are denied leadership positions compared to other races (Cheng 1996).

Asian American model minority women are portrayed as hypersexual and/or subservient (Espiritu 2008). In contrast to the sporting body, they serve as an exaggerated version of the home-bound white woman, making them a prized possession by men but also deserving of critique. Those with extremely thin bodies and white appearances receive the most attention within mainstream media and are read as the most natural by white audiences (Thakore 2013). Any discussion of Asian American women in sports is dominated by figure skaters and gymnastics, given those sports' highly racialized feminine performance culture (Rand 2012; Tuan 1999). Petite bodies in revealing uniforms, highly choreographed routines, and the need for precision fit the Asian American woman stereotype. When not emulating a white feminine ideal form, Asian American women can be harassed—even violently—for having foreign, hairy, ungraceful physiques (Gibson 1988). Such bodies stand in contrast to the lean, toned, hairless bodies of celebrated female athletes. It is no surprise, then, that Asian American women report less satisfaction with their "arms, breasts, height, eyes, and face" and lower body self-esteem in general than do white women (Mintz and Kashubeck 1999: 792). The authors argue such dissatisfaction stems from the racialization of white women's bodies as ideal. In other words, Asian American women's bodies represent extreme poles of femininity, leaving white women as the standard.

Sports Cultures versus Asian (American) Cultures

The controlling image of the model minority body deviates strongly from what is valued within mainstream sports, making sports the arena that Asian Americans cannot be read to populate. While there are many kinds of genders that one can perform, sports are the prime domain where hegemonic gendered boundaries of body and performance are drawn (Doyle 2013; Washington and Karen 2001). Sports reward a muscular masculinity. When the father quoted above claims that Indian children cannot hold their breath long enough and get tired too easily, he is saying that they cannot be sufficiently masculine, whether boys or girls. Boys who do not act in accepted masculine ways lose power within their social world. Girls who act in masculine ways, such as tomboys, may gain power and/or at least general respect from others (Halberstam 1998; Reay 2001). This is not to say that masculine behavior is always valued. Athletes' presumed gender and sexuality impacts how they are interpreted (Rand 2012). For instance, tomboys are criticized if they act like boys past a certain age. And even with girls' celebrated masculinity, certain gendered boundaries cannot be crossed, such as girls playing tackle football. Still, masculinity to varying degrees remains valued within sports.

This gender performance within sports is learned at a young age. A queer approach to sports, such as an emphasis not on one's speed or strength but instead on goals of inclusion and personal performance, could deconstruct this privileging of hypermasculinity (King 2008; Rand 2012). Instead, teachers rely on gendered assumptions in how they try to support girls and boys in athletics (Larsson, Fagrell, and Redelius 2009). The dominance in sports of some boys over other boys and of almost all boys over girls is taken as natural as youth get older. Traditional sports—and schooling in general—divide quickly into gendered divisions, even at the pre-kindergarten stage (Martin 1998). Everyday boys and girls participate in sports separately for the most part, reinforcing gendered norms and boys' sexist attitudes toward girls (Anderson 2008; Messner 2013). For these reasons, youth with a greater sense of standard bodily athleticism have higher levels of physical and general self-esteem (Findlay and Bowker 2009).

In addition to its gendered and heterosocial aspects, sports are highly racialized in the United States. African American men and women are read as hypermasculine and thus apt for athletics (Farred 2000). The success of white athletes is attributed to their more cerebral nature and hours of practice (Thangaraj 2010; Washington and Karen 2001). Sports that are more physical and aggressive, such as football and basketball, are seen as disproportionately populated by blacks due to natural rather than societal factors (Eitle and Eitle 2002).

While Asian Americans may aspire to the hegemonic version of masculinity, their racialization as the model minority positions them as imitators. They are deviant within the gendered and sexualized bodily regime, and so both physically and culturally outside of sports

(Thangaraj 2012). Eastern culture, embodied most thoroughly by Asian immigrant women (especially those "behind the veil"), presumably emphasizes cultural conservatism and bodily concealment. For instance, the popular film *Bend It like Beckham* portrays sports as in tension with ethnic cultural conservatism (Puar and Rai 2004). The United States serves as a tolerant, exceptional nation through its embrace of sports and endorsement of cultural assimilation. In other parts of the diaspora, sports are also read as means to counter stereotyped religious and ethnic sexism. Muslim women in Britain and Greece play basketball and see it as sign of their acculturation (Dagkas and Benn 2006; Samie 2013). The notions of meritocracy, peer support, and bodily performance within sports serve as rhetorical antidotes to Asian cultural conservatism and authoritarianism.

Part 2. Bees as Alternate Competitive Spaces

Bees as Nonnormative Competitions

Despite being the presumed model minority, youth who took part in the bees also claimed an affinity for and proficiency in sports. Scripps champion Anamika Veeramani started playing competitive golf after her bee career ended. One bee contestant said that he had to know how to play sports in order to avoid being stigmatized. Another's father was a huge sports fan. As another boy said,

> I think that my parents have exposed me enough to different sports that I think that I won't not be in able to fit in. But I think that it is more of a challenge to um actually play well. Because it's been, I mean I'm not that great at it, but I think that I know how to play a lot of them.

He recognizes a competitive disadvantage in athletic venues, so he turns to another form of competition that allows for more diverse forms of masculinity. Rather than bees being a natural outlet for youth's competitive drive, interest in them stems in part from the youth's perceived inability to excel in physical sports. Such enjoyment for the bees signals not simply youths' attraction toward words but also their recognition that the politics around sports cannot provide needed bodily recognition (Rand 2012). Youth (and their families) want to excel in something rather than be the Jacks or Jills of all trades. Sports works as an extracurricular interest for most of these youth, not as a passion. For a number of these youth, the bees become their passion.

As an alternative competitive space, bees helped solve the problem facing families of wanting to compete within a sports framework but feeling unable to do so due to the discourse around sports, families' body schemas, and essentialist assumptions. The bees provide a means for nonnormative gender performances while still within a sports logic that families desire. A competitive spirit is a fundamental motivation for this hyper-model minority to spend hours studying words. The youth claim to enjoy the studying process, even if they find it tiring and tedious. But a large part of their motivation is to win, not simply to learn. One teenage girl said,

> [The competitive element is] really important.
> *(Q): You're not just spelling for the sake of spelling. You're spelling to win?*
> Yeah! That's like a good 30 percent of it.

The more competitive youth commit significant time to studying for the bees. It is not uncommon for them to study for four hours a day during weekdays, after finishing school and their schoolwork, and eight hours on weekends as the bees approach. Even when not in "bee season," such as in the fall, committed youth spend an hour a day studying.

The bees deviate in productive ways from the hypergendered aspects of standard athletics, both in the preparation for them and the performances at the competitions. In traditional sports, men mostly serve as coaches, not only for boys but also for girls. In contrast, for bees both parents can coach the child(ren), thereby complicating the embodiment of sport knowledge and its respective gendered social formations. This is not to say that no gendered aspect is at play. Mothers seemed to do more tutoring than fathers. But this tendency stemmed not from a presumed feminine aptitude for spelling or teaching but from the gendered division of paid versus domestic labor that puts mothers at home and so more available to coach children when out of school. I observed a mother and her thirteen-year-old daughter sitting at their kitchen table after breakfast, working through word sheets from the popular bee-preparation book *Words of Wisdom: Keys to Success in the Scripps*

National Spelling Bee. They were preparing for an Indian spelling bee. Wearing casual summer clothes and petting their small, white, puffy dog, the daughter would spell the German-origin words her mother read out to her from a laptop computer. The daughter would note on paper any words she missed. This was a ritual they had done countless times before.

This parent-child moment was replicated in various ways by families throughout the day and across locations. *Spellbound*, the 2002 Academy Award–nominated documentary on the Scripps bee, profiles an Indian immigrant father coaching his son (and, before that, his daughter). A Scripps champion kept her practice memorabilia and shared with me the disposable paper placemat of an Italian restaurant that she had visited twenty years ago with her family. All over the menu she had written Italian-origin words. Her parents had taken the opportunity of being at an Italian restaurant to quiz her on related words. For spellers, every space allows for a teaching moment, not only a practice field, and no special equipment needs to be mastered and carried, just a pen and paper.

Beyond the act of preparing, the competitive performance at the bees also deviates from gendered sports expectations. Unlike traditional sports, boys and girls compete against one another rather than in single-sex constructs. Contestants wear casual clothes—jeans, shorts, Tee-shirts, dresses, sneakers, etc.—instead of gendered uniforms and equipment that often serve no functional purpose (Rand 2012). Rather than sex, the dividing markers are age and corresponding grade level. Either boys or girls can be the more masculine or the more feminine and still be completely competitive (see Halberstam 1998). One's cognitive abilities and years of practice matter in this case, not the physical skills one has developed. Such integration works against the hegemonic standards within traditional sports that privilege the most gendered persons on the field and in the locker room (Anderson 2008). For bees there is no locker room, no definitive backstage where boys or girls perform gender to one another and away from family. So, while mainstream sports are read as antidotes to traditional patriarchy within "Eastern" cultures, they actually further sexist and homophobic disciplinary regimes. Extracurricular activities that integrate the sexes, like spelling bees, can break down sexist assumptions (ibid.). Having said this, bees are not free of gendered practices. Boys and girls socialized separately during down time. But such a conventional division takes place "off the field" rather than being organized and enforced by the sport itself.

The nongendered body also finds support at these bees. While the ideal athletic body has well-defined muscles, zero body fat, no body hair, and no glasses, those at the bees carry a variety of body styles. Glasses are common. Few of the boys or girls, even those in junior high, would be described as physically intimidating. Instead, boys are often tall and lanky or of average and shorter height and of standard body appearance or slightly overweight by conventional norms. Girls at all ages range in body types from slim to large. Girls' bodies are not monitored and chastised as in traditional sports (Lenskyj 1990). In other words, the children had average physiques. Again, this is not to suggest that the youth did not carry their bodies in commonly gendered ways. At times, for example, boys wore sports gear and girls wore dresses and makeup. I heard girls compliment one another on the outfits they wore at the competition. Yet their ability to perform in the bees was not judged relative to their body types. In fact, having too muscular and coordinated a body could suggest that one did not take seriously enough the expectations of the bees. For instance, during a dialogue session about geography bees at the NSF finals, parents asked youth how they balanced preparation for the bees with other extracurricular activities. A tall, lanky teenage boy with glasses responded that he spent so much time studying for the geography bee that he dropped out of his school's soccer team, which was deemed much less important.[5] The nods with which parents reacted indicated their approval of cultivating a model minority body over a hypergendered one.

"The Brain Sport"

While bees affirm a model minority body in contrast to the gendered rules of traditional sports, sports proved to be a governing logic to them. Families do not reject the presumptions of sports. Instead, they want to embrace many of its characteristics. The bees provide a liminal space for families. It lets the hyper-model minority connect to the popular sports logic but without having the youth fail on the field.

Parts of the preparation and production of the bees mimic sports. While parents remain the most common tutors for spellers, "coaches"—as they are referred to by the youth and themselves—are growing in popularity. Many parents refer to themselves as coaches of their own children. Yet more and more adults work as for-profit coaches. Some are former Scripps champions and contestants, some are parents of strong contestants, and some are local educators who have turned to this entrepreneurial activity. One father of a highly successful speller quit his business and started coaching spelling and geography bee contestants full time. Most of his clientele are Indian, as is he. Families drive for over two hours twice a week to attend sessions at his home office. Spelling is not the only bee with coaches. The North South Foundation website has a link to "Coaching," which volunteers for its math bees have established. In geography, Kumar Nandur, aka "Coach Kumar," trains youth for free in Florida. Families traveled from as far as Ohio, Texas, and Virginia to attend his retreat for geography bee preparation.[6] At the 2013 North South Foundation finals, he hosted an education session for families, after which parents stood in line to introduce their children to him or to ask a particular question about strategies for the bee. As is common in other fields, as a position becomes more professionalized and moves out of the unpaid domestic sphere, it shifts from predominantly female to predominantly male.

In addition to coaches, there are materials specific to the bees that have become available and are seen as necessary tools for training, as with any specialized field. While the image of spellers combing through dog-eared dictionaries has merit, they now more often use spelling-bee-directed word lists, CDs, training videos, and the like that entrepreneurs have created and sell for a profit.

For those who make it to the Scripps National Spelling Bee, the sports analogy becomes even more heightened. Scripps is televised live for two days on the sports channel ESPN. As an ESPN producer told me, the bee is a somewhat unusual programming choice but still makes sense for ESPN to televise because it is highly competitive and suspenseful, much like its regular sports broadcasts. Extreme physical effort is not necessary for all "sporting" activities seen on the channel, such as the World Series of Poker and bowling. Nor is the presentation of a youth competition exceptional; the Little League World Series is televised on ESPN as well.

The production recipe that ESPN uses for traditional sports also applies to coverage of Scripps. In addition to televising the competition from different angles—moving between the speller at the microphone, the judges, the announcer, the families, the other contestants, and the audience at key moments—individual spellers' (as well as the pronouncer's) stories are highlighted so as to create narratives that further draw in viewers. The Scripps finals, involving approximately the top fifty contestants, are televised live in evening prime time on ESPN's main channel. Two anchors sit behind a constructed booth in the back of the ballroom where the competition is held. The anchors speak about the spellers and the categories of words they encounter, take the pulse of the anxiety-filled room, and interview children. The whispered tones of the announcers as spellers work through their words at the microphone are identical to the tones used during golf, diving, gymnastics, and other competitions. The presence of ESPN is frequently noted by parents and youth. During the first day of the competition, spellers and the families say they do not expect to win but hope to get far enough into the competition to "make it onto ESPN" the next evening. Consoling someone who made it to the finals but lost involves saying that at least s/he made it to ESPN, a channel that is uniformly thought of as "cool."

For those who do win, the sportslike experience heightens even more. After the confetti has fallen and the awards and trophies have been presented, reporters aim to get a brief interview with the winner, just as after major sports event. Moreover, like Super Bowl and World Series champions, the speller (along with her/his family) goes on to meet the president of the United States. One former champion said that the meeting with President Obama lasted for about twenty minutes, and they discussed (among other topics) why Indians excel at the bees. The winners also make appearances on late-night entertainment talk shows, on ESPN's main news program (*SportsCenter*), and on straight-news programs both nationally and in their local areas. Print and internet media also cover the accomplishment. Because the competition is televised nationally in prime time and subsequently covered in the media, past champions report being noticed by strangers afterward. Within the NSF and SASB competitions, former Scripps champions who come to run informational sessions and serve as judges are treated with extreme deference and awe, much like professional athletes at lower-tier sporting events. Youth and parents both line up to get their photographs taken with a champion and shake her/his hand.[7] The champions' parents are quizzed about their training regimens.

The sports logic within the media also guides SASB. Like Scripps, SASB is a televised, corporate-driven event. SASB is a for-profit venture directly run by the CEO, Rahul Walia, of its parent company, Touchdown Media. Rahul was looking for a product that would attract the Indian American audience, and thereby build support and credibility for Touchdown Media, a marketing and advertising agency that aims to link corporations to the South Asian American market. The spelling bee started as a tool to show corporate advertisers that he can connect with the client base.

> If you know you want to connect with this audience, let's do a spelling bee for them. For every South Asian child that is being represented on the national stage [at Scripps], I'm sure there are hundreds that are wanting to emulate [and are looking for a competition].

As for traditional sports, corporate sponsors make possible the competition of SASB. While NSF depends on hundreds of volunteers, SASB runs on just a few staff because it has financial support from Metropolitan Life Insurance, Air India, C2 Education, and Sony Television (which, as of 2013, broadcasts the bee once completed and edited). As in traditional sports, private corporations team up with SASB to offer awards to winners and contestants. As of 2013 the winner earns $10,000, sponsored by Metropolitan Life Insurance. Air India even gave two round-trip airline tickets to India to two contestants who had been attending the SASB finals for years.[8]

SASB does not just chase corporate sponsors. Corporations also chase spellers in the same way that sports celebrities are coveted by major advertisers and become lucrative "products" for the advertisers (Dinces 2011). For instance, on June 11, 2013, Touchdown Media hosted a reception in a New York City Indian restaurant in honor of the recent Scripps champion, Arvind Mahankali, an SASB alum. Representatives of SASB corporate sponsors were the main guests; along with past judges and family and friends, they were there to congratulate Mahankali and have videos and pictures taken with him, to be aired online and on Sony Television. At this event, corporate sponsors told me that they want to target the lucrative Indian American audience, stereotyped as wealthy, education focused, and family oriented, which fit their brands.

Like sports events, spelling bees must make good television in order to be broadcast. Sports leagues continually alter their rules to better engage the audience. Similarly, the spelling bee platform would not have risen in popularity if it did not attract an audience. In this way television production and corporate agendas have furthered the educational opportunities for Indian Americans, not the other way around. As Rahul said,

> The spelling bee does have a glamour quotient to it. It is an interactive kind of thing. A science contest or anything else math-related is going to be, you know, not as glamorous. . . . So I found that extremely interesting that something as, at that time what I used to consider mundane, could actually be a television event. . . . We want to take it to the UK and Canada. We want to do ground events there. [sic]

Bees become attractive to the community in part due to their availability, driven in part by corporate efforts to marry profit to "family values."

The resemblance of bees to traditional sports is not lost on the spellers and their families. They frequently compared bees to athletic competitions and drew upon sports analogies. Being a competitive speller is "like Olympic athletes!" said one youth, but harder.

> In the Olympics you get all those events and competitions [in your sport] outside of the Olympics. Basketball players play for sixteen years. But we only get five years of competing.

One father, as I passed him in the hallway and expressed sympathy for the fact that his son fell out of the SASB finals early, volunteered that spelling is the most "brutal of sports." If you make a mistake in golf, football, and most any other sport, you can make up for it. But in spelling, one mistake dooms you. One young person referred to the spelling bee as "the brain sport" and said that, as such, it is well suited for Indian Americans who are competitive but cannot excel in traditional sports.[9] Even individuals unassociated with bees talk about spelling as a sport. The Indian American comedian Hari Kondabolu has a routine on the Scripps National Spelling Bee, or "as I like to call it," he joked, "the Indian Super Bowl." As he told a reporter, "There aren't any South Asian athletes. I mean Jeremy Lin was Taiwanese-American. I took ownership of that. It's as close as we've gotten." Joking about the 2013 Scripps champion Mahankali's plan to compete in physics competitions after having won the spelling bee, Kondabolu declared, "He's a two-sport athlete!"[10]

Neoliberal Logics

The ability to claim bees as a legitimate sports alternative rests not only on its preparation and production but also on the neoliberal logic embedded within sports. Neoliberalism refers to the declining role of the state in securing the welfare of its residents, to be replaced by individual self-sufficiency and human capital development within an increasingly corporatized economy that stretches to markets abroad. People become entrepreneurs of themselves, investing in personal training that builds character and skills necessary for economic growth (Gordon 1991; Ong 2006).

Organized sports for both adults and youth have embraced and furthered the neoliberal ideology. It is taken for granted that youth should dedicate hours to sports training, which not only builds athletic skills but also creates disciplined, governed persons and bodies (Spaaij 2009). Such regulation of "moral" behavior is the explicit premise behind youth sports, especially for boys considered "at risk" (Anderson 2013). Similarly, parents of spellers promote spelling as a way for children to develop personal skills necessary for later schooling and work and to avoid adopting negative traits associated with delinquency. While winning is strongly desired, parents and youth both realize it is not likely, and so other benefits of competing are stressed (Friedman 2013). Spelling bees are more about creating the right kind of citizen than they are about the vocabulary. A couple of parents (of different children) and I were talking at the SASB finals. The first parent was speaking about her daughter:

> MOTHER: Winning and losing—they handle it so much better than, you know, people who never actually competed. [You learn] resilience.
> FATHER: Resilience and spirit.
> MOTHER: Seriously, man.

As another parent said about the real function of sports and bees,

> Playing a sport is not about getting the ball, it's about how you interact . . . it's about learning winning and losing, and you don't want to take that away.

Many parents echo this same point, that the worth of the bees comes from the hours training, of working towards a goal, of learning to sacrifice, of learning how to lose. As in traditional sports, the work sculpts not only the body but also the mind and spirit, turning children into governable persons with an unquestioned work ethic (Weeks 2011).

The hours now demanded for training means that youth specialize in specific sports at younger and younger ages rather than explore a range of sports, putting themselves at increased risk of injury.[11] The goal is to build up the body schema necessary to excel in a particular endeavor and effectively compete against peers who also have become more trained and focused. Preparation for the bees expects the same dedication and specialization at an increasingly young age. For instance, NSF starts at first grade but some parents petition to have their kindergarten students allowed entry. During a competition a child as young as age five or six was announced as a contestant; parents applaud in encouragement of someone so young already competing.

Within neoliberalism, private corporations rather than the state become individuals' "partners" in their self-growth. For example, NFL Play 60 is the National Football League's effort to encourage athleticism in youth, endorsed by the White House as a model to promote healthy bodies.[12] Corporations substitute for a lively civic sphere that would encourage exercise. Televised spelling bees, whether Scripps or SASB, are further examples of corporations promoting youth specialization. E. W. Scripps Company, which owns the National Spelling Bee, is a media corporation that owns television stations and newspapers across the country as well as a digital media platform. Before Scripps acquired the bee in 1941, local newspapers across the country rotated sponsorship of it. Scripps centralized the bee and placed it in the nation's capital to signify its status as a national event, abandoning any of its regional character. Scripps, a publicly traded company on the New York Stock Exchange, depends on the National Spelling Bee for part of its revenue, which its media outlets cover and promote.

Those who advertise on the spelling bee broadcasts also are quintessential neoliberal agents. For SASB, two main sponsors are MetLife, Inc., and C2 Education. As an insurance company, MetLife makes a profit out of helping individuals handle their individual and family economic risks through life insurance policies. C2 Education provides private tutoring for youth in preparation for scholastic exams as well as in preprofessional skills such as "time management" and "personal organization." Public education receives less attention and possibly support as a result.

After all the training and sacrifice by youth and their families, it is surprising that so few contestants remain bitter about losing. Having only one winner in sports leagues and spelling events is not questioned by participants but instead is considered appropriate, in part because sports and bees are regarded as meritocratic. Contestants supposedly are not judged by the color of their skin or their family's origin. With its multicultural cast of spellers, *Spellbound* argues that anyone can win the spelling bee. In the film, then National Spelling Bee pronouncer Alex Cameron expounds on the origins of the spelling bee in eighteenth-century America, a time of economic expansion made possible through educational achievement, virtues encapsulated in the bee (McArthur 2011). This belief in a system that offers people equal opportunity and choice to cultivate themselves as they see fit is the hallmark of neoliberal logic, one that allows the winners to have as much resources as they can without fault and which blames the losers for their loss. Among participants there is little discussion of how expensive it can be to adequately prepare for the bee, including the training materials, the time studying rather than assisting with domestic chores, the usefulness of having a parent who does not earn a wage outside the home so that (predominantly) she can train the child, and the costs of a dedicated coach.

One last way in which bees, like sports, uphold a neoliberal logic is their embrace of nationalism and patriotism as a means to validate its practices despite any detrimental effects. Within advanced capitalist systems, multinational corporations undermine citizens with the aid of government policies, in the form of tax codes, trade agreements, bankruptcy protections, union busting, and the like. Similarly, military interventions rarely serve the immediate needs of citizens. Nationalism and patriotism tie citizens to the state in emotional and ideological ways, preempting critique of the material costs imposed by neoliberal policies. Sports is well known to have become a nationalist endeavor. Beyond the rituals of elite air force planes flying overhead at important games and ordinary people singing the national anthem, politicians increasingly attend sports events and weigh in on sports news (Scherer and Koch 2010). Even sporting events that aim to subvert gendered or sexual axioms promote patriotism (Rand 2012). The same is true for spelling bees, which celebrate American English and have been regarded as an American pastime. In fact, the bee started as a way to promote and valorize American English over British English (McArthur 2011).

A Liminal Conclusion

The bees work as a liminal space that seems to resolve the contradictions facing their most ardent families: of feeling less adequate within hegemonic sports spaces while embracing and excelling in the same virtues of sports. More than being a "safe space" for those with the model minority body, the bees reconcile the hyper-model minority with the normative and valued logic of sports. We cannot understand the popularity of the bees among this group without understanding families' relationship to sports. Like any liminal encounter, the bees get their meanings, rituals, and symbols from their broader context, which provides a template of how to act (Gray and Thumma 1997; Turner 1969). In this case, they mimic sports events with their confetti, trophies, suspense, coaching preparation, single winner, celebrity adoration, production, and more. Underlying these symbols and rituals is the neoliberal ideology embedded within contemporary sports. By connecting these cultural dimensions to the model minority body, the bees validate the diasporic community's sense of themselves with their place in the United States.

Yet, as with all liminal spaces, these are temporary resolutions to social dislocations. While those few who become Scripps champions receive praise from their peers for having beaten so many challengers on national television, the rest return home relatively unnoticed, especially when having competed in Indian-only bees. These bees cannot overturn the hypergendered and sports logics that govern social lives. In fact, the bees affirm much of these logics and with that the primacy of sports and its gendered assumptions, which helped push Indian Americans toward alternative spaces like bees in the first place. By upholding a sports logic, the bees attract more youth but belie their queering potential.

NOTES

1 See, e.g., "Dinner for Tiger Joginder Singh," 1951, *South Asian American Digital Archive*. https://www.saada.org/item/20111222-568.

2 Kelly Whiteside, "USSF President Gulati Is Professor of the Pitch," May 1, 2006, *USA Today*. http://www.usatoday.com/sports/soccer/national/2006-05-01-gulati_x.htm?POE=click-refer.

3 U.S. Census Bureau, *2006–2010 American Community Survey*. http://www.census.gov/programs-surveys/acs/data/race-aian.html.

4 For instance, the porn industry portrays Asian American men as passive. Mainstream magazines and television convey this depiction as well. For instance, *Details* magazine in April 2004 had a spread asking "Gay or Asian?"—the point being that members of the two groups are identical in their effeminate styles, bodies, and fetishes (e.g., shaved balls).

5 Field notes, Durham, North Carolina, August 18, 2013.

6 Vicki Hyman, "They Know Where It's At: Indian-Americans Rule at National Geographic Bee," March 31, 2013, *NJ.com*. http://www.nj.com/news/index.ssf/2013/03/national_geographic_bee_story.html.

7 Field notes, San Jose, California, September 4, 2011.

8 Field notes, New Jersey, August 16, 2013.

9 The audience in the room applauded this remark. Field notes, New Jersey, August 15, 2013.

10 Elizabeth Blair, "Comedian Hari Kondabolu on Diversity, Race and Burger King," July 18, 2013, *National Public Radio*. http://www.npr.org/blogs/codeswitch/2013/07/18/203034882/comedian-hari-kondabolu-on-diversity-race-and-burger-king.

11 Tom Goldman, "Young Athletes Risk Back Injury by Playing Too Much," February 3, 2014, *National Public Radio*. http://www.npr.org/templates/transcript/transcript.php?storyId=269521744.

12 "First Lady's Let's Move! Campaign and NFL's Play 60 Campaign Team Up to Tackle Childhood Obesity," September 8, 2010, *White House/Office of the First Lady*. http://www.whitehouse.gov/the-press-office/2010/09/08/first-lady-s-let-s-move-campaign-and-nfl-s-play-60-campaign-team-tackle-.

REFERENCES

Anderson, Eric. 2013. "i9 and the Transformation of Youth Sport." *Journal of Sport & Social Issues* 37.1: 97–111.

———. 2008. "'I Used to Think Women Were Weak': Orthodox Masculinity, Gender Segregation, and Sport." *Sociological Forum* 23.2: 257–280.
Brandzel, Amy, and Jigna Desai. 2008. "Race, Violence, and Terror: The Cultural Defensibility of Heteromasculine Citizenship in the Virginia Tech Massacre and the Don Imus Affair." *Journal of Asian American Studies* 11.1: 61–85.
Chan, Jachinson. 2001. *Chinese American Masculinities: From Fu Manchu to Bruce Lee.* New York: Routledge.
Cheng, Cliff. 1996. "'We Choose Not to Compete': The 'Merit' Discourse in the Selection Process, and Asian and Asian American Men and Their Masculinity," in *Masculinities in Organizations*, ed. Cliff Cheng. Research on Men and Masculinities Series, Vol. 9. Thousand Oaks, CA: Sage Publications.
Coltrane, Scott, and Melinda Messineo. 2000. "The Perpetuation of Subtle Prejudice: Race and Gender Imagery in 1990s Television Advertising." *Sex Roles* 42.5–6: 363–389.
Dagkas, Symeon, and Tansin Benn. 2006. "Young Muslim Women's Experiences of Islam and Physical Education in Greece and Britain: A Comparative Study." *Sport, Education and Society* 11.1: 21–38.
Dinces, Sean. 2011. "'Flexible Opposition': Skateboarding Subcultures under the Rubric of Late Capitalism." *International Journal of the History of Sport* 28.11: 1512–1535.
Doyle, Jennifer. 2013. "Dirt off Her Shoulders." *GLQ: A Journal of Lesbian and Gay Studies* 19.4: 419–433.
Eitle, Tamela McNulty, and David J. Eitle. 2002. "Race, Cultural Capital, and the Educational Effects of Participation in Sports." *Sociology of Education* 75.2: 123–146.
Espiritu, Yen Le. 2008. *Asian American Women and Men: Labor, Laws, and Love.* Lanham, MD: Rowman & Littlefield.
Farred, Grant. 2000. "Cool as the Other Side of the Pillow: How ESPN's SportsCenter Has Changed Television Sports Talk." *Journal of Sport & Social Issues* 24.2: 96–117.
Findlay, Leanne C., and Anne Bowker. 2009. "The Link between Competitive Sport Participation and Self-Concept in Early Adolescence: A Consideration of Gender and Sport Orientation." *Journal of Youth and Adolescence* 38.1: 29–40.
Friedman, Hilary Levey. 2013. *Playing to Win: Raising Children in a Competitive Culture.* Berkeley, Los Angeles, and London: University of California Press.
Gibson, Margaret. 1988. *Accommodation without Assimilation: Sikh Immigrants in an American High School.* Ithaca, NY: Cornell University Press.
Gordon, Colin. 1991. "Governmental Rationality: An Introduction," in *The Foucault Effect: Studies in Governmentality*, ed. Michel Foucault, Graham Burchell, Colin Gordon, and Peter Miller. Chicago: University of Chicago Press.
Gray, Edward R., and Scott L. Thumma. 1997. "The Gospel Hour: Liminality, Identity, and Religion in a Gay Bar," in *Contemporary American Religion: An Ethnographic Reader*, ed. Penny Edgell Becker and Nancy Eisland. Lanham, MD: AltaMira Press: 79–98.
Halberstam, Judith. 1998. *Female Masculinity.* Durham, NC: Duke University Press.

Kim, Minjeong, and Angie Y. Chung. 2005. "Consuming Orientalism: Images of Asian/American Women in Multicultural Advertising." *Qualitative Sociology* 28.1: 67–91.

King, Samantha. 2008. "What's Queer about (Queer) Sport Sociology Now? A Review Essay." *Sociology of Sport Journal* 25(4): 419–442.

Larsson, Håkan, Birgitta Fagrell, and Karin Redelius. 2009. "Queering Physical Education: Between Benevolence towards Girls and a Tribute to Masculinity." *Physical Education and Sport Pedagogy* 14.1: 1–17.

Lenskyj, Helen. 1990. "Power and Play: Gender and Sexuality Issues in Sport and Physical Activity." *International Review for the Sociology of Sport* 25.3: 235–245.

Manalansan, Martin F., IV. 2003. *Global Divas: Filipino Gay Men in the Diaspora*. Durham, NC: Duke University Press.

Martin, Karin. 1998. "Becoming a Gendered Body: Practices of Preschools." *American Sociological Review* 6.4: 494–511.

McArthur, Rachel. 2011. "Out of Many, One: Spelling Bees and the United States National Spelling Bee." *English Languages: History, Diaspora, Culture* 2: 1–22.

Messner, Michael. 2013. "Reflections on Communication and Sport: On Men and Masculinities." *Communication & Sport* 1.2: 113–124.

Mintz, Laurie, and Susan Kashubeck. 1999. "Body Image and Disordered Eating among Asian American and Caucasian College Students: An Examination of Race and Gender Differences." *Psychology of Women Quarterly* 23.4: 781–796.

Mok, Teresa. 1998. "Getting the Message: Media Images and Stereotypes and Their Effect on Asian Americans." *Cultural Diversity and Mental Health* 4.3: 185.

Okihiro, Gary. 1994. *Margins and Mainstreams: Asians in American History and Culture*. Seattle: University of Washington Press.

Ong, Aihwa. 2006. *Neoliberalism as Exception: Mutations in Citizenship and Sovereignty*. Durham, NC: Duke University Press.

Ong, Paul, Edna Bonacich, and Lucie Cheng. 1994. *The New Asian Immigration in Los Angeles and Global Restructuring*. Philadelphia: Temple University Press.

Pascoe, C. J. 2011. *Dude, You're a Fag: Masculinity and Sexuality in High School*. Berkeley: University of California Press.

Puar, Jasbir K., and Amit Rai. 2004. "The Remaking of a Model Minority: Perverse Projectiles under the Specter of (Counter) Terrorism." *Social Text* 22.3: 75–104.

Rand, Erica. 2012. *Red Nails, Black Skates: Gender, Cash, and Pleasure on and off the Ice*. Durham, NC: Duke University Press.

Reay, Diane. 2001. "'Spice Girls,' 'Nice Girls,' 'Girlies,' and 'Tomboys': Gender Discourses, Girls' Cultures and Femininities in the Primary Classroom." *Gender and Education* 13.2: 153–166.

Samie, Samaya F. 2013. "Hetero-Sexy Self/Body Work and Basketball: The Invisible Sporting Women of British Pakistani Muslim Heritage." *South Asian Popular Culture* 11.3: 257–270.

Scherer, Jay, and Jordan Koch. 2010. "Living with War: Sport, Citizenship, and the Cultural Politics of Post-9/11 Canadian Identity." *Sociology of Sport Journal* 27.1: 1–29.

Shankar, Shalini. 2013. "Racial Naturalization, Advertising, and Model Consumers for a New Millennium." *Journal of Asian American Studies* 16.2: 159–188.

Spaaij, Ramón. 2009. "Sport as a Vehicle for Social Mobility and Regulation of Disadvantaged Urban Youth Lessons from Rotterdam." *International Review for the Sociology of Sport* 44.2–3: 247–264.

Sue, Stanley, and Harry H. L. Kitano. 1973. "Stereotypes as a Measure of Success." *Journal of Social Issues* 29.2: 83–98.

Thakore, Bhoomi. 2013. "Just Like Everyone Else? Locating South Asians in 21st-Century American Popular Media." PhD dissertation, Loyola University Chicago.

Thangaraj, Stanley I. 2013. "Competing Masculinities: South Asian American Identity Formation in Asian American Basketball Leagues." *South Asian Popular Culture* 11.3: 243–255.

———. 2012. "Playing through Differences: Black–White Racial Logic and Interrogating South Asian American Identity." *Ethnic and Racial Studies* 35.6: 988–1006.

———. 2010. "'Liting It Up': Popular Culture, Indo-Pak Basketball, and South Asian American Institutions." *Cosmopolitan Civil Societies: An Interdisciplinary Journal* 2.2: 71–91.

Tuan, Mia. 1999. "On Asian American Ice Queens and Multigeneration Asian Ethnics." *Amerasia Journal* 25.1: 181–186.

Turner, Victor. 1969. *The Ritual Process: Structure and Anti-Structure*. Chicago: Aldine.

Washington, Robert, and David Karen. 2001. "Sport and Society." *Annual Review of Sociology* 27: 187–212.

Weeks, Kathi. 2011. *The Problem with Work: Feminism, Marxism, Antiwork Politics, and Postwork Imaginaries*. Durham, NC: Duke University Press.

6

Mixed Martial Arts, Caged Orientalism, and Female Asian American Bodies

JESSICA W. CHIN AND DAVID L. ANDREWS

Introduction

The term "Asian American" was originally a pan-ethnic political category mobilized within the struggle for equal rights during the 1960s (Okamoto, 2006). However, like many expressions of radicalism during that time, the real and symbolic virulence of Asian Americans as a political category has been largely diffused and depoliticized by the hypercommodifying culture of late capitalism, wherein the celebration of racial or ethnic difference has become an important marketing strategy (hooks, 1992; Jameson, 1998). Not that the increased visibility of Asian American faces and characters within mainstream advertising, primetime television, or blockbuster movies should merely infer a heightened interest in engaging the not inconsiderable Asian American market (Shankar 2013, 2015). Rather, it is our contention that the elevated presence of Asian American Others within the popular media (including the emergence of a coterie of Asian American sport celebrities) is also, and perhaps more significantly, redolent of important transformations associated with the rise of a post-Fordist economic and cultural order. Prompted by the crisis of Fordist overproduction and the need to stimulate the consumer marketplace (Gartman, 1998), U.S. post-Fordist consumer capitalism has "fallen in love with difference" (Davidson, 1992, p. 199). Within this context, the racial and ethnic Otherness previously eschewed, or at the very least marginalized, by commercial interests has become an ever more noticeable aesthetic or stylistic dimension within the dominant regime of capital accumulation, and as a consequence, an ever more visible presence within American popular culture.

America's most celebrated athletes tend to be those who combine athletic excellence with carefully choreographed attitudes, values, and narratives that resonate with those of the general consuming public (that mythical, yet nonetheless influential cohort, residing somewhere in the Midwest of the American imagination). Unlike in previous epochs, post-Fordist America's economy of sport celebrities constitutes a distinctly multicultural domain, one in which racial and ethnic difference is *managed* for commercial expediency, rather than being *advanced* for sociopolitical transformation (or, indeed, *ignored* to realize a sociopolitical stasis). Hall described the post-Fordist turn to racial and ethnic difference as a "profound cultural revolution" responsible for the commercial mobilization and representation of the faces, cultures, and "languages of the margin," which has important implications for marginalized groups being able to "reclaim some form of representation for themselves." When it comes to the mediated representation of Asian American sport celebrities, we do not share Hall's sanguine view. There appears little likelihood of Asian American sport celebrities avoiding the Orientalizing and "imperializing eye" (Hall, 1992, p. 34) that has and continues to represent Asian American–ness in a manner complicit in the "reorganization of white supremacy and the ways it produced racial hierarchy" (Yu, 2003, p. 1408).

While numerous contributions to this volume demonstrate sport to be a vital and resonant space for the expression of Asian American communities' sense of collective identity and belonging, within this discussion, we offer an alternative viewpoint. It is our contention that the relatively recent emergence of the high-profile Asian American celebrity athlete (most visibly personified by Jeremy Lin, but also including such figures as Kristi Yamaguchi, Michelle Kwan, and Michelle Wie) has passively reinforced—as opposed to actively challenged and rendered anachronous—residual stereotypes pertaining to the nature of Asian American bodies and populations. As Leonard (2014) noted, the multiple discursive fields that combined to create the promotional vortex known as "Linsanity" incorporated:

> [p]art model minority discourse, part immigrant narrative, part American Dream, part anti-Black racism, part American exceptionalism, and part Cinderella story.... Whether talking race, culture, nation, or ethnicity, Lin offered a vehicle to rehash and recycle stereotypes galore. (p. 145)

In addition to invoking many of the tropes associated with the Asian American population at large, the Lin phenomenon is rooted in a specifically masculinist racial narrative that counters the pejorative representation of Asian American males as physically emasculated, passive, nerds (Kim, 2014; also see Wang, this volume). This racially essentialized subjectivity is reinforced through the positioning of Lin as the atypical Asian American male. The very atypicality of Lin as a high-profile male Asian American athlete is arguably accentuated by the relative preponderance of highly visible female Asian American athletes. Hence, in what we consider to be an interesting counterpoint to the Lin scenario, our general aim is to critically examine the construction and representation of female Asian American sport celebrities, specifically as it pertains to the intersecting racial/ethnic, gender, and national politics of the contemporary (Asian) American formation. This involves an explication of the Orientalist treatment of Asian American women within the popular media, followed by interrogations of the representation of Asian American female athletes operating both within stereotypically female sport cultures, and within the traditionally masculine preserve of mixed martial arts (MMA). Through this analysis, we hope to elucidate the precise and intersecting ways that female Asian American athletic bodies are raced and gendered, in ways that challenge and corroborate the representation and perception of Asian American women within U.S. popular culture.

I. Orientalism and Asian American Othering

This analysis is framed by Edward Said's (1994, 1979) concept of Orientalism. At its core, Orientalism refers to the longstanding Western logic rooted in the establishment of epistemological and ontological differences that positioned the Occident/Occidental in a position of supremacy over the Orient/Oriental (Schueller, 2001). Thereby, the authority of the West (the Occident) over the East (the Orient) was justified in the minds and consciences of Western imperial powers, through strategic representational practices involving "making statements about it, authorizing views of it, describing it, by teaching it, settling it, ruling over it: in short, Orientalism as a Western style for dominating, restructuring, and having authority over the Orient" (Said, 1979, p. 3).

In Foucauldian terms, Said demonstrated how the West's rendering visible of the Orient was attendant to its domination of it. Thus, the discursive production of the Orient is a constitutive element of the West's seemingly manifest social, cultural, political, economic, and ideological supremacy, highlighting the dependency of the West on constructing representations, or knowledge, of the Orient "for nothing less than its sense of self" (Darnell, 2013, p. 5). As Park and Wilkins (2005) noted:

> Through this process of Orientalism, large groups of people with diverse histories become oversimplified into one monolithic, subordinate and ahistorical category. These problematic constructions are perpetuated through visual images, verbal descriptors, and the selection of experts within the media. While Orientalism describes how western media, and other institutions, dominate through the cultural production of the eastern other, this reflexive process also means that the West defines its own culture, and sense of dominance, in relation to this constructed, subordinate "Orient." (p. 3)

At the heart of Orientalizing representational practices is the homogenized Othering of Oriental bodies, the reductive discursive caricaturing of an entire continent of diverse and heterogeneous peoples (Lowe, 1991; 1996) into "one or two terminal, collective abstractions" (Said, 1979, p. 155). These were generalized embodiments of Eastern difference: "European externalizations" (Ono & Pham, 2009, p. 43). The marginalizing and demonizing Western gaze has—as much through media and cultural expressions as political, legal, or economic edict—constructed the Oriental Other. Hence, according to the prevailing Orientalist binary, popular representations routinely depict the Oriental masses as comprising "mysterious, erotic, dark, dangerous" uncivilized bodies (Nayak & Maline, 2009, p. 256), unavoidably counterposed in relation to the embodied Occidental civility of the West.

While Said's original explication of Orientalism focused largely on the West's depiction of the cultures and peoples of the Middle East, within *Culture and Imperialism* (1994), he broadened the discussion to include a wider range of Orientalized Asian constituencies, and a broader array of nineteenth- and twentieth-century Orientalizing agents (including works of Western—predominantly, though by no means exclusively, U.S-originated—fiction, nonfiction, television, films, music, and theater). As he noted, highlighting the "crude, reductionist, coarsely racialist" Western representation of the Arab world in the post-1967 era, "films and television shows portraying Arabs as sleazy 'camel-jockeys,' terrorists, and offensively wealthy 'sheikhs' pour forth" (1994, p. 36). If anything, the mass media–propelled Orientalism Said identified is ever more virulent today. Though there are over 50 countries in the continent of Asia (and 16 culturally, economically, and politically distinct countries in East and Southeast Asia, more specifically), stereotypes enacted within, and through, popular culture and mainstream media tend to generalize across large swaths of Asian nations, erasing multiple, heterogeneous layers of history, identity, and experience (Lowe, 1991). Certainly, this is something identified and elaborated upon by numerous scholars interested in illuminating the Orientalizing of contrasting national populations and settings (cf. Brody, 2010; Keft-Kennedy, 2005; Klein, 2003; Little, 2008; Rosen, 2000; Schueller, 2001; Tchen & Yeats, 2014).

Within the U.S. context, the highly heterogeneous, hybrid, and multiplicitous Asian American population has been subject to a process of reductionist demonization at the hands of political, economic, legal, and cultural institutions alike. Most pointedly in terms of our focus, U.S. cinema, television, and print media have an established history of reducing Asian Americans to a singular ethnic group characterized by a strong work ethic, high level of intelligence, and bodies that are inherently weak and passive. Many communications studies confirm that the representation of Asian Americans in Western advertising, television, films, newspapers, magazines, and popular literature reinforce dominant ethnic-racial stereotypes that typically frame Asian Americans as the model minority, the minority group that has achieved great educational, social, and financial success due to high innate levels of intelligence, combined with an engrained work ethic (Hamamoto, 1994; Kawai, 2005; Paek & Shah, 2003; Shankar, 2013; Williams, Martins, Consalvo, & Ivory, 2009). According to Prashad (2000), within the context of U.S. Orientalism, the East (particularly in the form of the numerous variants of Asian American culture) is constitutive of the very racial/ethnic hierarchies that continue to inform American society and culture. Prashad focuses on South Asian Americans, but his position is equally applicable to South East or East Asian Americans, in that all these groupings "sign a social contract with a racist polity by making a pledge to work hard but to retain a social life at some remove from U.S. society" (2000, p. x). Unlike African Americans, members of these immigrant groupings may be valued by mainstream (read: white) American society for their work ethic and commitment to family structures and values (C. J. Kim, 1999; Xu & Lee, 2013).

As positive as it may appear, on one level the model minority stereotype leads to a myopic and subordinating view of diverse Asian American communities (e.g., assuming all groups of Asian Americans are financially and academically successful), while limiting the settings and positions in which Asian Americans are perceived as belonging (e.g., in business or medical settings, rather than competitive sports settings) (Taylor & Stern, 1997). The popular representation of Asian Americans as model minorities is also complicated by the enduring influence of negative stereotypes pertaining to Asian Americans, not least of which being the fact that they are "aliens." Through reference to "agents of orientalists" such as the traveling circus, Christian missionaries, and Indian lectures, Prashad (2000) identified how India is represented to the American consuming public less as "romantic and beautiful" than "hideous and barbaric." Hence, Asian Americans from the Indian subcontinent become, at least partially, dehumanized through their association with caricatured and scare-mongering depictions of this exotic, primitive, and barbaric land and culture. Such is also the case for Asian Americans whose antecedents descended from what are constructed and consumed as other equally anonymous, yet assumedly uncivilized and thereby potentially threatening, foreign lands. In this sense, the work ethic and drive associated with model minority status becomes a source of national anxiety. As Kawai noted, even as they exhibit the most model of minority behaviors, Asian Americans are widely perceived to be an alien threat in need of monitoring; they are "'forever foreigners' who divert from U.S. dominant cultural norms, are economic competitors, and thereby undermine the White nation" (2005, p. 110).

Within the popular American imagination, Asian Americans are positioned in highly bifurcated terms, either as a model minority or as a threat to American society (Hamamoto, 1994; Tchen & Yeats, 2014). It is in this sense that Asian Americans as the model, yet threatening, minority are racially triangulated as "'aliens' or 'outsiders' with regard to White Americans, but as 'superior' in relation to African Americans" (Kawai, 2005, p. 110). However, as a function of their visible racial Otherness and perceived cultural differences, they are never fully or unquestioningly accepted into the bosom of American society. They are always already peripheral, marginal, and subordinate to the American social, cultural, and political mainstream. This Orientalist Othering of the Asian American population is also highly gendered, with the typologies of representative Asian American male and female subjectivities circulating within popular discourse, offering interesting points of gender comparison. Of course, at its very core, Orientalism is both a racializing *and* gendering project, in that it emasculates Asian American culture through the positioning of the West as powerful, superior, and protector (masculine), and the East as vulnerable, inferior, and protectee (feminine) (Chou, 2012). This process of social and cultural emasculation is further compounded through the popular cultural castration of Asian American males through recourse to their perceived physical frailty, sporting inability, and predilection for feminine and feminizing occupations (Chou, 2012). In addition to representing them as emasculated, passive, and subservient (Kim, 2005), popular Western thought has simultaneously castigated Asian American males for being cunning, villainous, culturally unassimilable, and lacking the social and communication skills required for integration into mainstream American society (Ma, 1998; Zhang, 2010).

Whereas Asian American male bodies have been subject to a process of racial-cultural castration, leading to their widespread positioning as "asexual and nerdy . . . and ordinarily as physically unattractive" (Ono & Pham, 2009, p. 71), representations of Asian American females demonstrate a very different institutionalized discursive stability (Said, 1979). As the subject of the intersecting race, gender, and sexual Orientalist politics that seemingly define the Western (male) popular imagination, popular representations of Asian American females include the following hypersexualized subjectivities: "concubine, geisha girl, mail-order bride; dragon lady, lotus blossom, precious pearl" (Lu, 1997, p. 17). Ono noted the virgin-and-whore dialectic as dominating contemporary representations of Asian American women. In terms of the former, and unlike its male counterpart, the perceived frailty of the Asian American female body is positioned as part of its sexual allure: the "Lotus Blossom and Madame Butterfly" subjectivities evoking "depictions of women as sexually attractive and alluring and demure, passive, obedient, physically non-imposing, self-sacrificial, and supplicant (especially to white male suitors)" (Ono & Pham, 2009, p. 66). Complicating and contrasting with the "China doll" perception of Asian American female bodies as being "sexually exotic docile bodies" (Chou, 2012, p. 2), the "Dragon Lady" subjectivity represents a "feminized version of yellow peril" whose sexual availability and desire is conjoined with a sinister pragmatism and deceitfulness (Ono & Pham, 2009, p.66). As Kim and Chung (2005) noted, while differing in significant respects, both popular subjectivities "have served to stimulate the sexual voyeurism of White American males and the objectification of foreign, exotic Oriental women as their rightful property" (pp. 75–76). The articulation of this Asian American female dialectic has been identified within numerous cultural fields, including film, theater, television, and advertising (Kim & Chung, 2005; Marchetti, 1993; Shimizu, 2007). Within the remainder of this discussion, our aim is to critically illuminate its expression within contemporary sport culture.

II. The Representation of Asian American Female Athletes within Stereotypically Feminine Sport Cultures

Orientalist stereotypes used to represent Asian American women in popular media (discussed in the previous section) have many correlates in the production of Asian American female sport celebrities. Both male and female Asian American athletes have garnered much success in their sporting careers, but even as many of these athletes serve as American ambassadors on the international sporting stage, acceptance into the American public imaginary as full citizens has always only been partial and even that achieved only through continuous wrangling within the established racial and gender order (Fong, 2008). In the U.S. context, Asian American female athletes have been most visible at the elite level in figure skating and golf, with special attention given in the media to Kristi Yamaguchi and Michelle Kwan in figure skating and Michelle Wie in golf. Sportscasters, reporters, and media producers, in their presentation of Asian American female athletes, have effectively extended the narrative of the Asian American woman as different than and outsider to their European American counterparts, usually read as "white" (Tuan, 1999a, 1999b). Examples include the treatment of Kristi Yamaguchi as compared to Nancy Kerrigan, and of Michelle Kwan in relation to Tara Lipinski in the 1992 and 1998 Winter Olympic Games, respectively (Tuan, 1999b; Joo, 2012). An examination of the photos, commentary, and sponsorship opportunities reveals the ways in which Yamaguchi and Kwan were framed and positioned as less American than their more visibly white American teammates. This phenomenon was particularly evident in the resistance to accepting the face of Yamaguchi in favor of Kerrigan, who was more readily accepted as the "familiar" and "typical" "girl next door" in popular (sport) media (Fong, 2008; Tuan, 1999b). Though Yamaguchi and Kwan were both U.S. national champions—and Yamaguchi earned Olympic gold for the U.S.—their teammates were given clear preferential treatment by the media and sponsors.

While Asian American males who are successful in major sports are "illegible" in the sense that they complicate—and in many instances directly challenge—stereotypical understandings of male Asian bodies (Farred, 2006), Asian American female athletes located in spaces of stereotypically feminine sport cultures (e.g., involving little to no physical contact or use of heavy equipment) are perhaps read with greater ease because they generally perform within the parameters of the Orientalist framework. However, tensions still exist in the presentation of these athletes; for, even while essentialized meanings of Asian female (athletic) bodies persist, ethnic difference is continuously coded such that Asian exceptionalism and exoticism marks these bodies as different and subject to the Orientalist gaze (Said, 1979). For example, standing 6′1″, Michelle Wie commands a presence that challenges the stereotypical diminutive, lotus blossom image, but at the same time continues to instill a sense of awe in outside observers whose gaze is set on her physical appearance and performance as an ethnic Other (Billings, Angelini & Eastman, 2008).[1] Thus, while the participation and success of Asian American women in sports is becoming more visible, particularly in stereotypically feminine sports, this visibility has been accompanied by constant framing of the Asian American female body as an object of gaze.

In the current moment, Asian American female athletes are challenged by dominant narratives that may ebb and flow within a shifting sociopolitical context, but have consistently stayed the course in maintaining racial and ethnic markers of difference. This is partially due to the superficial alignment of Asian Americans with Asians of different national identities, positioning Asian Americans with Asians as a monolithic threat to the dominant racial order in U.S. sporting space.[2] Though the cases of Yamaguchi, Kwan, and Wie present evidence of racialized and ethnic difference impacting their acceptance and representation in popular sport media, an interesting counterpoint can be found in newly emerging sports that are less tied to traditional notions of femininity.

III. The Representation of Asian American Athletes within Women's Mixed Martial Arts

In this section, we examine the complex negotiation of Asian American female subjectivities within the sport of mixed martial arts (MMA) in the wake of a substantial growth in the popularity of fighting sports, especially among women, over the past decade (Luker, 2012). After providing a brief introduction to MMA and its corollary, women's MMA (WMMA), we analyze the production and management of Asian American female images and bodies on the internet, demonstrating the extent to which a complicated web of actors, including the fighters themselves, are complicit in the objectification of the female (Asian) body, perpetuation and commercialization of the Asian mystique, and reinforcement of a generic "Other" in MMA.

MMA and the Rise of Female Fighters

Mixed martial arts is defined in the Nevada Administrative Code (NAC) as "unarmed combat involving the use . . . of a combination of techniques from different disciplines of the martial arts, including, without limitation, grappling, kicking and striking" (chapter 457, section 285). MMA is a full contact sport that requires skills in at least two fighting styles, including, but not limited to, jujitsu, wrestling, boxing, karate, Muay Thai, and sando or sanshou. The worldwide draw of MMA comes from its popularity as both a form of entertainment and as an option for amateur and professional fight training, attracting men and women alike.

Much of MMA's popularity in the United States and around the world is due to the leading professional MMA organization, the Ultimate Fighting Championship (UFC). Started in 1993, the UFC is owned and operated by Zuffa, LLC. On its website, the UFC claims to be the "largest Pay-Per-View event provider in the world, broadcast in over 149 countries and territories, to nearly one billion homes worldwide, in 30 different languages." While women had been widely participating in MMA before the UFC's emergence, the organization's president, Dana White, saw little value in female bouts and declared in 2011 that women would never fight in the UFC (Wetzel, 2013). With the enormous market demand for MMA, there was increasing interest in women's fighting. Consequently, soon after dismissing the idea of female fighters, White announced the first UFC fight ticket to not only include, but also headline female fighters.[3] Granting permission for women to share a fight ticket with the men was a momentous shift on the part of White and the UFC. Not only did this mark recognition of women's fighting legitimacy, if not commercial draw, but it also served as a springboard for female fighters to become internet media sensations. News and videos of fights between women rapidly gained notoriety through YouTube and other social media and internet platforms, avenues through which fighting female bodies have been showcased in a variety of ways outside the UFC's Octagon.[4] The airing of such programs as *The Ultimate Fighter* (*TUF*), a reality show that follows the training and competitions of MMA fighters, led to further visibility for these athletes and their fighting skills. While *TUF* initially cast exclusively male fighters, the show had its first co-ed season in 2013, and for its twentieth season in 2014, *TUF* announced its first all-female cast (Tuttle, 2014).

In MMA, the presentation of female Asian Americans is informed by selective historical images of Asians and Asian Americans in popular literature, film, and television programs, which perpetuates an Orientalist gaze. Through a variety of online platforms, including social media, the athletes are introduced and promoted as individuals, each with their own unique fighting styles and character traits. However, the presentation of the athletes, through interviews, Twitter feeds, videos, pictures, and press releases, whether in their own voice or that of media reporters, reinforces abstract generalizations of female Asian Americans, emphasizing their physical beauty, work ethic, and family life. As anthropologist Constancio R. Arnaldo, Jr., demonstrates in his study of pugilist Manny Pacquiao's popularity in this anthology, the various internet circuits and "imagined communities" (Anderson, 1991) become places where bodies are multiply inflected with meaning.

The growth and development of women's mixed martial arts has been accompanied by an increase in the visibility and exposure of a wide spectrum of gender performances in sport in the United States. Women are increasingly challenging traditional gender norms in and through a variety of sporting spaces (Messner, 1988). A clear example is the participation of women in sports that involves punching, kicking, and choking other women, voluntarily putting themselves at risk of being struck, knocked out, and injured, to say nothing of the training requirements and changes in body mass and physical appearance, all of which are the norm in MMA and many other fighting sports. Other examples include women's participation in sports such as ice hockey, rugby, tackle football, and body building where physicality, power, and muscularity are emphasized, and female athletes readily display aggressiveness, toughness, and strength, attributes that are normally associated with definitions of masculinity rather than femininity (Bolin & Granskog, 2003; Cahn, 1995; Krane, Choi, Baird & Aimar, 2004; Lowe, 1998; Messner, 1988; Theberge, 2002). While women's participation in MMA may challenge the boundaries of established gender norms, they have by no means completely transgressed these boundaries. Significantly contributing to the barriers faced by women in MMA is the reality that MMA organizations like the Ultimate Fighting Championship are deeply entrenched in a culture of masculinity; further, major media outlets continue to frame MMA in sexist, heteronormative terms (Weaving, 2014).

Janet Martin, co-founder of Invicta FC, the only professional all-female MMA promotion, conducted research on the influence of negative stereotypes on the behavior of female MMA fighters (Martin, 2011). Adopting a survey from Davis-Delano, Pollack, and Ellsworth Vose (2009), who did a similar study on female athletes, Martin found three primary stereotypes to which fighters responded with apologetic behavior—actions performed as a defense against negative stereotypes or stigma. In Martin's study, negative stereotypes commonly identified by MMA female fighters included being identified as masculine and "manly," lesbians, and inferior to male athletes. Similar to many critical sports feminist studies, Martin's study concluded that maintaining the linkage of sports and masculinity in contemporary society increases the chances that "female athletes will be the target of negative labeling, stereotypes, and stigmatization based on gender, sexuality, and ability" (p. 30). In response, MMA athletes actively managed the stigma and stereotypes commonly associated with female fighters through apologetic behavior that included consciously making efforts to appear more feminine and avoid being labeled as a lesbian. "Female masculinity" was seen as dichotomous to the ways that conservative social actors overemphasized emblems of masculinity through male biological sex instead of a variety of practices (see Halberstam, 1998). Martin also found that while athletes responded to stigma and stereotypes with apologetic behavior, they also embraced a "heterosexy fit" identity, whereby the display of a tough, fit, athletic body is viewed as an acceptable presentation of a heterosexual, feminine body (Ezzell, 2009; Samie, 2013). Considering Martin's findings about perceptions of gender, apologetic behavior, and gender performance in MMA, and the findings regarding racial stereotypes and Orientalist presentations of Asians Americans in popular media discussed earlier, we continue with an examination of the mediated construction of Asian American female MMA fighters.

Asian American Knockouts: Negotiating Asian American Subjectivities

For women fighting in MMA, racial stereotypes are closely tied to notions of femininity and female physicality. Asian American martial artists in particular, because of their cultural, ethnic, and racial position, must negotiate a complex arrangement of stigma and stereotypes tied to race and gender. In other words, although Asian American athletes competing in professional MMA are not unique in their embodiment of power, strength, sexuality, and femininity when compared to other fighters, their ethnic and racial background opens them up to Orientalist tropes, complicating the negotiation of Asian American female subjectivities in MMA.

Professional MMA Asian American female fighters include Team Execution's Jenny Liou Shriver, Invicta's Miriam Nakamura, Jinh Yu Frey, and Michelle Waterson, and UFC's Shayna Baszler. Though the specifics of their ethnic background are rarely discussed, their educational background and work ethic are often highlighted (cf. model minority). From websites and interviews posted on the internet, for example, audiences learn that Jinh Yu Frey holds an associates' degree in nuclear medicine and a bachelor of science in radiological sciences, is a full-time graduate student working toward her master's of business administration, and works full-time at a cancer clinic (jinyufrey.com); Jenny Liou Shriver is a published poet and college professor who has earned a BS in biology, two master's degrees, and a PhD (Dave, 2014); and Shayna Baszler has earned two degrees, one in religion and the other in abnormal child psychology (Marq, 2012).

Standing 5′2″, at 105 lbs., Jinh Yu Frey is best known for her first-round knockout of Darla Harris at the Sugar Creek Showdown (SCS) in 2013; shortly thereafter, she accepted an offer to fight for Invicta FC. Frey received recognition as a formidable newcomer to MMA after a video was posted to YouTube featuring the blow she delivered to her opponent's head at SCS 18, ending the match with a KO in 24 seconds (Dicker, 2013). The video of the fight on YouTube has garnered over 2.3 million hits. Within the atom-weight division (105 lbs.), the lightest of the MMA weight classes, Frey joined veteran Michelle Waterson, who had been the reigning atom-weight champion until 2014. Waterson came to Invicta after having gained recognition as a cast member on *Fight Girls*, an MMA reality show on the Oxygen Network. Premiering in 2007, *Fight Girls* followed the training and competitions of women training in Muay Thai, a fighting style also known as Thai boxing.

Michelle Waterson has established herself as a serious contender in MMA, and according to Fightmatrix.com, as of March 2015 was ranked number three in the MMA's atom-weight fighter ranks. Though Waterson receives much press for her dominating presence in the fight cage, her popularity is also tied to her profile as a former model. Commonly referred to as the "Karate Hottie," Waterson was also a former Hooter's waitress, a powerful combination in portraying a hypersexualized image of femininity, and certainly not one that might easily pair with the image of a physically threatening mixed martial artist. On the internet, there is a seemingly endless array of pictures from Waterson's modeling days that correspond to, and indeed for some, affirm, the label Karate Hottie, elevating her status in the commercial, masculine world of MMA.

Although Waterson is known as a highly skilled fighter, an examination of the racialized and gendered discursive construction of her image and body by a variety of stakeholders shows how she is subjected to, and to a certain extent, complicit within, a hierarchal, disciplined space that reinforces the inferior position of women within the heteronormative, masculinist space of MMA; for it is in this setting that representations of Asian American women demonstrate a "discursive consistency" (Said, 1979) that continues a historical narrative of Asian American women as mysterious, beautiful objects of desire.

The use of the term "karate" as a generic descriptor of Asian martial arts is another aspect of how the name Karate Hottie perpetuates caricatures of Asian Americans, particularly to audiences that have limited knowledge of martial arts disciplines. Waterson's bio page on the Bikini Central Supermodels website features a poster of "Michelle Waterson The Karate Hottie!" The font of the poster's title and various captions—"Hi-YAH!!" "POW!" and "SHE'S THE BLACKBELT CHICK WITH THE SUPER KICK!"—is meant to look "Asian," with curves at the edges of the yellow, red, and black letters. In the center of the poster is an illustration of Waterson standing in a black sports bra and black bottoms with a martial arts black belt tied around her hips. Her closed right fist is held up against the open palm of her left hand in front of her chest; at the point of contact—where fist meets palm—is a cartoonish flash of light. The smaller pictures on the poster include illustrations of Waterson in "karate" poses—one of her squatting down with arms to the side, a second with one arm outstretched overhead grabbing her foot, and a third with one leg sticking straight out from her hip doing a front kick. On each side of the central picture she is posing in a red bikini, in more provocative poses. The background includes a drawing of a red building with Oriental-esque columns and roof edges. The caption underneath reads:

> She's lean, she's mean (ok, only when she's karate chopping) and she's one hot fighting machine. Meet Bikini.com Supermodel Michelle Waterson, The Karate Hottie—the most bodacious blackbelt this side of the Pacific! Think all martial artists look like Bruce Lee? We're confident that Michelle, with her genuine smile and gentle curves, will prove you all wrong. This petite athlete can rough you up in a way that'll definitely have

you asking for more. So put on your beginner's white belt, strap on some heavy padding, and get ready for some bruising of the most pleasurable kind.[5]

This particular description in conjunction with the illustrations described above entices, encourages, and reinforces innumerable racialized and sexualized images of Asian American women. The name Karate Hottie lends itself to images of a woman who is not only "lean," "hot," and "petite" with a "genuine smile and gentle curves," but can also use her "karate chopping" to provide "some bruising of the most pleasurable kind." The pictures and captions mock with great abandon the respected and honorable practices and traditions of kung fu, such as the fist-on-palm formation, and those of martial arts disciplines in general that have been established over centuries. In this respect, the marketing language, images, and overall presentation of Waterson are not simply racialized, but racist in intent, meaning, and content.

Waterson is not averse to the use of her nickname in the media, adopting the name herself for her Instagram and Twitter accounts: Michelle Waterson @KarateHottieMMA. Though she has herself embraced the label of Karate Hottie, she acknowledges that the label calls attention to her qualifications as a model rather than a fighter. In an interview with *Sports Illustrated* in 2013, she was asked how she would like to be marketed as an athlete, to which she responded:

> People are going to see me however they want to see me. Obviously, sex sells and what not. Part of that, as far as my image, was me. When I was first getting into it, I was working at Hooters and I was doing bikini competitions, photo shoots for calendars, and this and that. But it's not necessarily who I am now. If people want to view me as that and label me as that, that's perfectly fine. Because if that's going to get me in the door so people can actually see how skilled I am as an athlete, that's fine. I'll play the game. To me, people are going to judge you no matter what, no matter how you put yourself out there. In my opinion, they can judge however they want to. Hopefully, it's in a positive light. (Segura, 2013)

While Waterson would like to be known for her ability to compete as a professional MMA fighter, she recognizes that marketing and bringing attention to herself as the Karate Hottie is part of the "game" that requires women to overcome societal barriers to acceptance in the male-dominated world of sport. However, in her uncritical acceptance and support of the label Karate Hottie, Waterson becomes an active agent in reinforcing Orientalist views of Asian American women and their bodies at the same moment of challenge.

The representation of Waterson to the public achieves many purposes, primarily related to image, money, and marketing—critical components in supporting the success and sustainability of the women's side of MMA. In addition to her representation as a fighter and former model and Hooter's waitress, Waterson's role as mother and wife is also made very public through her own social media outlets and MMA-related commercial sites. Examples include article titles such as "Michelle Waterson—From Karate Hottie to MMA Mamma" (Wombat Sports, September 7, 2011); and her own Twitter posts: "My magical wedding at Hacienda Vargas! It was perfect" (July 19, 2012); "My hubby and I!" (July 30, 2012); "My baby araya!" (September 22, 2011); "my little beautiful [girl]" (October 1, 2011). Notions of motherhood and wifehood are closely tied to social constructs of femininity and prescribed gender roles, regardless of race. However, because stereotypes of Asian American women fall at extreme ends of a bifurcated schemata with fierce, manipulative "dragon ladies" on one end and submissive, often sexualized "China dolls" on the other (Lee & Joo, 2005; Prasso, 2005; Zhang, 2010), understandings of Asian American MMA mothers or wives become entangled in a highly textured web of sociocultural, political, and economic relations. To some degree, the presentation of these athletes as mothers and wives reinforces their femininity, displaying a caring and nurturing side as a balance to the violence enacted during fights that brings into question their feminine traits.[6]

It is important to note, however, that for Asian American women, demonstrating physicality through martial arts has not always meant a need to reconcile their femininity with the legitimacy of their place next to men. Within multiple media outlets, a popular image of Asian American martial artists is presented in the form of Chinese female warriors, skilled martial artists who have been allowed to freely demonstrate their strength and skills as fighters alongside their male counterparts. The presentation of female warriors in contemporary martial arts films demonstrates the extent to which they have made irrelevant Western notions of gender that have denied women's legitimacy in sporting spaces next to men. Examining cultural specificities related to the significance of gender of female knights in the world of *wuxia*, and the use of woman-warrior-as-spectacle in martial arts films, Cai explains:

> The Chinese female warrior, for example, presents a unique problematic. She falls largely outside the paradigms charted by the (critical Western feminist) approaches I have described. The martial arts (*wuxia*) discourse often marginalizes, or makes inadequate or irrelevant, the loci in which many feminist readings contest the inscriptions of the female and difference—namely, romance, home, maternity, family, sexuality, sexual preference, class, race, and age. Its genre conventions short-circuit familiar critical currents, displacing women from the recognized realms, allowing them to fight alongside men and to possess as much physical prowess as their male counterparts in a fictitious world. (2005, p. 443)

The representation of women in the *wuxia* discourse is different than Western representations that often repress the physicality of women and deny them equal status. Further, in MMA, audiences are challenged in similar ways to film audiences when "confronted with the complexities and fluidity of cultural representation brought about by transnational products" such as Asian and American martial arts heroines (Gomes, 2010, p. 169). In a critical examination of movie reviews of films that prominently feature Chinese swordswomen, Catherine Gomes (2010) notes that these women are often read through a Western-centered, rather than Asian-centered, lens that relies on a limited set of fabricated images and cultural references, thus limiting the ability to read these women outside of the Western gaze. Consequently, in their struggle "to make sense of the gendered 'foreign' woman" (p. 169), Chinese swordswomen, or martial arts heroines more broadly, are framed within the larger construct of Occident and Orient wherein their position as foreign Other is (re-) affirmed with each rendering. In addition, other critics of cultural popular representations of Asian American and Asian women have noted the relative ease with which "martial artistry tends to map smoothly onto Asian/Asian American women's bodies," thus attending to some of the unease that might otherwise present itself to audiences with localized and thus limited cultural reference points for understanding "women's physical fierceness" (Tung, 2004, p. 115).

In the case of Michelle Waterson, we can see many of these intersecting vectors at play, particularly the fluid, ambiguous presentation and reading of her public image and performance as a fighter, model, mother, wife, and Asian American martial artist. While videos of her fights bring to center stage her physicality and strength, others promote another (much different) side to her image, showcasing her humor and charisma. For example, in "10 Things You Didn't Know about Michelle Waterson," a promotional video for Invicta 10, produced by Invicta and widely shared through YouTube and on multiple MMA websites, Waterson responds to ten unrelated questions that reveal a little about her (e.g., her likes and dislikes). Within the span of the five-minute video, audiences are entertained by her smiles and giggles, as well as her imitation of Robert Downey, Jr., getting in a "karate chopping"–ready stance as body parts are flying around him in the movie *Tropic Thunder* (her response to the question of what is the funniest movie she's ever seen); her imitation of animal noises, including a dolphin and a peacock; and her singing part of Jason Mraz's popular hit "Lucky (I'm in Love with My Best Friend)," which she identifies as both her wedding song and her favorite song. Prior to the "10 Things" video, Invicta featured Waterson in another video, "Why I Fight: Michelle Waterson," in which we learn about her training background as well as the factors that motivate and inspire her to compete in MMA. In this video to promote Invicta 8, Waterson's image as a fighter is visually and aurally juxtaposed with her role as mother and wife, with the video cutting in and out of footage from her fights and pictures of her with her daughter and husband. In this two-and-a-half minute video, Waterson also explains that she fights because it allows her to face her fears and to "conquer them one by one."

In her journey to becoming the atom-weight champion, she gives much credit to her husband, explaining that she "wouldn't be able to fight if it wasn't for him." Through these videos, Invicta tells the story of Waterson and presents her as someone who is perhaps not as exotic as might have been thought had she been seen only in fighting mode—bloodied, kicking and punching at full force; rather, audiences can see that she shares many of the stereotypically feminine traits associated with demeanor and family values. The juxtaposition of the images sends the message that though perhaps at first glance they might not seem compatible, they are not only compatible but can also be complementary. Through this reconciliation, Waterson's image is carefully constructed and mediated to suit the commercial needs of the organization, making her body readable—and consequently, those of other Asian American female fighters as well. In this instance, another issue in the cultural production of Asian American images and bodies is revealed. For while we see the overt racialization of Waterson in material produced outside of MMA, within media directly associated with the promotion of MMA events and figures, race and ethnicity are not openly addressed. Rather, at a time when inclusion and multicultural understanding are high priorities in U.S. society, this banner is flown high when commercially expedient. In the process, difference is often celebrated in its erasure, which has significant consequences for Asian American female athletes.

In a study of Asian American and Asian diaspora literatures, Sheng-Mei Ma (1998) argues that within Chinese American literature, authors have worked to create an Asian American subjectivity that is distinctly separate from that of their immigrant counterparts, distancing themselves from dominant Orientalist stereotypes, perceptions, and discourse. Just as in the examples within literature provided by Ma, in MMA, this separation becomes problematic in that it requires an implicit acknowledgement of the Oriental Other to which they are compared.

> [T]his in-between status involves an excruciating dilemma: their unique Americanness derives in large measure from a resistance to Orientalist discourse, which in turn presupposes an acknowledgement and even an internalization of the vocabulary of Western constructions of themselves. (Ma, 1998, p. 2)

In the promotional Invicta interview videos described above, the presentation of Waterson's quirkiness, wit, and friendliness, which makes her relatable to a general audience, simultaneously stakes her claim to a space in the national American imaginary while casting off and substantiating ethnic and racial stereotypes of the socially awkward (i.e., nerdy) and unpersonable (i.e., Dragon Lady) Asian Other. Another consequence of this separation is the continued homogenization of

Asians, such that Asian American female martial artists still fall victim to a reductionist Orientalist gaze and the production of a generic Asian(ness) that caricatures an entire continent and its diverse representation of national and ethnic cultures (Lowe, 1991; 1996). In the process, the stories of immigration, access to resources, experiences of racialization and racism, and connection and disconnection from the category of Asian America are left out. The management of difference through strategic representational practices of these female athletes thus not only reproduces reductive narratives, but also reinforces racial, ethnic, and national hierarchies.

IV. Reflections

While Asian Americans experience marginalization across a spectrum of mainstream U.S. sports and newly emerging contact sports, the increasingly popular sport of MMA does not take exception to the perpetuation of established racial and gender norms. Asian American female MMA fighters have come to represent a collective abstraction that is informed by shifting commercial narratives about Asian American women in a multicultural society. Their presentation reflects the views and perceptions within contemporary American society that, although constantly evolving, continues to mark Asians as a minority Other, even as the visible presence of Asian American athletes is growing. An examination of the promotion and production of professional female Asian American MMA fighters reveals some of the many dynamic and complex processes of gendered racialization at play in MMA. Though we primarily focused on Michelle "Karate Hottie" Waterson in this chapter, including other fighters in the analysis would be instructive in further deconstructing the multiple sites of discipline that both regulate and complicate the negotiation of Asian American female subjectivity.

Though Asian American female fighters, like Waterson, have been able to excel in MMA and achieve success as women in a male-dominated sport, the production of their images, bodies, and identities remains constrained by the highly commercialized, masculine space of MMA (Weaving, 2014). Positioned within an integrated network of corporate and social power that regulates and disciplines the performative ethnic female body, these women must constantly negotiate their position at the intersection of perceived contradictions related to being physically aggressive female athletes and Orientalist codes that inform superficial markers of racial, ethnic, and national identity. For even as women show their affinity for and ability to succeed in a combat sport, the popularity of Asian American fighters has not been limited by a lack of femininity, sex appeal, or ethnic beauty tied to an Asian mystique. With the recent growth in professional women's MMA come new spaces and opportunities to reimagine traditional images of Asian American women. Indeed, it is within these new spaces that we must make a move to identify and break down the "cultural grammar that structures many of the racial discourses of the contemporary moment" (Kim, 2012), the cultural grammar that these fighters and the MMA community, in particular, work together to employ in reconfiguring the Orientalist narratives that continue to reinforce the inferior position of Asian Americans in their own home.

NOTES

1 Much attention was also paid to her age, as she started to play competitively at ten years old. She also drew attention for her participation on men's tours, which she also started to do at a young age (Billings et al., 2008).

2 See, for example, K.-Y. Kim's (2012) discussion of Korean golfers, especially in regard to the backlash against their increased presence on and domination of the LPGA tour.

3 The now infamous bout at UFC 157 was between Ronda Rousey and Liz Carmouche, held on February 23, 2013.

4 The Octagon is the 750-square-foot fight cage in which UFC bouts are held.

5 This website is currently offline, without a functional URL, and no archived version of it is accessible.

6 See Muller (2007) for her description of "family nights" at the Women's National Basketball Association, designed to counteract the "lesbian" and "butch" representation of female basketball players.

REFERENCES

Anderson, B. R. O. G. (1991). *Imagined Communities: Reflections on the Origin and Spread of Nationalism*. London: Verso.

Billings, A. C., Angelini, J., & Eastman, S. (2008). "Wie Shock: Television Commentary about Playing on the PGA and LPGA Tours." *Howard Journal of Communications*, 19(1), 64–84.

Bohn, M. (2013, Jan. 5). "Invicta FC Provides Refund and Free Live Stream for Invicta FC 4: 'Esparza vs Hyatt' after Payment Processing and Streaming Issues." *MMAmania.com*. http://www.mmamania.com/2013/1/5/3841062/invicta-fc-provides-refund-and-free-live-stream-for-invicta-fc-4.

Bolin, A., & Granskog, J. (2003). *Athletic Intruders: Ethnographic Research on Women, Culture, and Exercise*. Albany: State University of New York Press.

Brennand, T. (2014, Oct. 1). "Bethefittest Interview Jinh Yu Frey." *BeTheFittest*. http://bethefittest.co.uk/fitness-blog/bethefittest-interview-jinh-yu-frey.

Brody, D. (2010). *Visualizing American Empire: Orientalism and Imperialism in the Philippines*. Chicago: University of Chicago Press.

Cahn, S. (1995). *Coming on Strong: Gender and Sexuality in Twentieth-Century Women's Sport*. Cambridge, MA: Harvard University Press.

Cai, R. (2005). "Gender Imaginations in *Crouching Tiger, Hidden Dragon* and the Wuxia World." *positions*, 13(2), 441–471.

Chou, R. S. (2012). *Asian American Sexual Politics: The Construction of Race, Gender, and Sexuality*. Lanham, MD: Rowman & Littlefield.

Darnell, S. C. (2013). "Orientalism through Sport: Towards a Said-ian Analysis of Imperialism and 'Sport for Development and Peace.'" *Sport in Society*, 17(8), 1000–1014.

Dave. (2014, May 28). "Interview with the Brainiac Badass Jenny Liou." *FighterEmpire.com*. http://fighterempire.com/interview-with-the-braniac-badass-jenny-liou/.

Davidson, M. (1992). *The Consumerist Manifesto: Advertising in Postmodern Times*. London: Comedia.

Davis-Delano, L. R., Pollock, A., & Ellsworth Vose, J. (2009). "Apologetic Behavior among Female Athletes: A New Questionnaire and Initial Results." *International Review for the Sociology of Sport*, 44(2/3), 131–150.

De Souza, D. (2012, July 24). "Invicta FC President Shannon Knapp: Pioneer for Women's MMA." *MMA Corner*. http://themmacorner.com/2012/07/24/invicta-fc-president-shannon-knapp-pioneer-for-womens-mma.

Dicker, R. (2013, Aug. 14). "Jinh Yu Knockout of Darla Harris in MMA Bout Is a Hit." *Huffington Post*. http://www.huffingtonpost.com.

Ezzell, M. B. (2009). "'Barbie Dolls' on the Pitch: Identity Work, Defensive Othering, and Inequality in Women's Rugby." *Social Problems*, 56(1), 111–131.

Farred, G. (2006). *Phantom Calls*. Chicago: Prickly Paradigm Press.

Feder, A. M. (1994). "'A Radiant Smile from the Lovely Lady': Overdetermined Femininity in 'Ladies' Figure Skating." *Drama Review*, 38(1), 62–78.

Fong, T. P. 2008. *The Contemporary Asian American Experience: Beyond the Model Minority*. Upper Saddle River, NJ: Prentice Hall.

Ford, A. (2013, July 30). "Fightland Talks To: Invicta President Shannon Knapp." *Fightland* (blog). http://fightland.vice.com/blog/fightland-talks-to-invicta-president-shannon-knapp.

Foucault, M. (1977). *Discipline and Punish: The Birth of the Prison* (A. Sheridan, trans.). New York: Vintage Books.

Front Row MMA. (2012, July 23). "Shannon Knapp Talks about Invicta FC2 This Coming Weekend." http://frontrowmma.com.

Gartman, D. (1998). "Postmodernism: Or, the Cultural Logic of Post-Fordism." *Sociological Quarterly*, 39(1), 119–137.

Gomes, C. (2010). "Lost in Translation: American Critical Audience and the Transnational Chinese Swordswoman." In L. Dong (ed.), *Transnationalism and the Asian American Heroine: Essays on Literature, Film, Myth and Media* (pp. 168–186). Jefferson, NC: McFarland.

Grauer, Y. (n.d.). "Karate Hottie Interview." *Sherdog*. http://www.sherdog.com/events/Invicta-FC-5-Penne-vs-Waterson-27451.

Halberstam, J. (1998). *Female Masculinity*. Durham, NC: Duke University Press.

Hall, S. (1992). "The Local and the Global: Globalization and Ethnicity." In A. D. Smith (ed.), *Culture, Globalization and the World-System* (pp. 19–39). Minneapolis: University of Minnesota Press.

Hamamoto, D. Y. (1994). *Monitored Peril: Asian Americans and the Politics of TV Representation*. Minneapolis: University of Minnesota Press.

Hanson, S. L. (2005). "Hidden Dragons: Asian American Women and Sport." *Journal of Sport & Social Issues*, 29(3), 279–312.

Hemminger, B. (2013, Jan. 7). "Make It Right: Invicta FC President Shannon Knapp Interview Exclusive with MMAnia.com." *MMAmania.com*. http://www.mmamania.com/2013/1/7/3848872/make-it-right-invicta-fc-president-shannon-knapp-interview-exclusive.

Holden, E. (2013, Oct. 27). "Shannon Knapp Opens Up about Why Janet Martin Is No Longer with Invicta FC." *Examiner.com*. http://www.examiner.com/article/shannon-knapp-opens-up-about-why-janet-martin-is-no-longer-with-invicta-fc.

hooks, b. (1992). *Black Looks: Race and Representation*. Boston: South End Press.

Hsu, H. (2012). "Everyone Else's Jeremy Lin." *Amerasia Journal*, 38(3), 126–128.

Jameson, F. (1998). *The Cultural Turn: Selected Writings on the Postmodern, 1983–1998*. London & New York: Verso.

JasonDBK. (2012, Mar. 21). "Janet Martin Interview." *Promoting Real Women* (blog). http://promotingwomen.blogspot.com/2012/03/janet-martin-interview.html.

Joo, R. (2012). *Transnational Sport*. Durham, NC: Duke University Press.

Kawai, Y. (2005). "Stereotyping Asian Americans: The Dialectic of the Model Minority and the Yellow Peril." *Howard Journal of Communications*, 16(2), 109–130.

Keft-Kennedy, V. (2005). *Representing the Belly-Dancing Body: Feminism, Orientalism, and the Grotesque*. PhD thesis, School of English Literatures, Philosophy, and Languages, University of Wollongong. http://ro.uow.edu.au/theses/843.

Kim, C. (2014). "The Smell of Communities to Come: Jeremy Lin and Post-Racial Desire." *Journal of Intercultural Studies*, 35(3), 310–327.

Kim, C. J. (1999). "The Racial Triangulation of Asian Americans." *Politics and Society*, 27(1), 105–138.

Kim, D. Y. (2005). *Writing Manhood in Black and Yellow: Ralph Ellison, Frank Chin and the Literary Politics of Identity*. Stanford, CA: Stanford Univesity Press.

Kim, E., Walkosz, B. J., & Iverson, J. (2006). "USA Today's Coverage of the Top Women Golfers, 1998–2001." *Howard Journal of Communications*, 17(4), 307–321.

Kim, K.-Y. (2012). *Producing Korean Women Golfers on the LPGA Tour: Representing Gender, Race, Nation and Sport in a Transnational Context.* PhD thesis, University of Toronto. http://hdl.handle.net/1807/32791.

———. (2013). "Translation with Abusive Fidelity: Methodological Issues in Translating Media Texts about Korean LPGA Players." *Sociology of Sport Journal,* 30(3), 340–358.

Kim, M., & Chung, A. Y. (2005). "Consuming Orientalism: Images of Asian/American Women in Multicultural Advertising." *Qualitative Sociology,* 28(1), 67–91.

King, C. R. (2006). "Defacements/Effacements: Anti-Asian (American) Sentiment in Sport." *Journal of Sport and Social Issues,* 30, 340–352.

Klein, C. (2003). *Cold War Orientalism: Asia in the Middlebrow Imagination, 1945–1961.* Berkeley: University of California Press.

Krane, V., Choi, P. Y. L., Baird, S. M., & Aimar, C. M. (2004). "Living the Paradox: Female Athletes Negotiate Femininity and Muscularity." *Sex Roles,* 50(5/6), 315–329.

Lee, K., & Joo, S. (2005). "The Portrayal of Asian-Americans in Mainstream Magazine Ads: An Update." *Journalism & Mass Communication Quarterly,* 82, 654–671.

Leonard, D. J. (2014). "A Fantasy in the Garden, a Fantasy America Wants to Believe: Jeremy Lin, the NBA and Race Culture." In J. L. Conyers (ed.), *Race in American Sports: Essays* (pp. 144–165). Jefferson, NC: McFarland.

Little, D. (2008). "Orientalism, American Style: The Middle East in the Mind of America." In D. Little, *American Orientalism: The United States and the Middle East since 1945* (pp. 9–42).

Lowe, L. (1991). "Heterogeneity, Hybridity, Multiplicity: Marking Asian American Differences." *Diaspora,* 1, 24–44.

———. (1996). *Immigrant Acts: On Asian American Immigrant Politics.* Durham, NC: Duke University Press.

Lowe, M. R. (1998). *Women of Steel: Female Bodybuilders and the Struggle for Self-Definition.* New York: New York University Press.

Lu, L. (1997). "Critical Visions: The Representation and Resistance of Asian Women." In S. Shah (ed.), *Dragon Ladies: Asian American Feminists Breathe Fire* (pp. 17–28). Boston: Beacon Press.

Luker, R. (2012). "Shifting Interest by Age, Gender Gives MMA a Fighting Chance." *Street & Smith's Sports Business Journal,* 15(24), 17.

Ma, S. (1998). *Immigrant Subjectivities in Asian American and Asian Diaspora Literatures.* Buffalo: State University of New York Press.

Marchetti, G. (1993). *Romance and the "Yellow Peril": Race, Sex, and Discursive Strategies in Hollywood Fiction.* Berkeley: University of California Press.

Marq. (2012, Dec. 1). "Strong and Smart—The Invicta Fighters with College Degrees." *Wombat Sports.* https://wombatsports.wordpress.com/2012/12/01/strong-and-smart-the-invicta-fighters-outshine-ufc-fighters-on-college-degrees/.

Martin, J. (2011). "Girl Fight: Apologetic Behaviors among Female Mixed Martial Arts Fighters as a Reaction to Social Stigmatization, Stereotyping, and Labeling of Sports Participation." Unpublished BA thesis, Warren Wilson College.

Mastro, D. E., & Stern, S. R. (2003). "Representations of Race in Television Commercials: A Content Analysis of Prime-Time Advertising." *Journal of Broadcasting and Electronic Media*, 47(4), 638–647.

McElroy, K. (2014). "Basket Case: Framing the Intersection of 'Linsanity' and Blackness." *Howard Journal of Communications*, 25(4), 431–451.

Messner, M. A. (1988). "Sports and Male Domination: The Female Athlete as Contested Ideological Terrain." *Sociology of Sport Journal*, 5, 197–211.

MMAPayout.com. (2013, Jan. 7). "PPV Issues Hurt Invicta FC." http://mmapayout.com/index.php?s=PPV+issues+hurt+invicta+fc.

Morgan, J. (2014, June 30). "Making Money in MMA? UFC Champ Ronda Rousey Doing It the One Proven Way." *MMA Junkie*. http://mmajunkie.com/2014/06/how-to-make-money-in-mma-ufc-champ-ronda-rousey-doing-it-the-one-proven-way.

Muller, T. K. 2007. "The Contested Terrain of the Women's National Basketball Association's Arena." In Cara Aitchson (ed.), *Sport and Gender Identities: Masculinities, Femininities, and Sexualities* (pp. 37–52). London: Routledge.

Nayak, M. V., & Maline, C. (2009). "American Orientalism and American Exceptionalism: A Critical Rethinking of US Hegemony." *International Studies Review*, 11, 253–276.

Nevada Administrative Code. (n.d.). NAC 467.00285. "'Mixed Martial Arts' Defined." (NRS 467.030). Legislative Counsel, State of Nevada.

Okamoto, D. G. (2006). "Institutional Panethnicity: Boundary Formation in Asian-American Organizing." *Social Forces*, 85(1), 1–25.

Ono, K. A. & Pham, V. N. (2009). *Asian Americans and the Media*. Cambridge, MA: Polity.

Paek, H. J., & Shah, H. (2003). "Racial Ideology, Model Minorities, and the 'Not-So-Silent Partner': Stereotyping of Asian Americans in U.S. Magazine Advertising." *Howard Journal of Communications*, 14(4), 225–243.

Park, J., & Wilkins, K. (2005). "Re-orienting the Orientalist Gaze." *Global Media Journal*, 4(6), 1–15. http://www.globalmediajournal.com/open-access/reorienting-the-orientalist-gaze.pdf.

Prashad, V. (2000). *The Karma of Brown Folk*. Minneapolis: University of Minnesota Press.

Prasso, S. (2005). *The Asian Mystique: Dragon Ladies, Geisha Girls, and Our Fantasies of the Exotic Orient*. New York: PublicAffairs.

Przewoznik, J. (2014, June 12). "Invicta Atomweight: Jinh Yu Frey." *Knockout Lounge*. http://knockoutlounge.com/jinh-yu-frey/.

Rosen, S. L. (2000). "Japan as Other: Orientalism and Cultural Conflict." *Intercultural Communication*, 4, n.p. http://www.immi.se/intercultural/nr4/rosen.htm.

Said, E. (1994). *Culture and Imperialism*. New York: Random House.

———. (1979). *Orientalism*. New York: Vintage Books.

Samie, S. F. (2013). "Hetero-Sexy Self/Body Work and Basketball: The Invisible Sporting Women of British Pakistani Muslim Heritage." *South Asian Popular Culture*, 11(3), 257–270.

Schueller, M. J. (2001). *U.S. Orientalisms: Race, Nation, and Gender in Literature, 1790–1890*. Ann Arbor: University of Michigan Press.

Segura, M. (2013, March 27). "Invicta's Michelle Waterson Rediscovered Martial Arts in Thailand." *Sports Illustrated*. http://www.si.com/mma/2013/03/27/michelle-waterson-invicta.

Shankar, S. (2015). *Advertising Diversity: Ad Agencies and the Creation of Asian American Consumers*. Durham, NC: Duke University Press.

———. (2013). "Affect and Sport in South Asian American Advertising." *South Asian Popular Culture*, 11(3), 231–242.

Shimizu, C. P. (2007). *The Hypersexuality of Race: Performing Asian/American Women on Screen and Scene*. Durham, NC: Duke University Press

Shin, E. H., & Nam, E. A. (2004). "Culture, Gender Roles, and Sport: The Case of Korean Players on the LPGA Tour." *Journal of Sport & Social Issues*, 28(3), 223–244.

Tajima Creef, E. (1993). "Model Minorities and Monstrous Selves: The Winter Olympic Showdown of Kristi Yamaguchi and Midori Ito; Or: 'How to Tell Your Friends apart from the Japs' 1992-Style." *VAR Visual Anthropology Review*, 9(1), 141–146.

Taylor, C. R., & Stern, B. B. (1997). "Asian-Americans: Television Advertising and the 'Model Minority' stereotype." *Journal of Advertising*, 26(2), 47–61.

Tchen, J. K. W., & Yeats, D. (eds.). (2014). *Yellow Peril!: An Archive of Anti-Asian Fear*. London: Verso.

Theberge, N. (2002). "Challenging the Gendered Space of Sport: Women's Ice Hockey and the Struggle for Legitimacy." In S. Scraton & A. Flintoff (eds.), *Gender and Sport: A Reader* (pp. 292–302). London and New York: Routledge.

Tuan, M. (1999a). "Neither Real Americans nor Real Asians? Multigeneration Asian Ethnics Navigating the Terrain of Authenticity." *Qualitative Sociology*, 22(2), 105–126.

———. (1999b). "On Asian American Ice Queens and Multigeneration Asian Ethnics." *Amerasia Journal*, 25(1), 181–186.

Tung, C. (2004). "Embodying an Image: Gender, Race, and Sexuality in *La Femme Nikita*." In S. Inness (ed.), *Action Chicks: New Images of Tough Women in Popular Culture* (pp. 95–122). New York: Palgrave Macmillan.

Tuttle, C. J. (2014, Mar. 19). "UFC Announces The Ultimate Fighter (TUF) 20 Tryouts for April 28 in Las Vegas." *MMAmania.com*. http://www.mmamania.com/2014/3/19/5525092/ufc-the-ultimate-fighter-tuf-20-tryouts-april-28-las-vegas-mma.

Weaving, C. (2014). "Cage Fighting like a Girl: Exploring Gender Constructions in the Ultimate Fighting Championship (UFC)." *Journal of the Philosophy of Sport*, 41(1), 129–142.

Wetzel, D. (2013, Feb. 19). "Dana White's About Face on Women's MMA Became Official One Historic Night Last August." *Yahoo Sports*. http://sports.yahoo.com/news/mma—dana-white-s-about-face-on-women-s-mma-became-official-one-historic-night-last-august-045153399.html.

Williams, D., Martins, N., Consalvo, M., & Ivory, J. D. (2009). "The Virtual Census: Representations of Gender, Race and Age in Video Games." *New Media & Society*, 11(5), 815–834.

Yep, K. S. (2012). "Peddling Sport: Liberal Multiculturalism and the Racial Triangulation of Blackness, Chineseness and Native American-ness in Professional Basketball." *Ethnic and Racial Studies*, 35(6), 971–987.

Yu, H. (2003). "Tiger Woods Is Not the End of History: or, Why Sex across the Color Line Won't Save Us All." *American Historical Review*, 108(5), 1406–1414.

Xu, J., & Lee, J. C. (2013). "The Marginalized 'Model' Minority: An Empirical Examination of the Racial Triangulation of Asian Americans." *Social Forces*, 91(4), 1363–1397.

Zhang, Q. (2010). "Asian Americans beyond the Model Minority Stereotype: The Nerdy and the Left Out." *Journal of International and Intercultural Communication*, 3(1), 20–37.

WEBSITES CONSULTED
invictafc.com
jinyufrey.com
johnbaikephotography.com
twitter.com
ufc.com
wombatsports.wordpress.com

7

The Continued Legacy of Japanese American Youth Basketball Leagues

CHRISTINA B. CHIN

Introduction

Currently, Japanese American basketball leagues are thriving cultural and athletic organizations involving over 10,000 youth and adults participating in year-round leagues and tournaments in California (Watanabe 2008). The growth in the popularity and size of these leagues shows no signs of slowing down; there seems to be steady interest within the Japanese American community and the larger Asian American community as a whole. Despite a high degree of social integration by other measures—intermarriage, residential integration, language acquisition (Alba and Nee 2003; Zhou and Gatewood 2007), many third- and fourth-generation Japanese Americans continue to seek out and sustain co-ethnic spaces over racially mixed ones. The basketball court is one such important social site for co-ethnic socialization and intimacy.[1]

In this chapter, I explore why participants in Japanese American youth basketball leagues continue to collectively work together to create and play on a court of their own making. Specifically, I argue how members see sports as a cultural legacy that is not only reflected in the ethnic community, but also among generations of players in families. Instead of incorporating standard and stereotyped markers of ethnicity/ cultural identity that continue to frame Asian Americans as "forever foreign" (Lowe 1996), the chapter delves into inter- and intragenerational socialization through sport. Secondly, I demonstrate how these sites of play are part of a larger social frame where subtle racialized and gendered microaggressions position Asian bodies as smaller, weaker, and "forever foreign" to the game of basketball. In doing so, I contend that sports, particularly basketball, continues to be a space where Asians are not "becoming white" but rather an interesting social venue where they remain problematically depicted as foreign and invisible (Zhou 2004). As a result, Japanese American sports leagues continue to have a vibrant social and cultural presence, one that grows in popularity as more Japanese and Asian American families participate each year. Sport then constitutes a vacant site where social intimacies and sporting pleasures are ways to construct, perform, and manage Japanese American identity.

Methods

Research Site

As one of the oldest and largest Japanese American youth sports organizations in Southern California, the Pacific Coast Youth (PCY) basketball league is the center of my ethnographic fieldwork.[2] Started in the 1960s, the PCY was a purely volunteer-based organization run by a committee of elected members.[3] The league sponsors just over 30 male and female youth basketball teams with players ranging between the ages of 7 and 18. Moreover, the organization hosts an annual basketball tournament that is one of the largest in the region, drawing up to 400 teams in and around the Southern California areas as well as league participation from Northern California.

Although the PCY league does not hold or enforce any formal rules of racial or ethnic eligibility or quotas, the majority of participants are Asian American, with over half of the participants having full or mixed Japanese American heritage.[4] As I demonstrate later in this chapter, the racial composition of the league is connected to its larger historical legacy as an ethnic exclusive space and the current subtle racial exclusion of Asian Americans from other multiracial sporting spaces.[5]

Participant Observation

To capture the lived experiences and the meanings practitioners give to this ethnic basketball league, I conducted participant observation from December 2007 through June 2008. During this time, I followed a total of eight different teams—a boys' and girls' team in the third, sixth, ninth, and twelfth grades—for one season. By observing teams at varying ages, I captured "snapshots" of players at different stages in the "career life" of a league basketball player; it was common for players to join a team while they were in elementary school and continue playing through high school. Such an extended engagement with basketball illustrated to me the long histories and futures of Japanese American basketball that contest the normative understandings of Japanese Americans as never "American" enough.

To better understand the interactions, experiences, and activities from the perspectives of the players, coaches, family, and fans as they naturally occurred, I regularly attended weekend practices, games, and tournaments for both the junior season (second through seventh grade) as well as the senior season (eight through twelfth grade). These events gave me the opportunity to observe the nuanced interactions among members and capture their everyday lived sporting experience. To observe the organizational and political aspects of the league, I also attended monthly PCY commissioner meetings held at the local veterans' post. These meetings gave me insider knowledge of the internal and structural decisions regarding the management and organization of teams. I paid particular attention to guidelines, policies, and procedures regarding who could join and how new members were recruited into the organization, giving me detailed insight into the criteria that members used to delineate who was considered an "insider" and who they thought of as "outsiders" to the community.

Interviews

While participant observation captured the interactional experiences as they occurred in real time, I also conducted over 60 open-ended, in-depth interviews with players, family members, and league organizers to examine the lived experiences and personal opinions as they were told through the words and expressions of the participants themselves. Collection of interviews began in December 2008 and concluded in October 2009. Interviewees were selected first from the eight teams I had followed and expanded through a snowball sampling method to include members from different teams and age groups. All participants were given informed-consent forms and the parents of children under the age of 18 were asked permission before their children were interviewed.

To record the oral history of the PCY league, I interviewed some of the league founders and former players. From these oral histories, I gleaned information about the past to highlight the origins of the league, its initial goals, and early growth. League organizers were interviewed to gain a better sense of the bureaucratic, organizational, and political aspects of the league.

Interviews with current players, coaches, and family members captured how individuals experienced and constructed their sense of self—especially in relation to race, ethnicity, and gender—through participation in leagues like the PCY. Moreover, I interviewed participants who are also actively involved in nonethnic basketball leagues. These interviews offered a comparison between participation in the Japanese American league and those that were city sponsored.

Historical Legacy of Japanese American Sports Leagues

Japanese and Japanese Americans have had an especially long and successful sports legacy in the United States. Starting from the first immigrant arrivals, the *Issei* generation set in motion the first of many roots into the sports community particularly through their active involvement in sumo and baseball. As Ryan Reft has described in great detail earlier in this volume, Western sports arrived in Asia long before Asian American engagement with sport. Part of the affinity to sports is thus a larger history of sporting cultures and transnational connections between Japan and the United States. The second generation, the *Nisei* generation, continued to embrace baseball and basketball as popular pastimes, particularly in working-class communities where playing sports gave plantation and farm workers the opportunity to forget the hardships of tedious physical labor (Nakagawa 2001; Regalado 2012). Several historians have noted how discriminatory practices prevented some nonwhite groups from participation in professional or mainstream sporting spaces prior to the Civil Rights Movement (Burgos 2007).[6]

During this time, many Japanese athletes were barred not only from joining professional sport leagues, but also faced exclusion and segregation at the community level. As a second-generation Japanese American boy growing up in a predominantly white neighborhood in the 1930s,

Bruce, one of the PCY founders, was no stranger to the discrimination and prejudice directed against Japanese and other minority groups. Racial segregation was common in everyday life, including sports and recreational activities.[7] As Bruce revealed,

> I didn't like being Japanese being in an all-white town. So it was difficult being raised like that in a place where there was a lot of prejudice. We couldn't even go to the swimming pool because we had to wait till Monday for minorities—that's the only day we could go swimming.

The feeling of being treated as "less than" and having fewer privileges and rights to sporting activities than whites contributed to the racial divide and hierarchy that placed Asians and other racial groups on the bottom.

In the face of exclusion, Japanese Americans continued to create their own racial and ethnic leagues to parallel other white-only sports organizations. By the 1920s, several Japanese associations and churches on the West Coast began forming athletic organizations including the Japanese American Citizens League (JACL), the Japanese Amateur Athletic Union (JAAU) in San Francisco, and the Japanese Athletic Union (JAU) in Los Angeles. These organizations were instrumental in developing and expanding sports programs within the Japanese American community and cementing a cultural tradition of athletics.

American sporting cultures continued to play an active role during World War II, when the Japanese American community faced some of their most challenging times. In 1942, over 110,000 Japanese American men, women, and children, two thirds of whom were American citizens by birth, were systematically uprooted from their homes and transplanted to temporary "relocation centers" located at fairgrounds and horse-racing tracks located in desolate and remote regions of the United States. If sports were an outlet for entertainment, acceptance, and community organizing for the *Issei* and *Nisei* generations, sports activities served a similar purpose during these years of internment. With few freedoms and liberties during internment, Japanese and Japanese American internees were able to manage, coach, train, and field their own teams. These sports activities gave the community a growing sense of pride, unity, and empowerment even under oppressive confinement. Within this sporting space, Japanese Americans could offer their own renditions of citizenship and national identity. Japanese American men and women were quick to set up sporting activities and teams within the confines of their barbed-wire communities, including baseball and basketball teams.

Sports was a form of entertainment—an enjoyable way to pass the time, break up the boredom within the desolate confines of the camp, and challenge the dominant representation of them as national traitors who were "forever foreign" (Lowe 1996; Pearce 2005). Interned with his family in Poston, Arizona, Bruce spoke with me about his three-and-a-half-year experience living in the camp and the role that sports played during that time:

> Well, I can tell you what we did to keep ourselves occupied. I went in when I was 12 and I came out when I was 15, a sophomore in high school. Things were pretty much barren, pretty much nothing. You didn't know anybody. You didn't know how long you were going to be there. It was a frightening experience. You did not know what was going to happen to you and why you were there. . . . But they had a recreation department and you could go there and if you wanted to buy a baseball glove, you could order it there. If you wanted sports equipment there—a basketball, baseball, football—you could check it out and you took it to your block. Like I said, we found ways to keep ourselves occupied.

During this disruptive and often frightening experience, many interned youth like Bruce turned to sports as a social outlet to keep themselves grounded and stay "occupied." In this capacity, sports played a pivotal role in creating a degree of continuity and normalcy in a racially hostile world while forging new alliances and a sense of pride in their teams while offering internees "approaches for finding articulation, and preserving meaning in a senseless situation" (Nakagawa 2001).

The postwar era saw a rise in participation in more traditionally "American" sporting teams including baseball, basketball, golf, and bowling clubs. As Japanese Americans poured their hearts, interests, and efforts into these American sports, participation in more traditional Japanese sports (e.g., sumo, kendo, judo) declined. On the playing grounds, Japanese Americans could both validate their identity as Americans and prove themselves loyal to the country. By the 1980s and 1990s, the *Sansei* (third-) and *Yonsei* (fourth-) generation Japanese American were moving away from their inner-city niches into wealthier suburban communities, where new sports leagues and organizations were formed to meet their athletic and social needs. In Southern California alone, when there was once only the Nisei Athletic Union (NAU), by the end of the 1980s a dozen other organizations cropped up, including the JAO, FOR, CYC, CBO, and SEYO—an "alphabet soup" of athletic organizations (Niiya 2000). As the popularity of basketball began to grow on a national level, so did its popularity in Japanese American sports leagues. Especially given the long games in the summer sun, limited field space, and necessity for more equipment, interest in baseball began to wane and it soon took a backseat to the growing number of basketball teams being formed within the leagues. Plus, one cannot discount the effect the National Basketball Association's Los Angeles Lakers, with their wildly popular "Showtime" style of play, and the growing iconicity of Michael Jordan had in drawing various communities to basketball (Farred 2006; LeFeber 1999).

My findings demonstrate that interest in joining these leagues is intertwined with the desire to continue a cultural and familial legacy of athleticism—one that often spans several generations. Additionally, persistent racial barriers in the form of racial and gendered microaggressions continue to disadvantage young Asian players, who are frequently racialized as physically weaker, passive, and too "model minority" to play an aggressive contact sport like basketball. Collectively, these forces contribute to the thriving and persistent nature of Japanese American leagues.

Preserving Ethnic and Familial Legacies

For many PCY members, the appeal of participating in a co-ethnic league was rooted in a longing to participate and continue a history of sporting traditions that privileged Japanese heritage. While there were no official rules in the league's bylaws barring non-Japanese youths' entry into the league, organizing members expressed a strong desire to maintain a particular racial and ethnic boundary that gave preference to youth of Japanese ancestry. As Kathy, the PCY league secretary and third-generation Japanese American, explained to me:

> Well, there aren't any official rules about which kids from which race can join—it's more unwritten and unspoken. The committee tries to keep the tradition of the organization the same as when it started, which used to be all Japanese kids. We don't like to exclude others but our kids need a place so they can play basketball too. So we mostly accept teams with lots of Japanese kids—or at least Asian kids—who join.

Given the historical practice of exclusion of Japanese Americans in white sporting spaces, for members like Kathy, the preservation of "tradition"—to create a space so Japanese American youth could actively participate in basketball—was a top priority. Recognizing that some exclusion was necessary, Kathy underscores the continued need for athletic spaces for Japanese American youth. And while ethnic boundaries are expanding to include other Asian ethnic groups, the tradition of a predominately Japanese American or Asian American space must be maintained.

In addition to continuing the league's original mission, the tradition of sports participation was an activity that often spanned several generations in one family. While sitting on the sidelines during a third-grade girls' game, Susan, a third-generation Japanese American mother, explained how there were three generations of players who grew up playing in Japanese American leagues:

> It was my mother that started it all—she started playing when she was a young girl and continued to play well into her 40s. Then when she had me, she put me in a [Japanese American] league. And when Leila [her daughter] got old enough, we knew she would play too. If [Leila] has kids, I'm sure they will play ball too. That's just what this family does.

Susan's family was not unique in this regard. Sport was passed on in complex ways that challenged the dominant rhetoric of sporting lineage from father to son. In this capacity ethnic leagues provided various types of gender nonconforming practices that might not have always been possible in mainstream leagues (see also Yep 2009).

Moreover, some parents saw these sports leagues as a means to transpose their own childhood experiences into their own children's lives, including their social connections to other co-ethnics. For example, Jason, a father of two boys, grew up playing in a league just 15 miles away. He reminisced, "I remember how much fun I had playing JA ball and I wanted my kids to have that experience too. Some of my best friends came out of playing in these leagues. . . . I don't think I would be as connected to the [Japanese American] community if it weren't for these leagues." Much of the motivation for parents joining the PCY league was to re-create the possibility of a similar childhood—one that was infused with close friendships with other Japanese American youth and families. While youth would have the physical benefits of playing basketball two to three times a week, parents recognized the social potential these leagues had in fostering close ties to other co-ethnics, which was made harder by living in a predominately white community.

Finally, the PCY league maintained an ethnic legacy by also highlighting the contributions and sacrifices of previous generations of Japanese Americans off the court. Longer histories are often embodied in the sporting body and time is multiply embodied on the basketball court. In an effort to bridge generations of Japanese Americans together, the PCY league often created opportunities for youth to meet elders from the community, in particular a local Veterans of Foreign Wars (VFW) organization of predominately Japanese American war veterans. Through these interactions, youth were able to learn more about the legacy and accomplishments of older generation Japanese Americans. During our interview, Janice described her interactions with the veterans at a senior scholarship banquet; her conversations with them influenced her feelings about playing for PCY:

> We got to meet [veterans] there who fought in the wars and who have been serving the country. . . . I asked [the veterans], "Oh, what was the war like?" And hearing their perspective from someone who was there as opposed to something that you read or from a documentary or something, it's completely different. I think that putting on that jersey and

knowing that I'm representing [the veterans], that's kind of big because you're representing a group of people who went out there and fought for the country. Especially during World War II when Japanese Americans were shunned and people were like, "They're probably enemies and we shouldn't trust them."

Janice's remark demonstrates how playing for PCY—a league that was founded by several veterans—became a source of pride and honor that came with wearing her team's jersey. Participation in the league became more than just involvement in a game; as Janice reflected, "I'm representing some of the heroes of my community when I put on that jersey." The struggle, sacrifice, and legacy of the previous generations are honored and embodied among the youth who participate in the league.

Battling Microaggressions

In addition to a strong desire to continue the historical legacy of co-ethnic sporting traditions within their community and families, many PCY members felt that there was a continued need for ethnic leagues due to racial discrimination in the form of microaggressions. Racial microaggressions are subtle, everyday racialized insults directed toward people of color, often automatically or unconsciously, which serve to keep those on the margins in their place (Solorzano et.al 2000; Sue 2010). Often, the cumulative effect of racial microaggressions can lead to a host of negative experiences including psychological problems (e.g., depression, low self-esteem, anxiety), barriers in higher education, and racial battle fatigue (Ong et al. 2013; Sue et al. 2007). Racial microaggressions against Asian Americans often include embodiments of foreignness, model minority stereotypes that overemphasize intelligence or class, and a conflation of ethnic identities and groups. Moreover, because racial identities are often intertwined with gender, these microaggressions target Asian females as exotic while Asian men are typically emasculated (Shimizu 2007; Thangaraj 2015).

Many of the athletes and parents experienced racial microaggressions regarding players' physical size, often battling assumptions that Asian bodies were somehow smaller and ahtletically inferior than those of other racial groups. If black bodies are frequently read as physically dominating and naturally athletic (Brooks 2009), Asian bodies on the other hand are generally perceived as smaller, shorter, and less muscular. This can be seen when players reveal their involvement with basketball to others including teachers and school acquaintances. Laura, a skilled player on the twelfth-grade girls' PCY team and a starting player for her high school's varsity basketball team, recounted a typical reaction she might receive while wearing her basketball warm-ups:

> Random students would come up to me and ask what team I was on. And I would tell them the basketball team and they wouldn't believe me! ... They'd say, "Aren't you a little short to play?" ... And even teachers, when they'd come to watch [my games], they'd be all shocked that this little girl [gesturing to herself] can shoot some threes.

Students' disbelief in Laura's position on the team served as a subtle, yet consistent reminder that the basketball court was a foreign space for Asian athletes. PCY players like Laura were often told that they do not "look" the part of a "typical" basketball player—tall, white, or black. While most youth across all racial groups would struggle to meet the average height expectations of NBA and WNBA players, Asians in particular were seen as having atypical bodies for basketball—they "just didn't seem like the type" to play the game. Laura and many other players felt that their bodies were negatively scrutinized because they did not fit that stereotypical physical or racial mold.

The game of basketball has increasingly been seen as a space dominated by hypermasculine men and less feminine female players. For young Asian American males and females, their participation in the game heightened how their bodies were both racialized and gendered simultaneously on the court. This intersectionality often presented different challenges for players. For example, a particular salient racial microaggression for young Asian males was one that emasculated their style of play on the court as feminine, weak, and soft. Russell, a fourth-generation Japanese American player on the twelfth-grade boys' team, explained,

> When I walk out onto the court, I'm always [seen as] the underdog. ... People are not going to see me be the most athletic or strongest like

you would a black guy on the court. . . . It doesn't matter if you're tall. Look at me. I'm like six feet, which is considered tall in PCY, but because I'm kind of skinny and Asian, other people think I can't defend or play aggressively.

Many Asian boys like Russell routinely spoke of opposing players underestimating their abilities on the court as less threatening because of their race and gender. Yet, as underdogs, they were often not fiercely guarded and, as a result, were able to score more frequently and move the ball around.

Some Asian male players responded to these emasculating racial microaggressions by adopting a hypermasculine display of athleticism and aggression. In response to his underdog status, Russell confessed that he purposely adopted a "dirty" style of play—one that included giving hard fouls and sharply planted elbows while the referee's watchful gaze was turned elsewhere. Russell wanted other players to "think twice" about guarding him and to perhaps think differently of Asian players more broadly. While male athletes are expected to maintain performances of hegemonic masculinity in which they appear to be well-muscled, strong, unemotional, and hypercompetitive, some players felt more pressure to make a public display of their aggression and physical abilities to avoid fulfilling gendered stereotypes of Asian men as effeminate and weak. Similarly, in his study of South Asian American male basketball leagues in Atlanta, Thangaraj (2013) found that players challenged emasculating racial stereotypes by resorting to hypermasculine behaviors and beliefs including homophobia or misogyny that preserved conservative regimes of race, gender, and sexuality.

Players also experienced racial microaggressions that placed them into model minority stereotypes that emphasized an imagined preference for academics over sports. As Chuck, a ninth grader on the PCY boys team, explained, "A lot of people think, 'Oh, well [Asians] should be smart, they should be hitting the books, they should be doctors and all these other professions.'" Players were frequently assumed to be focused only on their academic pursuits, leaving little room or desire to be athletes. Mirroring the "model minority" narrative that paints an inaccurate picture of academic exceptionalism, Asian American youth like Chuck were expected to be studious and smart in the classroom—"the model worker, the overachiever, the math maniac, or the science/computer nerd" (Lee and Zhou 2004, 10). Yet, as model minorities, these youth were rarely seen as "jocks" who have the physical aggression, ability, or passion to be basketball players. In other words, Asian American youth could be scholars, but not ballers.

Conclusion

The legacy of sports activity is a lengthy and important one within the Japanese American community. From the first immigrants to the current generation of players, this chapter has demonstrated how youth sports has been a common thread to unify this ethnic group through a variety of social, political, and community transformations. Yet for each generation of athletes, race and gender continue to shape the experiences and identities of players. Denied access into white leagues, the early generations of Japanese immigrants rallied together to start their own ethnic leagues—a tradition that continued during their internment and as they rebuilt sporting communities after relocation and resettlement in predominately white suburban neighborhoods. Youth basketball played a significant and persistent social and political role as an outlet through which to reimagine a sense of belonging and participation in mainstream American cultural pastimes.

While discriminatory laws no longer keep Japanese or other Asian American youth confined to playing in Asian-only leagues (Yep 2009), my findings demonstrate the continued desire to seek out and participate in co-ethnic sporting spaces among later-generation Japanese Americans. For some athletes, to be authentically Japanese American means being an active member of a JA basketball league; the legacy of the community is imbedded onto the courts and in the stands. With a strong sense of pride and tradition associated with playing basketball, participation puts players in a social position to strengthen their identity and belonging to the Japanese American community, while those who do not play were often on the outskirts.

In many ways, the basketball court is still a space where many Asian Americans are racialized as foreign or invisible. Microaggressions on the court are part of the everyday experience of exclusion in a supposedly "postracial" society. Whether it is someone's surprise reaction or subtle jokes about size, Asian players frequently encounter racial and gendered microaggressions that reinforce stereotypic assumptions about their bodies and athletic ability. As a result, Asian youth continue to be racialized as physically smaller, inferior, effeminate, and weaker compared to other racial groups. Moreover, perpetuating the model minority myth, Asian American athletes are also subtly reminded that their place is more likely to be confined to academic pursuits rather than including athletic ones.

Yet in predominately Japanese American leagues like PCY, players and their families have created a counter-space—a site where deficit notions of people of color can be challenged and where a positive racial climate can be established and maintained (Chin 2015; Solorzano et al. 2000). On these courts, racial tokenism is erased and nonconformist gender ideologies can emerge. The PCY league makes it possible for young players to carry forward a legacy of sporting tradition that continues to create opportunities for play in a game that rarely recognizes them as athletes. Their play and social network offers a much more expansive version of American identity than the one they experience outside of co-ethnic spaces.

NOTES

1 Portions of this chapter have been previously published in *Amerasia Journal* (see Chin 2015).

2 All names have been changed to protect the identity of participants and the organizations involved.

3 The PCY league is connected to the Southern California Sports Association (SCSA), an athletic youth organization that oversees the PCY along with eight other Japanese American and Asian American youth sports leagues.

4 This percentage was determined through informal interviews with families and by examining the names and photographs of players in the tournament handbook and team yearbook.

5 See also Thangaraj (2015).

6 For a sociological investigation of Asian discrimination, U.K. society, and sport, see Burdsey (2007).

7 See Carrington (2010) and Burdsey (2011).

REFERENCES

Alba, Richard, and Victor Nee. 2003. *Remaking the American Mainstream: Assimilation and Contemporary Immigration*. Cambridge, MA: Harvard University Press.

Brooks, Scott. 2009. *Black Men Can't Shoot*. Chicago: University of Chicago Press.

Burdsey, Daniel. 2011. "That Joke Isn't Funny Anymore: Racial Microaggressions, Color-Blind Ideology and the Mitigation of Racism in English Men's First-Class Cricket." *Sociology of Sport Journal* 28:3, 261–283.

———. 2007. *British Asians and Football: Culture, Identity, Exclusion*. London: Routledge.

Burgos, Adrian, Jr. 2007. *Playing America's Game: Baseball, Latinos, and the Color Line*. Berkeley: University of California Press.

Carrington, Ben. 2010. *Race, Sport and Politics: The Sporting Black Diaspora*. Thousand Oaks, CA: Sage Publications.

Chin, Christina B. 2015. "'Aren't You a Little Short to Play Ball?': Japanese American Youth and Racial Microaggressions in Basketball Leagues." *Amerasia Journal* 41:2, 47–65.

Farred, Grant. 2006. *Phantom Calls: Race and the Globalization of the NBA*. Chicago: Prickly Paradigm Press.

Lee, Jennifer, and Min Zhou. 2004. *Asian American Youth: Culture, Identity, and Ethnicity*. New York: Routledge.

LeFeber, Walter. 1999. *Michael Jordan and the New Global Capitalism*. New York: W. W. Norton.

Lowe, Lisa. 1996. *Immigrant Acts: On Asian American Cultural Politics*. Durham, NC: Duke University Press.

Nakagawa, Kerry. 2001. *Through a Diamond: 100 Years of Japanese American Baseball*. San Francisco: Rudi Publishing.

Niiya, Brian. 2000. "Sport in the Japanese American Community—An Introduction," pp. 14–67 in *More than a Game: Sport in the Japanese American Community*, edited by Brian Niiya. Los Angeles: Japanese American National Museum.

Ong, Anthony D., Anthony L. Burrow, Thomas E. Fuller-Rowell, Nicole M. Ja, and Derald Wing Sue. 2013. "Racial Microaggressions and Daily Well-Being among Asian Americans." *Journal of Counseling Psychology* 60:2, 188–199.

Pearce, Ralph. 2005. *From Asahi to Zebras: Japanese American Baseball in San Jose, California*. San Jose, CA: Japanese American Museum of San Jose.

Regalado, Samuel O. 2012. *Nikkei Baseball: Japanese American Players from Immigration and Internment to the Major Leagues*. Urbana: University of Illinois Press.

Shimizu, Celine Parreñas. 2007. *The Hypersexuality of Race: Performing Asian/American Women on Screen and Scene*. Durham, NC: Duke University Press.

Solorzano, Daniel, Miguel Ceja, and Tara Yosso. 2000. "Critical Race Theory, Racial Microaggressions, and Campus Racial Climate: The Experiences of African American College Students." *Journal of Negro Education* 69, 60–73.

Sue, Derald Wing. 2010. *Microaggressions in Everyday Life: Race, Gender, and Sexual Orientation*. Hoboken, NJ: Wiley.

Sue, Derald Wing, Jennifer Bucceri, Annie I. Lin, Kevin L. Nadal, and Gina C. Torino. 2007. "Racial Microaggressions and the Asian American Experience." *Cultural Diversity & Ethnic Minority Psychology* 13:1, 72–81.

Thangaraj, Stanley I. 2015. *Desi Hoop Dreams: Pickup Basketball and the Making of Asian American Masculinity*. New York: New York University Press.

———. 2013. "Competing Masculinities: South Asian American Identity Formation in Asian American Basketball leagues." *South Asian Popular Culture* 11:3, 243–255.

Watanabe, Teresa. 2008. "Los Angeles' Little Tokyo to Finally Get Its Gym." *Los Angeles Times*, September 24.

Yep, Kathleen S. 2009. *Outside of the Paint: When Basketball Ruled at the Chinese Playground*. Philadelphia: Temple University Press.

Zhou, Min. 2004. "Are Asian Americans Becoming White?" *Contexts* 3:1, 29–37.

Zhou, Min, and J. V. Gatewood. 2007. "Transforming Asian America: Globalization and Contemporary Immigration to the United States," pp. 115–138 in *Contemporary Asian America: A Multidisciplinary Reader*, edited by Min Zhou and J. V. Gatewood. New York: New York University Press.

PART IV

Refugees, Pacific Islanders, and Sport

8

Hmong Youth, American Football, and the Cultural Politics of Ethnic Sports Tournaments

CHIA YOUYEE VANG

The December 12, 2011, edition of *Sports Illustrated* ran a story titled "How to Become an American." It traced the migration of Hmong refugees to the small town of Magazine, Arkansas, and celebrated the fact that despite being "tiny Asians," Hmong boys had utilized an unexpected channel to assimilate into American society—playing football. Sixteen-year-old Charly Moua was quoted saying, "I like football because I can knock over bigger kids." While engaging with this supposed anomaly, the article went between transnational spaces and global circuits by discussing the United States' secret war in Laos and the Hmong people's subsequent displacement. It subsequently contrasted the experiences of refugee parents with second-generation youth in a part of the country with few Asian Americans. The presence of Hmong boys on J. D. Leftwich High School's football team was said to have not only "created an intriguing image for the Magazine program but also forced coaches to radically rethink the physical configuration of a football player." The parents' hard work and sacrifices raising more than 120,000 chickens for Tyson Foods was juxtaposed against the boys' unexpected contributions to the school's state championship in 2010. The article concluded with Charly assertively stating, "There's a tradition now here with *Asian* kids, and the parents are really behind us, and we try to do well, because of all they [parents] went through to get here."[1]

This chapter explores Hmong refugee experiences, their community formation, and sports participation to provide valuable insight into how particular waves of Hmong immigration to the U.S. challenge the space of "Asian America," which itself has gone through many transformations from the unassimilable "yellow peril" to the model minority. Arriving at America's gates during a time of increased Asian immigration and culture wars, Hmong refugees from Laos became the antithesis of the Asian American model minority. Unlike the highly skilled Asian immigrants who entered to fill U.S. jobs with a shortage of American workers,[2] images in popular media highlighted the Hmong's agrarian background and illiteracy, welfare dependency, low education attainment, and inability to assimilate. The achievements of *Time* magazine's 1987 Asian American whiz kids were seemingly beyond reach for Hmong refugee youth. Excluded from the "model minority myth" of high-achieving Americans of Asian descent, they became part of the "Other Asian."[3] They were seen as failed and unlikely Asian American subjects as a result of their segmented assimilation toward the lower end of the socioeconomic ladder.[4] Unlike the earlier post-1965 wave of professionals, most Hmong refugees possessed limited transferable skills. Like Vietnamese and Cambodian refugees who struggled to adjust to their new environments, Hmong were racialized as dangerous, prone to crime, and uncontrollable. Consequently, if they entered the public consciousness, it would generally be through academic studies of youth violence and media coverage of crime related activities. In opposition to such racializations, the *Sports Illustrated* story turned a new page for Hmong Americanization. An examination of Hmong American identity formation through the cultural politics of sports demonstrates the strategic ways in which they are defying popular images of Hmong American boys and young men as gangbangers or thugs and girls and women as docile victims of patriarchal Hmong culture. Sport opens up ways to reshape racial dynamics and offer other renditions of individual and collective identities.[5] I argue that U.S. sport becomes that realm where these young individuals negotiate identities and their racializations. Moreover, their participation in football and other organized sports invokes different notions of time and space in performing Asian America that challenges the dominant framings of the "model minority."

Migration and Place Making

U.S. empire building is intimately connected to Hmong and Hmong American history. The Moua family settled in the U.S. as a direct result of American imperialism in Southeast Asia during the Cold War era. Thus, Hmong America must be situated in the time of the Vietnam

War that shaped their spaces of identity making in the United States. From the early 1960s through the end of the Vietnam War, the Hmong became entangled in U.S. covert operations in Laos in support of the war effort in Vietnam. Supplied and trained by the U.S. Central Intelligence Agency, the Hmong clandestine army numbered a few hundred in the early 1960s and increased to more than 40,000 by the late 1960s. They faced severe losses during and after the war. An estimated 17,000 died on the battlefield and more than 50,000 civilians perished.[6] Following U.S. disengagement from Southeast Asia, those who had collaborated with Americans feared for their lives and sought a way out. The exodus began as a trickle as military elites made what many thought was a temporary escape from the risk of retribution, and grew in scale and level of desperation as conditions rapidly deteriorated. Thousands crossed the Mekong River to seek asylum in Thailand and were eventually administered into United Nations–sponsored refugee camps. Since 1975, more than 130,000 Hmong refugees have settled in the United States and by 2010 the Hmong American population had increased to more than 260,000.[7]

U.S. refugee resettlement policies initially dispersed them throughout the country, but through chain migration they, in due course, established ethnic enclaves in several key states, including California, Minnesota, Wisconsin, and North Carolina. As displaced people with limited resources and few transferable skills, most Hmong initially confronted tremendous difficulties adapting to life in the United States. While poverty, isolation, language issues, racism, and violence plagued their lives, a strong sense of ethnic identity and community building emerged parallel to these daily struggles. Movement across state borders over the last few decades resulted in more Hmong Americans residing in the Midwest than any other region. The Twin Cities (Saint Paul and Minneapolis, Minnesota) became the largest concentration of Hmong in the nation. In small towns like Wausau, Wisconsin, Hmong Americans constitute 10 percent of the population. Although California has the largest Hmong population, as people of Asian descent, they blend in more easily with the state's diverse Asian demographic composition. On the contrary, Hmong represent the largest Asian groups in Minnesota and Wisconsin, which have not only enabled them to amass political power but also changed the racial landscape of predominantly white Midwestern cities. Because the smaller places in the Midwest are not usually designated as Asian American destination cities, the Hmong had become representatives of Asian America. The phenomenon of migrating to Southern states to work in the poultry industry, as the Moua family had, began in the early 2000s.[8] Driven by entrepreneurial spirit and dreams of owning land, hundreds flocked to the South to purchase poultry farms and start cattle businesses, thus creating many small and mostly rural communities consisting of extended family members.

The adaptation of Vietnam War refugees (those from Cambodia, Laos, and Vietnam) has been a significant topic among academic scholarship and community studies within the literature on immigrant incorporation during the last few decades.[9] The knowledge produced in the immediate postwar period followed what Yên Lê Espiritu called "rescue and liberation."[10] These earlier studies characterized them as helpless and demoralized refugees who were victims of the Vietnam War in need of care to be provided by Americans. Researchers often portrayed refugees as passive subjects to be rescued, focusing on a moral responsibility of the West to lend a helping hand to refugees "voting with their feet" to escape communism. Studies after arrival then shifted to refugees as problems to be solved.[11] Gang involvement and delinquency became subjects of many scholarly studies and popular media representation that further contributed to this racialization of refugees. Clint Eastwood's 2008 film *Gran Torino* is an example of the ways in which popular culture serves as space for Hmong to negotiate and perform ethnic identity. Rather than seen as embracing the white middle-class values associated with the model minority, Hmong Americans and other Southeast Asian Americans are stereotyped as problem minorities holding on to their traditions.[12]

Hmong American contributions to U.S. society during the short time that they have been in the country are notable in the areas of education, business, and civic engagement, but these have been overlooked in social science research's and the popular media's emphases on problems. Since Choua Lee's pioneering election to the Saint Paul school board in 1991, Hmong in California, Minnesota, and Wisconsin have continued to successfully run for local and state political offices. Educational attainment has enabled many to hold important positions in both the public and private sectors. Moreover, their concentration in certain U.S. locations has helped to ensure that other Americans have thriving jobs and businesses. The scholarship on them has recently begun to shift to better reflect the dynamic Hmong American community, but there is a gap in knowledge about the diverse ways in which Hmong Americans are reproducing ethnic culture and re-creating new identities in diasporic locations. This analysis of sports participation through an insider lens makes visible the development over time of a distinctive Hmong Americanization process that has remained under the radar of researchers.

Role of Sport in U.S. Society and Asian Americans

If sport reflects culture and patriotism, then what does Americans' obsession with it suggest about American culture and citizenship? Commitment to professional sports and demonstration of preference for one team over another is ubiquitous in American society. The enormous sports memorabilia and team uniform industries in addition to the millions of dollars that spectators spend each year makes participation in some ways necessary to prove one's Americanness. Americans' daily fascination with sport plays an intimate role in making kids from all walks of life dream of being the next star. Consequently, the role of sport in U.S. society has shifted to reflect an increase in organized, adult-controlled activities and a decrease in unstructured pickup games at the park.[13] From professional teams, collegiate teams, and K–12 school teams to select and recreational neighborhood programs, it is easy to make the case that sport is an integral part of U.S. society. Delaney and Madigan write, "Sport is as much a part of American society and culture as are other social institutions such as family, religion, politics, economics and education. . . . Athletic contests are important to the socialization of youth, to the integration of disparate groups and social classes, to physical and mental well-being, and to the enhancement of community pride."[14] American society may be "inundated with images and ideas about sport," but different segments of the U.S. population experience sport differently. The heterogeneous Asian American communities, accordingly, have different relations to sport.[15]

Significant barriers exist that have resulted in fewer Asian Americans participating in sport. The problem, as Kathleen S. Yep demonstrated, is the "simultaneity of hyper-racialization and de-racialization in sports discourse" where different racial groups were positioned in relation to each other in the broader society.[16] Asian American athletes are treated as "novelties" and prevalent racism in sports programs deters them from participating.[17] However, there is, as Yep and España-Maram demonstrate, a longer historical engagement with mainstream sport. On the other end of the spectrum, Asian American men, in particular, have historically been regarded as weak and physically nonnormative (Thangaraj 2015). As David L. Eng contended, "the Asian American male is both materially and physically feminized within the context of the larger U.S. cultural imaginary."[18] This has had an enduring impact on how athletic institutions view Asian American abilities, which has likely contributed to Asian American parents discouraging their children from participation in certain sports. The latter is important since it has been found that parents influence the sport participation rates of children "by serving as role models, providers of experience, and interpreters of experience by transmitting values and norms of sport participation."[19] The strongest predictor of participation is the value that parents place on sport participation. If parents do not value the role of sports in their children's lives, then they would not support their children taking part in sports programs. For example, Soumya Palreddy's study of South Asian American sport involvement found that acculturation significantly contributed to parents seeing value in sports.[20] Moreover, sometimes parents come with high commitment to sports, but they are not necessarily mainstream U.S. sports.

The valuation Asian American students place on sports is also impacted by the high expectations their parents have in regard to their academic pursuits. School sports may impede educational progress of ethnic minority youth who are already academically marginalized because it distracts them from their studies.[21] Interviews with Hmong American youth reveal that Hmong parents do believe participating in sport would negatively impact their schoolwork. John, a university sophomore, shared that his father refused to allow him to play on the high school soccer team because he did not believe John could do well in both.[22] Interestingly, however, he was permitted to play with his cousin's team that competed in Hmong tournaments. John explained his father's rationale: "My dad thought that if I played for the school, I would just go join gangs and not keep up with my homework. When I play with my cousins, who are all older than me, he thinks it's fine because they will look after me when he's not around" (interview with author, 2014).

Youa concurs with John. Her parents worried about letting her join the volleyball team during high school. As a high-achieving student, she was able to convince them to let her play. The condition was that if she received any grade lower than an A minus, she would quit the team. Not only was Youa able to maintain a high grade-point average, but she also excelled on the court. As the only Asian American player on the team, she was voted most valuable player during freshman year by her all-white teammates. Youa recalled:

> Because we live in a pretty white neighborhood and there are few Asian people, I guess my parents were afraid that I wouldn't be accepted. Before I joined sports, I was quiet and no one really noticed me except my teachers because I was a good student. I love volleyball and I had played with my cousins at Hmong tournaments so I was actually better than a lot of the white girls I played with. They were of course all taller than me but I had a lot of skills that they didn't. When all the other parents started to compliment about me to my parents during games, they started to understand why I wanted to play. It's like they don't see me as just a quiet Asian girl who's smart. It made me feel good, like I was just one of them." (interview with author, 2014)

Youa's experience is complex but not out of the ordinary because sport has been found to play a significant role in immigrants' adaptation to their new culture.[23] Though studies have found that first- and second-generation Asian American high school students are more likely to be involved in academic school-based extracurricular activities than in school sports, Youa's ability to outperform her peers enables her to be treated as "one of them."[24] The tension she struggles with stems from the social and cultural perceptions of Asian Americans as "quiet" and "not athletic," which can influence how Asian Americans perceive themselves and subsequently influence their decisions about which school activities to pursue.[25] Asian American women, in particular, are invisible in sport literature in part because of simplistic stereotypes of them as submissive and subservient.[26] Unlike Youa, Nhoua grew up in inner-city Milwaukee and attended a racially diverse public school. With the reputation of being able to "play soccer like the boys," Nhoua was named an all-conference player throughout her high school career, which contributed to her positive outlook and school pride. She continued to compete in Hmong tournaments while in college and led a team of mostly Hmong American young women along with several Hispanic/Latina team members (interview with author, 2008).

Participation in school athletic programs contributed to Hmong youth's sense of belonging in those specific contexts. Linsanity, or the excitement over professional basketball player Jeremy Lin, in 2012 certainly created an Asian American hypervisibility in sport that also heightened debates about race, ethnicity, and gender. Many Asian Americans are passionate basketball players who participate in ethnic specific and pan-Asian-American tournaments each year (see Thangaraj 2013; Chin 2012). Whether in small pickup games, rec leagues, or the National Basketball Association, Asian American basketball players outside co-ethnic or racial spaces have not been taken seriously. Lin's success on the courts made a dent in the stereotypes against Asian athletes in general.[27] More importantly, as Kathleen S. Yep articulated regarding Lin, "In many ways, Linsanity created opportunities. It made transparent the perception and construction of heteronormative Asian American masculinities in mainstream discourse. . . . [Sport] has been used in specific ways to regulate and empower Asian American and Pacific Islander communities."[28] Although his rise to stardom was certainly a phenomenon that Hmong boys and men who are sports fans followed, few interviewees mentioned him as their role model. In fact, when asked about their role models, interviewees frequently mentioned other Hmong Americans they knew personally or mainstream sport stars.[29] Although Hmong Americans embrace mainstream U.S. sport and normative sporting heroes on many levels, they still create, embrace, and desire their own pantheon of co-ethnic heroes.

Embracing America's Game

Why have Hmong youth become fascinated with American football? Football is said to strike a most responsive chord in the American psyche; indeed, "no other American sport consistently draws fans in the numbers that are attracted to football."[30] At the same time that the boys in Magazine, Arkansas, made news headlines, other Hmong American high school football players were noticed. In Snellville, Georgia, Brookwood High School's kicker Erick Yang's change from soccer to football made him an "overnight sensation." Erick is quoted, "I never knew football would be so much fun. Yes, I'd love to play college football. I just find football more exciting than soccer. There are more people at the games, and I love the adrenaline rush."[31] In Wausau, Wisconsin, D.C. Everest High School's star safety, Jerry Lee, was the keynote speaker at the city's Hmong History Month luncheon. Unlike Erick, who came to football later, Jerry started in middle school. Jerry's invitation to be the luncheon speaker is an unlikely blending of what is Hmong and American because "American football and Hmong history do not often get paired together."[32] Like Erick Yang, Sacramento, California's Grant High placekicker, Charlie Vue, did not play football until high school, but he became an effective player. His coach stated, "The kid never played football and never kicked before. He's been so terrific in his first two years."[33] Significant in these experiences is the greater attention that these athletes receive playing football, which generally draws more fans than other high school sports. As "overnight successes," they have the potential to offer more visibility as role models both on and off the field. Although placekickers are not seen with the positive valence of masculinity to the same degree as players at other positions where there is much more frequent and intense contact, these players were now a part of an "imagined community" (Anderson 1991) of football players, where they took pleasure in the masculine ethos and its respective positive valence of toughness.

Acceptance of football has led more boys and young men to the game. In Saint Paul, at least a couple of Hmong players are on the high school football roster and in schools with high Hmong concentration like Harding and Johnson High on the East Side, nearly a quarter of the names are Hmong.[34] Two Hmong Americans are football coaches in the Twin Cities. At Saint Paul's Harding Senior High School, Elliot Vang was hired as assistant coach to help "introduce Hmong to America's game," according to one area newspaper.[35] While attracting athletes from other cultures to the game was said to be important, both Vang and the head coach, Dave Zeitchick, emphasized that Hmong identity was not the primary factor. Vang stated, "I think I was hired as a coach, first and foremost. . . . I do not think the fact that I was Hmong had anything to do with it. Now that I'm here, I do want to pave the way and show the Hmong population that there are ways to get into athletics and achieve success." Though 20 percent of Harding High School's 1,009 students were Hmong, Dave Zeitchick stated, "I didn't think about the significance of him being Hmong." Vang's statement is significant—he goes on to say that he wants to use organized school athletic programs to encourage Hmong boys and young men to participate in sports. Although his ethnic identity may not have played a role in his hiring, the increase in Hmong boys joining high school teams can be attributed to a wider acceptance of football. To be sure, college football is on the minds of young Hmong Americans and they continue to chase NFL dreams no matter how distant they may seem.[36]

What are the pleasures Hmong boys are getting from playing such a physical game? How is this part of and against the "thug" racialization? Long did not want to follow in the footsteps of his older brother, who played club soccer at the highest level. He was a solid soccer player, but the increasingly competitive nature of U.S. youth soccer meant that he would not be given much playing time. When he entered high school in 2012 in a suburb of Milwaukee, he tried out for the football team. Long explained:

> When I was in middle school one of my best friend's brother played for the high school football team so I went to some of their games. It was so exciting! It's like the whole school was there. The band played and everyone at the game seemed to be having so much fun. I had been to my brother's soccer games and it's mostly just the families of the players there. I dreamt of being able to run down the football field and having hundreds of people cheering for me! (interview with author, 2014)

The number of spectators certainly set football apart from soccer, but it is clear from Long's observation that the resources schools dedicate to football, like the school band's presence, create a certain kind of excitement that is lacking at soccer games. In conversations with several parents of Hmong football players during a game in Saint Paul, they enthusiastically shared why they support their sons. "I got hooked on football while in college. My roommate, who was white, watched it all the time. I think it's great that my son's playing football. Unlike me, he has so much school pride. When I was in high school, the Hmong kids, we didn't even care about homecoming and things like that," exclaimed Pao, a man in his mid-40s. Mao, a mother of five sons and one daughter, was watching her second-oldest play. She revealed that she knew very little about football before her son joined the team. She said, "My boys are so crazy about football! They are not like other Hmong boys who prefer soccer. I still don't really understand everything after two years of watching. I know something good has happened when I hear the people around me cheer. Sometimes they are quite rowdy, but that's okay because we're all here to cheer for our team." Mao's husband, Bill, added, "I like that Hmong parents are now coming to watch the kids play. We feel like it's our school, our team, and not just coming to school and going home" (interviews with author, 2014). These comments are illustrative of the changing perspectives of Hmong Americans about the role of organized sports as a means of staking out their Americanness. What these individuals expressed reinforces Charly Moua's earlier point about the importance of parental support and demonstrates Hmong Americans' multigenerational interaction with U.S. sports.

Ethnicity and Sports Tournaments

To understand the increasing popularity of American football among Hmong Americans, it is equally important to place it within the context of Hmong American ethnic sports tournaments and explore the ways in which they influence the reconfiguration of ethnic boundaries.[37] When the refugees first arrived in the U.S., many were isolated and yearned to be with others from their ethnic group. As people settled in various parts of the country, they began to organize sports tournaments that served multiple purposes. These sports festivals stitch Hmong communities together and enable organizers and attendees to exert ethnic pride, negotiate gender, and demonstrate a sense of belonging in a multitude of U.S. communities as reflected by state-based and city-based teams. As such, they are one of the ways in which Hmong Americans construct "imagined communities."[38] Although these events frequently occur at public parks and county fairgrounds, the attendees are almost exclusively Hmong Americans. Tournaments are often held on U.S. holidays, most commonly Memorial Day, the Fourth of July, and Labor Day. This practice begs us to rethink the extent to which these tournaments become a site for Hmong Americans' exertion of ethnic power and control over their cultural meanings and negotiation of national spaces. Instead of participating in mainstream activities surrounding these holidays, Hmong tournaments become a site for challenging the structure of American society and creating new positions of dominance within Asian America.

In Midwestern states with large populations, tournaments are held on weekends as soon as the grounds dry in the spring and they may occur as late as October. In warmer areas like the California Central Valley, they may take place almost year-round. Tournaments may be sports competitions alone or they may be a part of New Year celebrations and other community events. Event names range from Saint Paul's "Hmong Freedom Celebration and Sports Festival" to the "Asian Memorial Festival" in Green Bay, Wisconsin, "Hmong Michigan Soccer Tournament" in Fraser, Michigan, "NW Arkansas and NE Oklahoma Hmong New Year Sports Tournament" in Rose, Oklahoma, "Hmong Southeast Puavpheej Easter Spring Festival" in Newton, North Carolina, and "Hmong International New Year" in Fresno, California.[39] At the same time that Hmong sports events are used to build ethnic community, they reveal the multiple marginalities that they experience as an ethnic group. They may draw a few hundred people in the case of small towns in southern states to more than 50,000 in locations with large Hmong populations like the Twin Cities and Fresno.

Attendees of small events consist primarily of those from the surrounding communities, but large events appeal to teams and spectators from around the country. Moreover, in recent years, Hmong soccer teams from France, Laos, Thailand, and Australia have competed in the Twin Cities Fourth of July tournament—in the 2014 tournament, 150 teams participated.[40] Clearly, playing soccer for Hmong men allows them to perform a global cosmopolitanism.[41] The persistent practice of including "Hmong" in event names disrupts Asian American panethnicity, while the sporadic use of "Asian" without "Hmong" connotes Hmong Americans' power to selectively define themselves. In large Hmong tournaments, ethnic Lao teams have also competed for years, in addition to many teams that included a few non-Hmong players. Korean, Vietnamese, and Cambodian teams have also occasionally participated. Within the last decade, former refugees from Burma/Myanmar have begun to take part in the Twin Cities tournament. Although organizers do not exclude other Asian groups, referring to it as a "Hmong" event erases the diverse groups' involvement. On the contrary, the common use of the term "Asian" in some event titles in Wisconsin represents an underlying power that organizers have by claiming "Asian America" as a Hmong space. Although attended mostly by Hmong Americans, these "Asian" festivals reflect the reality that Hmong are the largest Asian ethnic group in most Wisconsin cities. As indicated earlier, their position at the bottom of the Asian American socioeconomic ladder excludes them from model minority status. As a result of their marginalization in mainstream U.S. society as pan-ethnically Asian American and dislocation within Asian America as a result of their social location as refugee Americans, the sporting contests constitute a crucial means to perform identity in fields of power. The emphasis on "Hmongness" is an illustration of not only ethnocentric viewpoints, but is also is direct response to their positioning within the Asian America landscape. Through the structuring of sporting spaces as almost exclusively Hmong American, isolation serves the purpose of providing a time where they can selectively claim "Asianness" on their own terms.

Parallel to this experience is the sustained popularity of soccer and volleyball among Hmong Americans. While women's volleyball teams have been an integral part of ethnic tournaments, soccer teams became common only since the early 2000s. Women's volleyball teams share courts with men's teams, but as a sport that is viewed as appropriate for women to play, their presence on the court does not create the same tension as soccer. The globalization of soccer makes its appeal to Hmong Americans not surprising. As Eduardo P. Archetti articulated, "[soccer] is a powerful masculine expression of national capabilities and potentialities" (1999: 15).[42] At most tournaments, women's teams play only after all of the men's games have taken place. Veteran soccer player Nhoua described how female competitors are commonly treated by tournament organizers: "It's so unfair that they [the organizers] make us wait hours to play. They are unorganized and they never start on time. They would tell the women's teams to be there at a certain hour, but then we would have to wait until a field becomes available. They do not take the women's teams seriously. Our prizes are ALWAYS less than those for men's teams" (interview with author, 2014).[43] This disparity in access to time on the sporting pitch reveals how men come to stand in for the diaspora in particular ways in relation to women. Men, through their perceived muscularity and aggression, stand for the strength and resolve of these communities (see Burdsey 2007). Such procurements come at the expense of relegating women's sports to a marginalized status.

Soccer is consequently no longer the sport of choice for Hmong women, due in part as well to the shift of Hmong girls' and young women's interest in flag football. Based on traditional American football, flag football does not emphasize size and physical strength, and instead favors players who can move quickly. Chor explained her shift from soccer to flag football: "My dad said he didn't want me to look like a boy. Some of the girls who play soccer look tough and they are very strong. In soccer you have to keep running and fighting for the ball, so you do have to be strong" (interview with author, 2012). Her decision was also influenced by her father's opinion of Hmong women who played soccer. Chor's decision to find a "safer" sport may explain women's decreased interest in soccer, but Nhoua's frustration revealed that the ways in which tournament organizers treat women's games likely influenced its decline.

At ethnic tournaments, the number of women's flag football teams is more numerous than soccer teams. A key question that observers pose is why flag football has grown in popularity among second-generation Hmong Americans. As Kazoua explained, "I play flag football because my brothers play. I used to just watch them, but then I got interested in it and a bunch of my friends and I just formed our own team. I've never played soccer but I think soccer is harder" (interview with author, 2014). Although both soccer and flag football require agility, soccer, as Chor stated above, is perceived as more physically demanding than flag football, thus the latter is considered more appropriate for women and girls. Flag football allows women to claim an Americanness that is clear and specific. It is said to break barriers because it "gives independence."[44] Players' improved skills have resulted in spectators as well opponents delivering praise, such as the following *Hmong Sports Forum* post:

> I think that one of the greatest teams of all times is Blitz! They've gone so far! They give a good fight and never back down. You can see it on the field how much they wanna win! And their QB is amazing! They play as a team. In some of the women teams, you can spot only a couple of good players. But with blitz, you notice all of them and their plays. I really enjoy watching and playing this team. (female, Aug. 1, 2013 at 8:31 a.m.)[45]

Teenagers and older women play together, which creates opportunities for younger women to have role models. In 2007, when women's flag football was just starting at Hmong tournaments, *Hmong Today* reporter Marilyn Vang wrote, "[M]any of the players . . . didn't play a sport before agreeing to play flag football. . . . Even if these ladies play a tough game, they really are nice and approachable; maybe that's the difference between male and female football players."[46] This "nice girls" image may no longer hold sway. Examining the reasons why reveals that the sport has its own challenges. Asked to rank the top 20 Hmong women's flag football players, a female player summed it up: "maybe girls don't rank each other due to the fact that whatever happens on and off the field doesn't stay there (IT GETS TOO PERSONAL). LOL [laugh out loud] Creates too much drama with what's being said about the ranks. SAD to Say but it's just the truth" (female, Aug. 7, 2013, at 11:12 a.m.).[47] Other posts further illustrate the contentious reality of Hmong women's flag football. "I used to coach, sometimes I question their heart. Do they want to play and learn or just want to look good out on the field for guys. As patient as I am it's hard to teach girls who never learned how to play, play" (male, August 14, 2013, at 10:02 p.m.). Another male commented, "[T]eaching girls how to play football and [getting] them to understand some of it is not easy. Some get it, most never will. . . . A lot of girls also are just there for the social bonding" (male, July 5, 2013, at 11:34 p.m.). Another contributor to *Hmong Sports Forum* seems to suggest that Hmong culture and lack of opportunities to play sports are to blame for girls' ineffectiveness. He writes, "I would like to see more girls play flag football. . . . I believe the biggest problem is the way girls are brought up in our Hmong culture. I shouldn't say it's a 'problem,' it's more like an unfortunate reality. Not enough girls are exposed to sports and many parents don't support their girls playing sports" (male,

Aug. 14, 2013, at 8:46 p.m.). The "drama" on and off the field partially explains male perspectives about Hmong women's flag football experiences, but enduring gender inequality within Hmong culture cannot be overlooked. The "unfortunate reality" of girls' position in many Hmong families limits their access to athletic opportunities, and consequently, they lack the support to play. More troubling is the questioning of girls' intentions on the field. Kazoua reveals that it is not only male gaze that is of concern to her. She explained, "One time when we finished playing in Oshkosh [Wisconsin], I was walking with three of the girls from my team. We went past some girls who (they were in high heels!) gave us weird looks. I can't really describe it, but it's the kind of look that says, 'You are doing something girls shouldn't be doing.' We didn't care about them. We just kept walking" (interview with author, 2014). Given the "weird looks," why do Hmong women and girls continue to play flag football? Mai Yia's remarks are representative of the many who continued to play and recruit new players: "We play because we can! This is America. We can do anything we want. It's a free country!" (interview with author, 2014).

Managing Hmong American identity often means the collapsing of Hmongness and Americanness through the simultaneous presence of mainstream American sport and Hmong sport. In recent years, ethnic tournaments have incorporated other sports that reflect a desire, on the one hand, to integrate into U.S. society and an interest, on the other, in incorporating an "authentic" Hmong sport. An example of the former is the inclusion of tennis and golf competitions annually at the large Freedom Celebration and Sports Tournament in Saint Paul. Incorporating sports that are considered more elite and upper class not only reflects the increasingly diverse Hmong American population, but also reveals how a segment of the Hmong community attempts to demonstrate a sense of belonging in the United States. Unlike soccer, volleyball, and flag football, elite mainstream sports competitions need to take place away from the main playing fields at Saint Paul's Como Park. For example, the golf tournament is held at a golf course miles away. Consequently, these competitions do no attract large numbers of spectators, and thus, they do not incite the same enthusiasm that sports held at the park do, in particular the men's soccer championship match.

Unlike these elite mainstream sports, "Hmong top spin," or *tuj lub*, is provided space on the main playing fields. Top spin came on the scene among older Hmong American men within the last decade. Though not a Hmong invention, it was played by Hmong men for over a hundred years before their migration to the United States. A cone-shaped wood top tied to a bamboo stick with a string allows players to swing and spin their tops.[48] In competitions, knocking off opponents' spinning tops determines the winner. The game's popularity is not limited to ethnic tournaments. Players often gather in local parks, or on top spin courts like the one built in Westminster, Colorado, for the growing Hmong population.[49] This insertion of a "Hmong sport" into a mainstream public space presents contradictions to immigration integration narratives. Instead of simply assimilating into local communities, Hmong Americans have advocated for local communities to accommodate them. The game's popularity is growing in Saint Paul so much that its mayor, Chris Coleman, announced in August 2014 that he planned to use public funds to build a *tuj lub* court.[50] As David Eng has articulated, such accommodation occurs because "we are able both to reformulate and to transform the conditions under which we claim our identities and communities . . . while we are continually subjected to institutional structures of material and physic domination, we can also assert our rights as racialized subjects to contest and to alter these significant conditions."[51] Interestingly, however, these spaces are exclusively male. Women may watch but they do not *yet* actively participate.

Conclusion

The transformations within ethnic tournaments help to provide context for the ways in which Hmong boys' and young men's success at American football has been heralded as the best illustration of how they are becoming American. Exclusion from Asian America compelled them to create Hmong spaces to make sense of their lives. From small gatherings to large community events attended by thousands from across the country, they are spaces for performing ethnicity, but more importantly, they serve as venues for demonstrating cultural, social, economic, and political changes. Vendors selling a plethora of items from Asia and "Hmong food" create an environment that allows visitors to experience "Asia." Hmong American boys are making inroads into American high school football teams, and young women are challenging normative gendered behaviors by playing flag football and soccer in schools and at ethnic sports tournaments. As an ethnic minority group without a nation of its own, it is not unusual that much attention is given to individuals whose achievements stand out from Hmong Americans' ubiquitous characterization in popular and academic discourse as unassimilable illiterate farmers.

Sports are clearly not new to Hmong Americans because of the history of soccer and volleyball in ethnic specific tournaments in states with large Hmong American populations, but these sports lack football's status. Because football is the quintessential American sport, drawing more spectators than any other, Hmong boys' embrace of it has changed the landscape of what it means to be Hmong American. It is also a space where they can simultaneously challenge the contours of Americanness, Asian American–ness, and Hmong American–ness. If playing football is a way to demonstrate one's Americanness, then they have found an opening to do so. In the process, Hmong football players articulate Americanness and its respective sensibilities differently from those who participate in other mainstream and ethnic sports. As a result, we must be attentive to how fluid the categories of Hmong America, Asian America, and America are.

NOTES

1 Charles P. Pierce, "How to Become an American," *Sports Illustrated*, December 12, 2011, http://sportsillustrated.cnn.com/vault/article/magazine/MAG1192874/2/index.htm (accessed January 6, 2013).

2 Vijay Prashad, *The Karma of Brown Folk* (Minneapolis: University of Minnesota Press, 2000).

3 Angela Reyes, *Language, Identity, and Stereotype among Southeast Asian American Youth: The Other Asia* (Mahwah, NJ, and London: Lawrence Erlbaum, 2007), 1.

4 Alejandro Portes and Min Zhou, "The New Second Generation: Segmented Assimilation and Its Variants," *Annals of the American Academy of Political and Social Science* 530 (November 1993): 74–91.

5 See Ben Carrington, "Introduction: Sports Matters," *Ethnic and Racial Studies* 35(6) (2012): 961–970; Ben Carrington, *Race, Sport and Politics: The Sporting Black Diaspora* (Theory, Culture and Society Book Series), (London and Los Angeles: Sage, 2010).

6 Jane Hamilton-Merritt, *The Hmong, the Americans and the Secret War for Laos, 1942–1992* (Bloomington: Indiana University Press, 1999), 334.

7 Chia Youyee Vang, *Hmong America: Reconstructing Community in Diaspora* (Chicago: University of Illinois Press, 2010), 1. France, Canada, and Australia accepted Hmong refugees but in significantly smaller numbers.

8 Ibid., 65.

9 See Mimi Nguyen, *The Gift of Freedom: War, Debt, and Other Refugee Passages* (Durham, NC: Duke University Press, 2012).

10 See Yên Lê Espiritu, "Toward a Critical Refugee Study: The Vietnamese Refugee Subject in US Scholarship," *Journal of Vietnamese Studies* 1(1–2) (February/August 2006): 410–433; Yên Lê Espiritu, "The 'We-Win-Even-When-We-Lose' Syndrome: U.S. Press Coverage of the Twenty-Fifth Anniversary of the 'Fall of Saigon,'" *American Quarterly* 58(2) (June 2006): 329–352.

11 Ibid.

12 See Stacey Lee, "More than 'Model Minority' or 'Delinquents': A Look at Hmong American High School Students," *Harvard Educational Review* 71(3) (2001): 505–528; Ruben G. Rumbaut and Kenji Ima, *The Adaptation of Southeast Asian Refugee Youth: A Comparative Study. Final Report to the Office of Resettlement* (San Diego: San Diego State University, 1988); Mary Bulcholtz, "Styles and Stereotypes: The Linguistic Negotiation of Identity Among Laotian American Youth," *Pragmatics* 14(2/3) (2004): 127–148.

13 Sandra Spickard Prettyman and Brian Lampman (eds.), *Learning Culture through Sports: Perspectives on Society and Organized Sports* (2d. ed.) (Lanham, MD: Rowman & Littlefield, 2006), ix.

14 Tim Delaney and Tim Madigan, *The Sociology of Sports: An Introduction*, (Jefferson, NC: McFarland & Company, 2009), 3.

15 See Linda España-Maram, *Creating Masculinity in Los Angeles's Little Manila: Working-Class Filipinos and Popular Culture, 1920s–1950s*, (New York: Columbia University Press, 2006); Sameer Pandya, "The Jeremy Lin Discussion," *ESPN*, February 18, 2012, http://espn.go.com/espn/commentary/story/_/id/7581502/the-racial-complexion-jeremy-lin-discussion, (accessed September 22, 2014); Christina Chin, *Hoops, History, and Crossing Over: Boundary Making and Community Building in Japanese American Youth Basketball Leagues* (2012), Ph.D. diss., University of California-Los Angeles, https://escholarship.org/uc/item/2jg049zx#page-1Samuel O. Regalado, *Nikkei Baseball: Japanese American Players from Immigration and Internment to the Major Leagues* (Urbana-Champaign: University of Illinois Press, 2013); Stanley Thangaraj, "Competing Masculinities: South Asian American Identity Formation in Asian American Basketball Leagues," *South Asian Popular Culture* 11(3) (2013); Daniel Burdsey, Stanley Thangaraj, and Rajinder Dudrah, "Playing through Time and Space: Sport and South Asian Diasporas," *South Asian Popular Culture* 11(3) (2013).

16 Kathleen S. Yep, "Peddling Sport: Liberal Multiculturalism and the Racial Triangulation of Blackness, Chineseness and Native Americanness in Professional Basketball," *Ethnic and Racial Studies* 35(6) (2012): 971–987.

17 C. Richard King, "Asian Americans in Unexpected Places: Sport, Racism and the Media," in Prettyman and Lampman (eds.), *Learning Culture through Sports*, 174–180.

18 David L. Eng, *Racial Castration: Managing Masculinity in Asian America* (Durham, NC: Duke University Press, 2001), 2.

19 Soumya Palreddy, "Sports Participation among South Asian Americans: The Influence of Acculturation and Value of Sport" (2012), Ph.D. Diss., University of Wisconsin–Milwaukee, http://dc.uwm.edu/etd/192, 57.

20 Ibid., 138.

21 Jay Cloakley, *Sport in Society: Issues and Controversies* (10th ed.) (Boston: McGraw-Hill, 2004).

22 Throughout the chapter, I use pseudonyms for individuals I interviewed to ensure confidentiality.

23 Cloakley, *Sport in Society*.

24 Anthony A. Peguero, "Immigrant Youth Involvement in School-Based Extracurricular Activities," *Journal of Educational Research* 104 (2011): 19–27.

25 Grace Kao, "Group Images and Possible Selves among Adolescents: Linking Stereotypes to Expectations by Race and Ethnicity," *Sociological Forum* 15 (2000): 407–430.

26 Sandra L. Hanson, "Hidden Dragons: Asian American Women and Sport," *Journal of Sport & Social Issues* 29(3) (August 2005): 279–312.

27 Sean Gregory, Natalie Tso, and Vanessa Ko, "Linsanity!," *Time*, February 27, 2012, 42–45.

28 Kathleen S. Yep, "Linsanity and Centering Sport in Asian American Studies and Pacific Islander Studies," *Amerasia Journal* 38(3) (2012): 135–136.

29 It should be noted that although they were not on the cover, the story on Hmong football players appeared in *Sports Illustrated* slightly more than a year before Jeremy Lin was on the cover in February 2012. Starting in the early 1990s, Hmong boys' basketball tournaments were organized in community centers and high school gymnasiums. All-Hmong basketball tournaments and leagues were organized by players.

30 Allan Dundes, "Into the End Zone for a Touchdown: A Psychoanalytical Consideration of American Football," in Robert R. Sands (ed.), *Anthropology, Sport, and Culture* (Westport, CT: Bergin & Garvey, 1999), 201.

31 See Michael Carvell, "Brookwood's Erick Yang Is an Overnight Sensation in Football," *Atlanta Journal Constitution*, October 13, 2010, http://www.ajc.com/news/sports/high-school/brookwoods-erick-yang-is-an-overnight-sensation-in/nQk5s/ (accessed March 10, 2014); Ben Beitzel, "Kicking Convert: Broncos' Yang Transitions from Soccer to Football with No Problem," *GWINETT Daily Post*, December 1, 2010, http://www.gwinnettdailypost.com/news/2010/dec/01/kicking-convert-broncoso39-yang-transitions-from/ (accessed March 10, 2014). In 2011, Erick Yang was reportedly a walk-on kicker for Michigan State, but in 2014, he was on the Creighton University soccer team.

32 "Hmong Football Star at Ease in Two Cultures," *Wausau Daily*, April 25, 2010, http://www.wausaudailyherald.com/article/20100425/WDH0101/4250437/Hmong-football-star-ease-two-cultures (accessed March 10, 2014).

33 "Placekicker Charlie Vue Is a Favorite of Grant's Alberghini," *Sacramento Bee*, August 24, 2011, http://blogs.sacbee.com/preps/archives/2011/08/placekicker-cha.html (accessed March 22, 2014).

34 Wameng Moua, "Hmong Football Players—in St. Paul High Schools Today and in the NFL Tomorrow?," *Twin Cities Daily Planet*, October 24, 21012, http://www.tc-dailyplanet.net/news/2012/10/24/hmong-football-players-st-paul-high-schools-today-and-nfl-tomorrow (accessed March 22, 2014).

35 Tim Leighton, "Prep Football: Highland Assistant Coach Elliott Vang Helps Introduce Hmong to America's Game," *Pioneer Press*, August 26, 2013, http://www.twincities.com/sports/ci_23949378/prep-football-highland-assistant-elliott-vang-helping-introduce (accessed March 23, 2014).

36 Boua Xiong, "St. Paul Man Kicking His Way to an NFL Dream," *KARE 11 News*, March 12, 2014. http://www.kare11.com/story/news/features/2014/03/11/kicking-toward-an-nfl-dream/6308041/ (accessed March 23, 2014).

37 This author has attended many events across the U.S. during the last 30 years and competed in volleyball and soccer tournaments as a teenager.

38 Benedict Anderson, *Imagined Communities: Reflections on the Origin and Spread of Nationalism* (rev. ed.), (New York: Verso, 1991).

39 "Puavpheej" means proof or evidence that something is true or will take place.

40 Tim Post, "150 Soccer Teams from around the World Compete at Hmong Freedom Celebration," *MPR News Blog*, July 4, 2014, http://www.mprnews.org/story/2014/07/04/hmong-freedom-celebration (accessed September 23, 2014).

41 Eriberto P. Lozado, Jr., "Cosmopolitanism and Nationalism in Shanghai Sports," *City & Society* 18(2): 207–233.

42 I use "soccer" to be consistent with how Americans refer to this sport.

43 General descriptions in this section draw on participant observations and informal interviews with women soccer players in Green Bay, Oshkosh, and Milwaukee, Wisconsin, and Saint Paul, Minnesota, 2006–2014.

44 Dan Olson, "For Hmong American Women, Flag Football Breaks Barriers." *Minnesota Public Radio News*, June 28, 2013, http://www.mprnews.org/story/2013/06/28/news/for-hmong-american-women-flag-football-breaks-barriers (accessed March 22, 2014).

45 *Hmong Sports Forum*. http://hmongfootball.proboards.com/ (accessed October 12, 2014). Those who post must be members of the forum. Gender information is available on the site.

46 Marilyn Vang, "Hmong Girls Play Football," *Hmong Today*, August 08, 2007, http://www.tcdailyplanet.net/article/2007/08/08/hmong-girls-play-football.html (accessed October 12, 2014).

47 *Hmong Sports Forum* for this and following three quotations.

48 In the U.S., players use cut-off golf clubs instead of bamboo sticks.

49 Westminster Parks and Recreation, "Skyline Vista Park—Top Spin Court, 2595 W. 72nd Ave.," n.d., http://www.ci.westminster.co.us/ParksRec/Parks/ParkLocations/SkylineVistaParkTopSpinCourt.aspx (accessed April 30, 2014).

50 Joe Kimball, "St. Paul Is Looking to Build a Tuj Lub Court. So What Exactly Is Tuj Lub?," *MINNPOST*, 09/22/14, http://www.minnpost.com/sports/2014/09/st-paul-looking-build-tuj-lub-court-so-what-exactly-tuj-lub (accessed October 3, 2014).

51 Eng, *Racial Castration*, 28–29.

9

Lin, Te'o, and Asian American Masculinities in Sporting Flux

DAVID LEONARD

I was captivated by Linsanity; not so much because of Jeremy Lin's play—my loyalty and fandom begins and ends with the Los Angeles Lakers—but by the spectacle, the transnational media blitz, and the narratives trafficked alongside of his play.[1] I followed Lin's career while he was at Harvard. Long before the Linsanity phenomenon ended, the media was already framing his place in basketball lore: as an Asian American Michael Jordan (who was imagined as an African American Horatio Alger), the personification of the American Dream, and evidence of American exceptionalism. In sum, Linsanity was rife with cultural, racial, and national meaning.[2]

While never attracting equivalent global interest and international stardom, Mantei Te'o has been the subject of significant media attention in recent years. Even before the media turned his football career and personal life into a site for gossip and sensationalism, media interest was significant. Narratives of religion, immigration, and American exceptionalism anchored his place within the sporting landscape. Although his positioning was distinct from that of Lin as a result of his ethnicity as a Samoan American (Pacific Islander), the differences between basketball and football, and the varied racial demographics of the two sports, their stories are bound together by several tropes and discursive articulations.

With each, the meaning of an athleticized Asian Pacific Islander body inside a sport world marked by blackness is central. To look at Linsanity and the spectacle of Te'o is to look at race, gender, and sexuality, to look at the dialectics of Asian and black sporting bodies. There are many reasons to explore Linsanity and the Te'o storm. Each tells us about the ways that sports are celebrated as sites of upward mobility.

With Lin and with Te'o the media discourse consistently situated their rise within a narrative of the American Dream, celebrating sports as the vehicle for economic and cultural ascension (Uperesa and Mountjoy 2014; Leonard and King 2011; Farred 2006; Gems 2006). Similarly, they are bound together by a narrative that imagines sports as the great assimilator, as a means of individual and communal integration within the (white) American fabric. While Lin, as a first-generation (Taiwanese) Asian American, and Te'o, as a Hawaiian-born Samoan, embody the trope of sports as site of assimilation and Americanization, the narrative surrounding each speaks to the ways athletic participation and success are seen as means to and evidence of acceptance. The stories of globalization, colonization, and transnational commodity culture are equally prominent in their parallel stories. The popularity of basketball in Taiwan and football among Pacific Islanders speaks to the efforts by the NBA, the NFL, and their media partners to cultivate consumers and potential talent throughout the globe. And finally, a significant link rests with the ways that sports functions as a site and space for the authentication of a heterosexual masculinity (Thangaraj 2015). In each case, questions around masculinity (and athletic success) within the media discourse, which seemingly reads both Lin and Te'o through dominant understandings of masculinity (Thangaraj 2012; Ferber 2007; King & Springwood 2001; Messner 1995), are wrapped in discourses of blackness within a sport landscape. In other words, their athletic success and their value as cultural/financial/ideological commodities are defined by their connection with blackness.

Linsanity was the perfect storm of race, basketball, media, social media, and the national imagination (Kang 2010a, 2010b; Wang 2012; Zirin 2012). Yet at the center of Lin's international rise was his masculine (and homoerotic) appeal. The celebration of Lin as a challenge to the denial of masculinity to Asian American males simultaneously reflects the ways in which black masculinity is defined in and through basketball culture. While surely offering fans the often-denied sporting masculinity within the Asian body, the power of Jeremy Lin rests with his ability to mimic a basketball style, swagger, and skill associated with black ballers. Pride emanates from the style of masculinity performed by Lin, which derives from stereotypical constructions of black masculinity. Fulfilling a narrative of a "white American fantasy of an athletic prowess that can trump African-American hegemony in the league" (Farred 2006, p. 56) and the appeal of a masculinity defined by its association with blackness, the celebrations and various forms of public adoration of Asian and Asian American bodies are wrapped up in these ideas of race, gender, and nation.

One year later, America saw the ascendance and national fawning over an Asian Pacific Islander athlete, Notre Dame's Manti Te'o. Dominating on the collegiate national stage in America's most physical game, at one of the most physically demanding and taxing positions—linebacker— Te'o exuded all the requisite skills and physicality to be celebrated as a "real man." Succeeding on the gridiron with speed and style despite his size (by linebacker standards he is not big), Te'o reached heights that few Asian Pacific Americans had achieved in terms of football stardom. Unlike many of his Pacific Islander brethren, he was defined not by his size or his space-eating place on the offensive and defensive lines, but instead through athletic abilities whose description oscillated between the rhetoric of "work ethic" afforded to white athletes and the "innate aggressiveness" and perceived natural ability afforded to black athletes.

Like Lin, his appeal was wrapped up in a narrative about masculinity and his place within the national imagination. This all came to an end amid reports about a hoax or a fake online relationship with another man (whom he thought was a woman), which complicated the myth of American sport as "postracial." It was this intersection of gender and sexuality that inflected a particular racial formation. From challenging hegemonic notions of Asian American masculinity to embodying the feminized undesirable other, Te'o's football, economic, and cultural future was put in question. According to Andy Hutchins (2013), "That's an indication that it won't be every American who embraces the first football player with the confidence to identify as gay, and that at least some of us are still deeply uncomfortable with the idea that people who exude masculinity might also be sexually interested in men." In other words, Te'o no longer fit the template required for hegemonic masculinity and American football iconicity, particularly for an Asian Pacific Islander athlete. Given the hegemonic homoeroticism of sports culture, Asian American and Pacific Islander bodies and identities already are multiply and differently seen as queer, illegible masculine subjects (Eng 2001; McCune 2014b). Sporting cultures work to contain disruptive identities or those sporting subjects that offer multiple nonnormative readings. In thinking about both surveillance and containment, it is important to look at the ways that populations already seen as queer are marked as antithetical to an authentic sporting masculinity. In these moments, these are bodies read against, through, and alongside an essentialized inscription of a hypermasculinized and an uber-heterosexualized black athletic body.

This chapter thus looks at the racialized gender constructions of Jeremy Lin and Manti Te'o, by focusing on media narratives and the spectacle surrounding each of them. Focusing on the ways that sporting landscapes define, circumscribe, and constrain masculine formations, I argue that, in each athlete's case, both the meteoric rise and the backlash (especially against Te'o) are wrapped up in the expectations and masculine desires surrounding sporting cultures. Those expectations and desires reflect the proximity between hegemonic definitions of masculinity, with its emphasis on "physical force and control, occupational achievement, familiar patriarchy, frontiermanship, and heterosexuality," and particular relations to blackness and sporting cultures (Trujillo 2000). In other words, definitions of an authentic inscription of masculinity find validation and legitimation through "sportscape" (McCune 2014a). Sports provide a space for the performance of these hegemonic definitions of masculinity by which "the male body comes to represent power, and power itself is masculinized as physical force, speed, control, toughness, and domination" (Trujillo 2000). Yet sports also "allow men to watch and dissect other men's bodies in fetishistic detail, a space for starring without homosexuality alleged or feared" (Miller 2001, p. 26). In the homoerotic sports world and in the presence of queer athletic bodies, racialized athletic bodies serve to prop up heteronormative schemas, affirming hegemonic understanding of gender, sexuality, and race; the normalization of a narrow understanding of masculinity maintains racial, gendered, and sexualized binaries (Miller 2001). Not surprisingly, for African Americans, this results in the inscription of a hypermasculine body that produces fear, which in turn leads to surveillance and demands for control (Leonard & King 2011); for Asian Americans and Pacific Islander (AAPI) men, the invisibility of sporting bodies reifies dominant stereotypes about masculinity, one that sees Asian men as feminine and fragile and athleticized bodies as physical and dominating.

Throughout history, the legibility of a sporting masculinity for AAPI has been elusive. Inside and outside the sport arenas, certain Asian American bodies were always seen as fragile, queer, and nonnormative (Eng 2001; Shah 2001; Thangaraj 2013; Pandya 2013; España-Maram 2006), while Pacific Islander bodies received contradictory registers of "Othering" that included innate toughness (Smith 2005; Uperesa & Mountjoy 2014). The illegibility of AAPI athleticism contributes to the ubiquitous framing of Asian American and Pacific Islander masculinity as fraught with femininity, queerness, and fragility coupled with an inability to be controlled; to be Asian is to be at a distance from hegemonic definitions of masculinity. On the flip side, to be black is to be an athleticized body. Reflecting the entrenched racial sporting scripts, the predominance of the white racial frame (Feagin 2010), and the long-standing racial ideologies about body and mind, savage and civilization, and white and black, understandings of athleticism, body, and physicality are wrapped in racial discourse. That is, on many sporting fields, blackness is imagined as the benchmark of a desired physical masculinity, as long as it's controlled and disciplined. Whereas the black athlete is imagined as athletic, naturally gifted, creative, innovative, powerful, physically intimidating, muscular, extemporaneous, improvisational, and physically superior—"he's a beast"—white athletes are celebrated for their intelligence, ability to follow rules, respect for tradition, work ethic, and team orientation (Rhoden 2006; Boyd 2003; Dyson 2001; King & Springwood 2001; Boyd 1997; Hoberman 1997; Brooks 2009)—"he's a team leader," "he's cerebral."

On the other hand, contemporary AAPI bodies are either illegible or evidence of physical weakness, the unassimilable foreign body, and the pathology of a community that lacks real men that are able to dominate physically. While this is a post–Civil Rights Movement and post–1965 Immigration Act phenomenon, throughout U.S. history Asian Americans were seen as the "yellow peril." In the story of race in America, Asian Americans have been seen as a threat to white femininity, as a disruptive cultural intrusion, and a polluting body. The efforts to imagine Asian Americans as foreign, as not able to assimilate, and as culturally disruptive function in multiple ways, one of which has been the continued erasure of Asian American success in basketball, boxing, and baseball during the early twentieth century (Arnaldo & Thangaraj 2014;

España-Maram 2006; Regalado 2012). Asian Americans, who outside of the sporting realm has long been imagined as "nerdy," intelligent, the "model minority," and as all about the mind, are "illegible" as athletes, especially as physically dominant forces on the court and field. When present, the bodies of athleticized Asian Americans are illegible in many contexts, and the athletes rendered as "intelligent" players whose morality and cultural values may be beneficial within sporting cultures.

On rare occasions, athletic success is linked as much to body as mind, resulting in a narrative that allows the Asian athlete to be read through traditional inscriptions of masculinity and heterosexual sporting bodies. In some ways, both Lin and Te'o found space within those traditional sporting narratives usually reserved for white athletes. It is no wonder that Lin and Te'o captivated the national attention and were celebrated both inside and outside Asian American communities. Their mastery and success in the masculinized world of sports and their proximity to, if not dominance over, black bodies within the NBA and NFL compel attention.

In a post-1965 context, racial discourse regularly pits Asian Americans and African Americans against one another within the labor force and educational realm (which shapes conversations about sports). For Asian Americans, success is linked to educational attainment and a cultural emphasis on hard work, school, and activities of the mind. At one level, both Lin and Te'o's successes are linked to their intelligence, their values (religion), and their educational priorities. For example, Te'o's dominance on the gridiron, like that of Junior Seau, was attributed to his values. "But it will be his leadership, humility, unwavering determination and fortitude that people will long remember about this Mormon athlete who chose to take his talents all the way from Laie to South Bend, Ind., and wear the golden helmet as a Notre Dame captain," wrote Dick Harmon (2012). "That kind of leadership is in his blood and is found in his Samoan roots. In a year where that culture lost an icon in NFL legend Junior Seau, Manti Te'o may have just stepped on the stage and set a new standard." Explaining his exceptional college career, Harmon locates its foundation in his religion, the Catholic values of Notre Dame, and his Samoan "roots" and bloodlines. In another piece, Mark Lazarus (2012) celebrated Te'o's "maturity" and "obedience" as why he had emerged as one of the nation's best players: "*Obedient.* That's the word Brian Te'o uses to describe his son. Coachable is another way of putting it. He always knows his role, always does what he's told." Similarly, in a piece on Dat Nguyen, the Asian American one-time linebacker for Texas A&M and the Dallas Cowboys, Abe Levy (2012) described him as "a talented but undersized football player" who far exceeded expectations as an athlete. Citing his religiosity, "his work ethic and passion for the game," Levy attributed Nguyen's football success to his values rather than his physical prowess. On the other hand, Asian American athletes' successes and/or shortcomings are linked to their ability to tap in to blackness; their athleticism is linked to their proximity to blackness. While the "model minority myth" is predicated on their distance from blackness, athletic success derives from a closeness with and a mimicking of black athletic bodies.

This relationship to blackness is rooted in a history of Asian Americans being positioned against African Americans (Bow 2010). Rosalind Chou and Joe Feagin locate the emergence of model minority narratives as a counter to the radicalism, protest movements, and identity politics that proliferated during the mid-1960s:

> Largely in response to African American and Mexican American protests against discrimination, white scholars, political leaders, and journalists developed the model minority myth in order to allege that all Americans of color could achieve the American dream—and not by protesting discrimination in the stores and streets as African Americans and Mexican Americans were doing, but by working as "hard and quietly" as Japanese and Chinese Americans supposedly did. (2008, p. 13)

Commenting on the meaning and context of the model minority stereotype, Hiram Perez, in an essay about Tiger Woods, depicts the rhetoric surrounding the "model minority" discourse as simply homogenizing the Asian American by deploying stereotypes and celebrating Asian American accomplishments but "disciplin[ing] the unruly black bodies threatening national stability during the post-civil rights era" (Perez 2005, p. 226). Thus, the model minority discourse operates through the juxtaposition of Asian Americans' (homogenized) identities, cultures, and experiences with those of African Americans. According to Anita Mannur, "in recent years Asian Americans have been praised (in contrast to blacks and Latinos) for having 'assimilated' so well." In other words, Asian Americans are a "model minority because they are hard workers, they do not make a fuss, and are not loud" (Mannur 2005, p. 86). Asians sit between whiteness and racial otherness within the dominant racial discourse. "Whites' use of Asian Americans as a measuring stick for other Americans of color is highly divisive, for it pits groups of color against each other, as well as isolates Asian Americans from white Americans" (Chou & Feagin 2008, pp. 17–18). The dominant discourse posits, as historian Vijay Prashad (1998) has shown, Asian Americans as "all brain" in opposition to African Americans who are read as "all brawn." Such a binary positions African Americans as having pathological cultures and uncontrollable bodies that can only be domesticated and contained within the realm of sport. Asian Americans are represented, in turn, without any athletic, bodily abilities (see Thangaraj 2013).

Asian Americans with the ability to "play like black guys," to talk trash and walk with swagger, and to be physically dominating thus have an understandable appeal; unlike Yao Ming (Farred 2006), any number of baseball players, or several very successful AAPI lineman, Lin and Te'o are just as physically assuming as their black counterparts. Belying the model minority discourse, which often imagines Asianness as "disciplin[ing] the unruly black bodies threatening national stability during the post-civil rights era," the cultural power exhibited by Lin and Te'o comes from their (partial) embodiment of the "unruly black body." It comes from their consumptive practices of cultural blackness (Kelley 1997). With this in mind, this chapter examines dominant constructions of Asianness, blackness, masculinity, sexuality, and sporting cultures, venturing beyond the field to look at the cultural and societal investment in these Asian American athletes and what that tells us about race, gender, and identity.

Blackness and Linsanity

The success and national visibility achieved by Jeremy Lin has both inspired Asian Americans and has been driven by the adoration and pride he elicits from some within the community. Whether on Twitter, Facebook, or in the stadiums, it is clear that Lin is not simply a national phenomenon but a treasure for the Asian American community.

According to Jamilah King (2012), "his moment in the spotlight is an important time to reflect on how the country views its Asian American athletes." Whereas past Asian athletes like Yao Ming and Ichiro Suzuki captured the global Asian diaspora's imagination, Lin is the most widely recognized Asian American athlete on the American team sport scene. Timothy Dalrymple (2012) highlighted the appeal of Lin to Asian American males:

> He particularly has a following amongst Asian-Americans. And some Asian-American young men, long stereotyped as timid and unathletic, nerdy or effeminate or socially immature—have fought back tears (which may not help with the stereotype, but is understandable under the circumstances) as they watched Jeremy Lin score 25 points, 7 assists and 5 rebounds for the New York Knicks.

In "Asian Americans Energized in Seeing Knicks' Jeremy Lin Play," J. Michael Falgoust (2012) elucidated Lin's cultural power within the Asian American community by quoting the thoughts of several different people:

> "I don't care about the outcome. I just want to see him in action. He's as good of an Asian American athlete as there is"—Rose Nguyen

> "I'm so proud. I don't care if he is Chinese or Korean. I had to see him ... my boyfriend has been talking about him so much"—Christine Lee

> "I'm really excited. He breaks so many stereotypes. And my friends are just as excited. If you go to my Facebook feed, it's all Jeremy Lin. I like that he plays smart. But then he's from Harvard. So that is expected. He is also humble. He reminds me a lot of Derrick Rose, who's always crediting teammates"—Andrew Pipathsouk

Andrew Leonard similarly argued that Lin's popularity among Asian Americans is emblematic of the power of social media and also the pride that athletic success produces among Asian Americans, otherwise seen as "nerds" not "jocks." While problematically invoking the language of "genetics" in a way that erases Lin's tremendous athleticism and speed and fails to account for his mental mistakes (as evidenced, for example, by his high rate of turnovers), Leonard concluded that Lin inspires Asian American kids who yearn for a masculine role model given persistent invisibility and anti-Asian racism within the public square. "He's a triumph of will over genetic endowment, a fact that makes him inspiring to an entire generation of Californian kids restless with their model minority shackles," wrote Leonard. "I have seen tweets urging Jeremy Lin to run for the Republican nomination for the Michigan senate seat, tweets warning that the only American jobs in danger from Asians are those belonging to New York Knick starting point guards, and even a tweet riffing off Kobe Bryant's self-identification as 'black mamba'—Jeremy Lin is suddenly the 'yellow mamba.'" Lin trended number one on Twitter on three successive game days amid Linsanity; he was a top-ten searched item on Sina Weibo and was the talk of the sports world for several days during the peak of his ascendance. For this moment, it was Jeremy Lin's world and we were all just living in it.

The pride and possibility evoked by Linsanity points to the broader erasure and invisibility of Asian Americans within popular culture. "Asians are nearly invisible on television/movies/music, so any time I see an Asian on TV or in the movies, I feel like I've just spotted a unicorn, even though usually, I see them being portrayed as kung-fu masters/socially awkward mathematical geniuses/broken-English-speaking-fresh-off-the-boat owner of Chinese restaurant/nail salon/dry cleaners," wrote one blogger (quanimal 2012). "Anyway, this phenomenon is 10x worse in sports. While there has been some notable progress with Asians in professional baseball, Asians are all but non-existent in the big three sports in the US (football, basketball, baseball)." Lin breaks down, or at least penetrates, the walls that have excluded Asian Americans from popular culture. The pride, adoration, and celebration involved in Linsanity reflect this history of exclusion, a history of erasure and invisibility. The efforts to link Lin to Nike's "Witness" campaign is illustrative in that we are all witnesses, maybe for the first time in history, of an Asian American sports hero, someone who challenges and defies expectations and stereotypes.

Amid the invisibility of the Asian American athlete is a history of feminization of Asian American males and the erasure of the Asian

American athlete (King 2012; Wang 2012; Franks 2000). There is also a focus on the male athlete as the symbol of success and strength within Asian American communities that fails to account for female Asian American success in basketball. When present within media and popular culture, Asian American men have been represented as asexual, weak, physically challenged, and otherwise unmasculine. The entry of Lin into the dominant imagination reflects a challenge to this historic practice given the power of sports as a space of masculine prowess and as a key site for embodying national identity. Whether his emergence was responded to with shock or celebration, Lin's cultural power rests in his juxtaposition to the stereotyped Asian American male. According to Timothy Dalrymple (2012), sports commentators' "astonishment at the sight of Jeremy Lin outperforming the other players, their consistent references to how exhausted he must be, and how 'magical' a night he's having (rather than a natural result of talent and hard work) suggests that they've bought into the stereotype of the physically inferior Asian-American male."

Lin's ascendance while with the Knicks is not simply about success or dominance within the sports world, a place defined by masculine prowess and idealized male bodies. It reflects the cultural and gendered meaning of basketball. Lin is excelling in a world defined by black manhood, an identity that white racial frames construct through physicality, strength, speed, and swagger. Unlike other players who burst onto the American scene (Yao Ming, Yi Jianlian, Wang Zhizhi), Lin is a guard, who has found success because of his athleticism and skills as opposed to any "freakish" stature. "The best part is how viscerally pleasurable it is to watch Lin play: His game is flashy, almost showoffy, and requires him to have guts, guile and flair in equal measure," wrote Will Leitch (2012). "The drama of it is, it's obvious, what's most fun for him. It is all you could possibly want as a feel-good story."

In other words, Lin's appeal comes from his ability to ball like a street player, to face off against and dominate black players at "their own game." According to Todd Boyd, basketball is rife with racial binaries, through which basketball aesthetics defined as "black" or "white" convey hegemonic understandings of intelligence, athleticism, body, and creativity:

> Textbook basketball is akin to classical music, wherein performance is centered on the replication of a supposedly superior style.... Those who operate in the tradition of textbook basketball can be clearly linked to the recurrent Western ethos of replication. Playground basketball, on other hand, is much like jazz in the sense mastery of form depends upon one's ability to improvise, to create on the spot, to engage in full-court transition games that foreground style. (1997, p. 114)

Lin, thus, challenges the racial exclusivity of playground basketball, demonstrating that there is a place at the table for his nonblack body; his swagger, fearlessness, physicality, toughness, and attitude puts him in this new category (Brooks 2009; Thangaraj 2012, 2013). This is not to say that the media discourse did not traffic in the stereotypical inscriptions of Asian American masculinity. They did, positioning Lin as someone who could knock down a three-pointer, be a "hustler" on court, and solve math equations. His success was been attributed to his intelligence generally, his "basketball IQ" specifically, and even his religious faith (Beck 2012; Engel 2012; Falgoust 2012; Gaines 2012; O'Neil 2009; Torre 2010; Yu 2012; Wright 2012; Yang 2012; Zaldivar 2012). His athleticism and the hours he spent honing his skills on the court were less central to the narrative, although his proximity to and success alongside his black counterparts furthers his place as the embodiment of a desirable hegemonic masculinity. In other words, his talents were legible as an expression of his hard work; his skills were evident in his intelligence and "cerebral qualities." Unlike black hoopsters, he was understood as a "textbook" baller even as his worth and value on the court and as a cultural and ideological commodity outside the arena was defined in relationship to a "legible" (Neal 2013) black masculinity.

While surely offering fans the sporting masculinity often denied to the Asian body, the power of Jeremy Lin rests with his ability to mimic a basketball style, swagger, and skill associated with black ballers. "Through no fault of his own, Lin stands at a bombed-out intersection of expected narratives, bodies, perceived genes, the Church, the vocabulary of destinations and YouTube," wrote Jay Caspian Kang, who is Asian American, about Lin's electrifying play at Harvard. "What Jeremy Lin represents is a re-conception of our bodies, a visible measure of how the emasculated Asian-American body might measure up to the mythic legion of Big Black superman" (quoted in King 2012).

Writing about Yao Ming, Grant Farred reminds us about these issues:

> The body of the athlete, which has a long history of standing as the body of the nation, is simultaneously reduced and magnified in the Yao event, in its micro-articulation (Asian-American), it is asked to refute the myth of the feminized ethnic by challenging—and redressing the historic wrongs endured—those "American" bodies that have dismissed the physicality of the Asian male. As representative of the Chinese nation, Yao is expected to remain a national subject even as his basketball heritage seems difficult to unlearn and continues to disadvantage him in the NBA. . . . In his representation of the "Chinese people," Yao will not become an NBA—which is to say "African American"—player. He will not trash talk, he will not develop an "offensive personality," in more senses than one, and to his detriment, he will not become more "physical." (2006, p. 62)

Lin is confined by this trap, so his wagging tongue (that was blue during one game), his trash talk, his swagger, his reverse layups, his flashy speed, and his ability to dunk all confirm that Lin isn't just a basketball player but a *baller*. The celebration of Lin is thus wrapped up in the dominant configurations of blackness and how hegemonic visions of black masculinity confer a certain amount of power on him. For Lin, his entry into the realm of professional basketball does not follow the dominant discourse of assimilation into whiteness but reflects how blackness affords possibilities for expressing and claiming American masculinity.

According to Dave Zirin (2012), Lin's power comes from his transgressive play: "Asian-Americans, in our stereotypical lens, are supposed to be studious and reserved. We would expect nothing less than that the first Asian-American player would be robotic and fundamentally sound; their face an unsmiling mask." While Lin was not the first Asian American to play professional basketball in the U.S. (he was preceded by Rex Walters, Wataru Misaka, and Raymond Townsend), Zirin's analysis points to the larger ways that race operates in this context. Lin is appealing because he defies people's expectations about Asian Americans, because he is excelling and playing in a way that people expect from and authentically associate with black players. The dominant cultural practices of sport tell us how Asian American bodies are confined to only certain expressions. Lin's ability to express swagger was seen as an impossibility, as incompatible to an essentialized Asian subject. In Zirin's words, "Instead, we have Jeremy Lin threading no-look passes, throwing down dunks and, in the most respected mark of toughness, taking contact and finishing baskets." From this perspective, we see how race not only defines Lin, but the NBA as a cultural space. His power stems from his ability to "become" black within the national imagination as a baller, yet remain outside the prison/prism of the black-white binary. Or as Oliver Wang (2012) noted, the fanfare around Lin illustrates how "hegemonic masculinity is constructed whereupon whiteness hides behind a cloak of black desire." The yearning for visible Asian American athletes, particularly in basketball and football, reflects the acceptance of hegemonic definitions of masculinity and the ways that blackness, black bodies, and black masculinity operate in these spaces. Irrespective of the celebratory narratives that identified Lin as transformative, as a challenge to dominant stereotypes regarding Asian American masculinity, and as the embodiment of a major step on a pathway toward cultural, political, and social integration, Linsanity offered more "fools gold." Linsanity, under the guise of disruption and counterdiscourse, did more to reify the categories of race, gender, and sexuality. The assumed disruption of legible AAPI masculinity in fact legitimized dominant understandings of both black and Asian masculinity. Moreover, the efforts to attribute Lin's success to his values, his religion, and his proximity to a heterosexual hypermasculine blackness affirm the value of a certain type of heterosexual manhood at the cost of excluding queer subjects and women.

Te'o: The Hoax of Unfulfilled Masculinity

If basketball provides a place to perform a desirable masculinity through athleticism, physical talents, humiliation of others, mastery over an opponent, and a swagger, football is the embodiment of an idealized sporting masculinity. As hegemonic masculinity is defined through muscularity, dominance, power, militarism, and violence, football offers the ideal place to celebrate it. In a study by Michael Messner et al., the authors conclude that contemporary sports culture offers rewards and penalties (disciplinarity) for those athletes who embody the "right" kind of masculinity. Sport is a means of training boys into the proper kind of national heteronormative masculinity. By "right," they mean demonstrating levels of aggression, physicality, and violence, as well as a willingness to overcome injury:

> Athletes who are "playing with pain" or "giving up their body for the team" are often portrayed as heroes. Commentators laud athletes who engage in dangerous plays or compete while injured; conversely, they sometimes criticize athletes who remove themselves from games due to injuries, often raising questions about their manhood. For example, a SportsCenter commentator asked, "Could the Dominator be soft?" when an NHL goalie decided to sit out a game due to a groin injury. (Messner et al. 1999: 6)

Similarly, Eric Anderson and Edward M. Kian, in "Examining Media Contestation of Masculinity and Head Trauma in the National Football League," describe a culture in which the most important choices are really about embodying a desired masculinity; playing through injuries is just another constructed litmus test as to whether or not one is a "real man":

> It is these same discourses, including phrases like "man up," "no pain, no gain," and "pain is temporary, pride is forever," that encourage men to position their own bodies as an expendable weapon of athletic war. The discourse encourages athletes to conceal all fear in the pursuit of glory. Similarly, in the event of injury, football players must not show signs of pain or distress; instead, they must talk about returning to the game as soon as possible. (2012: 155)

To be a real man is to not only play football, but to do so without regard for safety; to be a real man is to stay out on the field, to disregard pain and long-term harm as any warrior would do. To be a real man is to ring an opponent's bell, to knock him out, leaving you and him in a state of delirium. Football celebrates vicious hits; along with the media, the NFL offers viewers entry into a world that is all about violence and pain.

The acts of pleasure and desire are embedded within the violence. The NFL discourse circulates highlight packages based around the most violent and physically dangerous, which in many ways are the reels of masculinity. Alongside a culture that questions a players' commitment and manhood when he puts his health in front of anything else, it also sends the message each and every day that football is all about the performance of an idealized hypermasculinity. In a culture where "complaining about pain is tantamount to weakness" and "playing hurt is as common as a forward pass," it is no wonder that guys "choose" to play hurt, to conceal injuries, to "risk" their long-term health for a game (McLaughlin 2011). As with the NBA, the visibility of black bodies, and the larger history of white supremacist imaginations of black masculinity, infects the ways we think about violence and masculinity on the gridiron.

It is within this context that I want to reflect on the importance of Manti Te'o, whose ascendance didn't simply mark the entry of an AAPI athlete onto the national landscape, but the arrival of an idealized Pacific Islander male athlete. His legibility as a football player (and not a lineman, a basketball player, a baseball star) offered a particularly powerful inscription of masculinity, one that situated him in relationship to dominant understandings of blackness in the NFL, one defined by physical dominance, fearlessness, invulnerability, heterosexuality, and power. Unlike Lin's Taiwanese/Chinese American body, which in many ways was seen as antithetical to the NBA's blackness prior to Linsanity, the Pacific Islander American body was already positioned in proximity to dominant inscriptions of blackness (Uperesa 2014; Gems 2006; Franks 2000). Within football discourses, Pacific Islanders are often inscribed as naturally big, athletic, and innately built for sport. "Polynesian players have also been racialized in ways that help them enter this line of work but restrict them from others," writes Fa'anofo (Lisaclaire) Uperesa. "They are stereotyped as genetically gifted with size, girth and quickness suitable for football, as well as violent impulses that can be channeled into success on the field by virtue of their respect for authority, instilled by discipline and socialization in hierarchical Samoan society" (2014, p. 283). The tropes applied to both Samoan and black football players through the discourses of "genetic advantages" and "cultural deficits" requiring disciplinarity and punishment are crucial.

Similarly, narratives around African American and Samoan football players often highlight childhood poverty and difficult circumstances early in life, celebrating football as providing the requisite values and discipline to secure the American Dream. Hegemonic narratives often focus on values and adversity as central to the Pacific Islander athletic experience. A *60 Minutes* segment, "American Samoa: Football Island," noted that as of 2010 there were 30 Samoans in the NFL and 200 playing Division 1 football—from an island of 65,000 people:

> It seems they do well despite the adversity. But getting cut up on lava rock and playing in sneakers without equipment are the keys to their success. Samoans are born big, but the island makes them tough.
> This is a place where kids use machetes to do their chores. Come to think of it, it's a place where kids do chores. Seventeen-year-old Aiulua Fanene does a day's work before school, under the direction of his father, David.
> "He's cooking in this house. He's cleaning in this house. That is something that kids back on the mainland would not believe if they didn't see it," Pelley told David Fanene.
> "That's how he's been brought up. Discipline . . . Obedience should be involved in this house and I am expecting my children to obey us," he said. (Pelley 2010)

With Te'o, the narrative highlighted each of these stereotypical tropes of hypermasculinity. As a linebacker, with a "motor," physical power, and ferocity, Te'o was often described in terms usually reserved for black NFL players. His childhood roots and his values were equally prominent as explanations for his football success and as points of focus for why his story mattered.

At the same time, his place at Notre Dame, with its cultural position in American football lore, and his status as a linebacker known for ferocious hits and fearlessness, added to his appeal. His tattoos and his swagger contributed to his positioning as a manly linebacker who in any given play could knock a quarterback out cold. While his Mormon religiosity and his intelligence were invoked as evidence of exceptionality, seemingly playing on the legible stereotypes of Asian American athletes, much of the sports discourse focused on the violence and power he brought to the game. Nicknamed "The Terminator," Te'o was known for his physical dominance on the field.

For example, on SB Nation, one post emphasized his perfect mix of intelligence, toughness, and physicality:

> Wrap-up tackling. Like I said, he can make the big hits, but notice how he makes each tackle. It seems like his hands are made of glue, because every time he gets to the guy with the ball, he wraps them up, or make a safe, big hit. The only way I can describe it is an interview with Patrick Chung [a hard-hitting Pats safety:] he says he always goes for the safe tackle, but when the big hit opportunes [sic] itself, he takes the right angle and lays the guy out. That was my impression of how Manti tackles his man. He takes a very good angle, and doesn't let the guy slip from his grasp. (Jack'sAxe 2011)

His counterpart at USC, Soma Vainuku, described him as follows: "He's physical, he's smart, he's their best linebacker. I think he's probably one of the best linebackers in the NCAA right now" (Moura 2011). This sort of celebratory tone was common in discussions of Te'o during his college career. Having received ample awards and leading Notre Dame's defense, he had the potential to be a superstar on and off the field, a role model, and on the Mount Rushmore of Asian American and Pacific Islander athletes. That all changed when reports surfaced that he had been "catfished"[3] and, furthermore, that his online "girlfriend" was in fact a man. The spectacle surrounding the "hoax" and resulting rumors that he was gay changed the narrative around Te'o. The legibility of Te'o, wrapped up in dominant inscriptions of blackness and Samoanness, was destabilized with these reports, in part because his body no longer was seen as physical, as hypermasculine, as dominating on and off the field, and as heterosexual (Diaz 2011; see also Thangaraj 2015). He was vulnerable, fragile, and human, qualities illegible within the NFL, particularly among its physically assuming black and brown bodies.

No longer a physically intimidating linebacker, someone defined by invulnerability and fearless, he became a joke, a feminized victim no longer worthy of celebration. His embodiment of an idealized masculinity and his challenges to both the invisibility of Samoan athleticism and the hypervisibility of the feminized Asian Pacific Islander body was disrupted by the hoax. "But Te'o's story is also ripe for questioning. . . . A great football player having a purely online relationship makes us wonder about him and his sexuality and should make us wonder *why* we wonder about those things," writes Andy Hutchins (2013). "A great football player being Catfished (and having this revealed just two months after MTV first aired *Catfish*) makes us wonder how susceptible we are to forged identities, and how the Internet has affected how we communicate." Having complicated the illegibility of the Asian Pacific Islander linebacker, or the physically dominating Asian body, the intersection of race, gender, and sexuality within the hoax narrative proved to be difficult for Te'o to overcome within both sport media discourses and his positioning in the NFL (as evidenced by how his draft status plummeted). Just as Linsanity waned alongside Lin's own success, Te'o's utility as a marker of masculinity, of physical dominance within a space defined by blackness, lessened with reports about the hoax. Being catfished, along with speculation about his sexuality, put him on the outside looking in at the fabric of American sports culture. Documentary filmmaker Byron Hurt further revealed how the hoax impacted the legibility of Te'o as a football player:

> The image of male athletes in general, but football players specifically, is that of being straight, tough, invulnerable, impenetrable. Athletes are hyper concerned with their masculine identity and how other men perceive their masculinity. Even though a player may not have negative attitudes toward a gay teammate, they have trouble aligning themselves with [them] because they don't want to be perceived as gay themselves. No straight man who's insecure about his masculinity wants to take that kind of risk. (quoted in King 2013)

That is, athletes as a whole, and most specifically in football, rugby, and hockey, are celebrated for being invulnerable, fearless, and willing to wreak havoc without any regard for their bodies. Those are the qualities of an authentic manhood, one worthy of celebration and adoration. Just as penetration by fear or pain are undesirable on (and off) the gridiron, just as the entry of weakness and vulnerability are incompatible with an idealized masculinity, football and its production of masculinity must also be a site devoid of desire for penetrating and being penetrated by the penis.

The mainstream media's renditions of Lin's and Te'o's racialized bodies illuminate how equivalence and uniformity do not exist within Asian America; the homogenized Asian American/Pacific Islander body is an illusion. Rather, both athletes offer different inscriptions of a legible AAPI identity. While sports offers a staging ground for similar narratives of "rags to riches," meritocracy, and the power of hard work, obedience, dedication, and religiosity, their racialized, gendered, and sexualized bodies are situated in distinct ways. While the representations afforded to the Chinese/Taiwanese/Asian American body and the Samoan/Hawaiian/Pacific Islander body, as well as the signifiers associated with basketball and football, are distinct, what binds them together is the shared juxtaposition with blackness. To understand Lin and Te'o is to understand the very distinct ways that their athleticized bodies are mapped onto blackness. Each has different relationships to blackness within the "sportscape," colored by race, gender, and sexuality, which further demonstrates the varying means by which Asian American communities are simultaneously complicated and essentialized. Across two different mainstream U.S. sports, we have a way of seeing how Asian American identity is fragile, always in flux, and conversant with historical racializations of Asian Americans in the United States.

NOTES

1 At the time of writing this article, Jeremy Lin had signed with the Houston Rockets, leaving the New York Knicks. In summer 2014, he was traded to my Los Angeles Lakers.

2 I would like to thank the editors—Stanley I. Thangaraj, Constancio R. Arnaldo, Jr., and Christina B. Chin—for their support and editorial feedback. This piece is reflection of their guidance, care, and analytical insights. Thank you to Robert Reese for his editorial assistance and support.

This chapter includes and builds on an essay by D. J. Leonard, "A Fantasy in the Garden, A Fantasy America Wants to Believe: Jeremy Lin, the NBA and Race Culture," pp. 144–165 in *Race in American Sports: Essays* © 2014, edited by James L. Conyers, Jr. By permission of McFarland & Company, Inc., Box 611, Jefferson NC 28640. www.mcfarlandpub.com. It also includes and builds on an essay by D. J. Leonard, "Masculinity, the NFL, and Concussions," which appeared in the *Feminist*

Wire (May 12, 2012, http://www.thefeministwire.com/2012/05/masculinity-the-nfl-and-concussions/).

3 This is when a person develops an online romantic relationship with another person who isn't who they claim to be. It is an act of deception.

REFERENCES

Abelmann, N., & Lie, J. (1995). *Blue Dreams: Korean Americans and the Los Angeles Riots*. Cambridge, MA: Harvard University Press.

Anderson, E., & Kian, E. M. (2012). "Examining Media Contestation of Masculinity and Head Trauma in the National Football League." *Men and Masculinities*, 15 (2), pp. 152–173.

Arnaldo, C., Jr., and Thangaraj, S. (2014). "Asian American Athletes." In *Encyclopedia of Asian American Society*, ed. Mary Danico. New York: Sage.

Basu, R. (2013, February 3). "To Understand Manti Te'o, Learn of His Culture, Religion." *Deseret News*. Retrieved April 29, 2014, from http://www.deseretnews.com/article/765621628/To-understand-Teo-learn-of-his-culture-religion.html.

Beck, H. (2012, February 8). "From Ivy Halls to the Garden, Surprise Star Jolts the N.B.A." *New York Times*. Retrieved December 10, 2012, from http://www.nytimes.com/2012/02/08/sports/basketball/jeremy-lin-has-burst-from-nba-novelty-act-to-knicks-star.html?_r=2&hpw.

Billings, A. C. (2004). "Depicting the Quarterback in Black and White: A Content Analysis of College and Professional Football Broadcast Commentary." *Howard Journal of Communications*, 15 (4), pp. 201–210.

Bow, Leslie. (2010). *Partly Colored*. New York: New York University Press.

Boyd, T. (1997). *Am I Black Enough for You?: Popular Culture from the 'Hood and Beyond*. Bloomington: University of Indiana Press.

———. (2003). *Young, Black, Rich and Famous: The Rise of the NBA, the Hip Hop Invasion and the Transformation of American Culture*. New York: Doubleday.

Brooks, S. (2009). *Black Men Can't Shoot*. Chicago: University of Chicago Press.

Bruce, T. (2004). "Making the Boundaries of the 'Normal' in Televised Sports: The Play-by-Play of Race." *Media, Culture & Society*, 26 (6), pp. 861–879.

Buffington, D. (2005). "Contesting Race on Sundays: Making Meaning out of the Rise in the Number of Black Quarterbacks." *Sociology of Sport Journal*, 22, pp. 12–31.

Chang, J. (1993). "Race, Class, Conflict, and Empowerment: On Ice Cube's 'Black Korea.'" *Amerasia Journal*, 19 (2), pp. 87–107.

Chou, R. S., & Feagin, J. R. (2008). *The Myth of the Model Minority: Asian Americans Facing Racism*. Boulder, CO: Paradigm Publishers.

Cole, C. L. (2001). "Nike's America/America's Michael Jordan." In *Michael Jordan Inc.: Corporate Sport, Media Culture and Late Modern America*, ed. D. L. Andrews. Albany: State University of New York Press.

Cole, C. L., & Andrews, D. L. (2001). "America's New Son: Tiger Woods and America's Multiculturalism." In *Sports Stars: The Cultural Politics of Sporting Celebrity*, ed. D. L. Andrews & S. J. Jackson. New York: Routledge.

Dalrymple, T. (2012, February 6). "Jeremy Lin and the Soft Bigotry of Low Expectations." *Patheos*. Retrieved December 10, 2012, from http://www.patheos.com/blogs/philosophicalfragments/2012/02/06/jeremy-lin-and-the-soft-bigotry-of-low-expectations/.

Denzin, N. (2001). "Representing Michael." *Michael Jordan Inc.: Corporate Sport, Media Culture and Late Modern America*, ed. D. L. Andrews. Albany: State University of New York Press.

Diaz, V. M. (2011). "Tackling Pacific Hegemonic Formations on the American Gridiron." *Amerasia Journal*, 37 (3), pp. 2–25.

Dyson, M. E. (2001). "Be Like Mike? Michael Jordan and the Pedagogy of Desire." In *Michael Jordan Inc.: Corporate Sport, Media Culture and Late Modern America*, ed. D. L. Andrews. Albany: State University of New York Press.

Eng, D. (2001). *Racial Castration*. Durham, NC: Duke University Press.

Engel, J. F. (2012, February 16). "Lin's Success Should Be No Surprise." *Fox Sports*. Retrieved December 9, 2012, from http://msn.foxsports.com/nba/story/Jeremy-Lin-New-York-Knicks-success-based-on-foundation-of-hard-work-021612.

España-Maram, L. (2006). *Creating Masculinity in Los Angeles's Little Manila*. New York: Columbia University Press.

Falgoust, J. M. (2012, February 8). "Asian Americans Energized in Seeing Knicks' Jeremy Lin Play." *USA Today*. Retrieved December 10, 2012, from http://usatoday30.usatoday.com/sports/basketball/nba/story/2012-02-08/Asian-Americans-flock-to-see-Jeremy-Lin-play/53017410/1.

Farred, G. (2006). *Phantom Calls: Race and the Globalization of the NBA*. Chicago: Prickly Paradigm Press.

Feagin, J. (2010). *The White Racial Frame: Centuries of Racial Framing and Counter Framing*. New York: Routledge.

Ferber, A. (2007). "The Construction of Black Masculinity: White Supremacy Now and Then." *Journal of Sport and Social Issues*, 31 (11), pp. 11–24.

Franks, J. (2000). *Crossing Sidelines, Crossing Cultures: Sport and Asian Pacific American Cultural Citizenship*. New York: University Press of America.

Gaines, C. (2012, February 7). "Faith and Uphill Battles Could Make Jeremy Lin: The NBA's Tim Tebow." *Business Insider*. Retrieved December 9, 2012, from http://www.businessinsider.com/faith-and-uphill-battles-could-make-jeremy-lin-the-nbas-tim-tebow-2012-2#ixzz2EgAE5pNT.

Gems, G. (2006). *The Athletic Crusade: Sports and American Cultural Imperialism*. Lincoln: University of Nebraska Press.

Harmon, D. (2012, December 7). "A Mormon Kid from Hawaii, Notre Dame's Manti Te'o Inspires Many." *Deseret News*. Retrieved September 27, 2014, from http://www.deseretnews.com/article/865568352/Dick-Harmon-A-Mormon-kid-from-Hawaii-Notre-Dames-Manti-Teo-inspires-many.html?pg=all.

Hartmann, D. (2007). "Rush Limbaugh, Donovan McNabb, and 'A Little Social Concern': Reflections on the Problems of Whiteness in Contemporary American Sport." *Journal of Sport and Social Issues*, 31 (1), pp. 45–60.

Hoberman, J. (1997). *Darwin's Athletes: How Sport Has Damaged Black America and Preserved the Myth of Race*. Boston: Houghton Mifflin.

Hughes, F. (2010, July 26). "Former Harvard Standout Lin Ready to Prove Himself with Warriors." *Sports Illustrated*. Retrieved December 10, 2012, from http://sportsillustrated.cnn.com/2010/writers/frank_hughes/07/26/jeremy.lin.warriors/index.html#ixzz2Eg9iaV9e.

Hutchins, A. (2013, January 28). "Why the Manti Te'o Girlfriend Hoax Story Matters." *SB Nation*. Retrieved April 29, 2014, from http://www.sbnation.com/college-football/2013/1/28/3915364/manti-teo-hoax-girlfriend-story.

Jack'sAxe (2011, October 5). "A Look at Manti Te'o, ILB from Notre Dame." *Silver and Black Pride*. Retrieved April 29, 2014, from http://www.silverandblackpride.com/2011/10/5/2471605/a-look-at-manti-teo-ilb-from-notre-dame.

Kang, J. K. (2010a, January 14). "Jeremy Lin Puts the Ball in Asian Americans' Court." *Los Angeles Times*. Retrieved December 10, 2012, from http://articles.latimes.com/2012/feb/21/entertainment/la-et-jeremy-lin-20120221.

———. (2010b, January 14). "The Lives of Others." *Free Darko*. Retrieved December 10, 2012, from http://freedarko.blogspot.com/2010/01/lives-of-others.html.

Kelley, R. D. G. (1997). *Yo' Mama's Disfunktional!: Fighting the Culture Wars in Urban America*. Boston: Beacon Press.

King, C. R., & Springwood, C. F. (2001). *Beyond the Cheers: Race as Spectacle in College Sport*. Albany: State University of New York Press.

King, J. (2012, February 8). "The Subtle Bigotry That Made Jeremy Lin the NBA's Most Surprising Star." *Colorlines*. Retrieved December 10, 2012, from http://colorlines.com/archives/2012/02/jeremy_lin.html.

King, J. (2013, February 28). "NFL Teams Are Breaking Their Own Rules by Asking if Manti Te'o Is Gay." *Colorlines*. Retrieved September 27, 2014, from http://www.colorlines.com/articles/nfl-teams-are-breaking-their-own-rules-asking-if-manti-teo-gay.

Lapchick, R. (2001). *Smashing Barriers: Race and Sport in the New Millennium*. Lanham, MD: Madison Books.

Lazarus, M. (2012, December 12). "Notre Dame Linebacker Manti Te'o Always Has Been Special." *Sun Times*. Retrieved September 27, 2014, from http://www.suntimes.com/sports/16758168-419/notre-dame-linebacker-manti-teo-always-has-been-special.html#.VCmY2ktlyaI.

Leitch, W. (2012, February 7). "The Jeremy Lin Show Is Just Getting Started, Folks." *New York Magazine*. Retrieved December 10, 2012, from http://nymag.com/daily/sports/2012/02/jeremy-lin-show-is-just-getting-started.html.

Leonard, A. (2012, February 8). "Jeremy Lin's Social Media Fast Break." *Salon*. Retrieved December 10, 2012, from http://www.salon.com/2012/02/08/jeremy_lins_social_media_fast_break/singleton/.

Leonard, D. J. (2003, summer). "Yo: Yao! What Does the 'Ming Dynasty' Tell Us about Race and Transnational Diplomacy in the NBA?" *Colorlines*, pp. 34–36.

Leonard, D. J., & King, C. R. (2011). *Commodified and Criminalized: New Racism and African Americans in Contemporary Sports*. Lanham, MD: Rowman & Littlefield.

Levy, A. (2012, November 16). "Refugee, Football Player Credits Faith for New Life in S.A." *My San Antonio*. Retrieved September 27, 2014, from http://www.mysanantonio.com/news/local_news/article/Refugee-football-star-practices-his-faith-4045087.php.

Liu, L. W. (2012, February 14). "Why Jeremy Lin's Race Matters." *CNN.com*. Retrieved December 10, 2012, from http://www.cnn.com/2012/02/13/opinion/jeremy-lin-race/index.html.

Mannur, A. (2005). "Model Minorities Can Cook: Fusion Cuisine in Asian America." In *East Main Street: Asian American Popular Culture*, ed. S. Davé, L. Nishime, & T. G. Oden. New York: New York University Press.

Martin, Michel (2010, February 4). "Asian-American Ivy Leaguer Has Tall Hoop Dreams." *NPR*. Retrieved December 10, 2012, from http://www.npr.org/templates/story/story.php?storyId=123368990.

McCune, J. (2014a). "Another Missed Shot: After Collins, the NBA and the Politics of Identities." Paper presented at Jason Collins in the American Sportscape: Race, Gender, and the Politics of Sexuality Symposia, Washington University, April 11, 2014, St. Louis, Missouri.

———. (2014b). *Sexual Discretion: Black Masculinity and the Politics of Passing*. Chicago: University of Chicago Press.

McLaughlin, E. (2011, July 1). "Film Aims to Show Football's Culture of Playing despite Concussions." *CNN.com*. Retrieved April 29, 2014, from http://www.cnn.com/2011/US/07/01/nfl.concussions.bell.rung/index.html?_s=PM:US.

Messner, M. (1995). *Power at Play: Sports and the Problem of Masculinity*. Boston: Beacon Press.

Messner, M., et al. (1999). "Boys to Men, Sports Media: Messages about Masculinity." *Children Now*. Retrieved April 29, 2014, from http://library.la84.org/9arr/ResearchReports/boystomen.pdf.

Miller, T. (2001). *Sportsex*. Philadelphia: Temple University Press.

Moura, P. (2011, October 20). "Manti Te'o a True Threat for Trojans." *ESPN.com*. Retrieved April 29, 2014, from http://espn.go.com/blog/los-angeles/USC/post/_/id/9555/manti-teo-a-true-threat-for-trojans.

Murrell, A. J., & Curtis, E. M. (1994). "Causal Attributions of Performance for Black and White Quarterbacks in the NFL: A Look at the Sports Pages." *Journal of Sport & Social Issues*, 18, pp. 224–233.

Neal, M. A. (2013). *Looking for Leroy: Illegible Black Masculinities*. New York: New York University Press.

Niven, D. (2005). "Race, Quarterbacks and the Media: Testing the Rush Limbaugh Hypothesis." *Journal of Black Studies*, 35, pp. 684–694.

Omi, M., & Takagi, D. Y. (1996). "Situating Asian Americans in the Political Discourse of Affirmative Action." *Representations*, 55, pp. 155–162.

O'Neil, D. (2009, December 10). "Immigrant Dream Plays Out through Son." *ESPN.com*. Retrieved December 10, 2012, from http://sports.espn.go.com/ncb/columns/story?columnist=oneil_dana&id=4730385.

Pandya, S. (2013). "Situating Vijay Singh in (Asian) America." *South Asian Popular Culture*, 11 (3), pp. 219–230.

Pelley, S. (2010). "American Samoa: Football Island." *CBSNews.com*. Retrieved October 1, 2014, from http://www.cbsnews.com/news/american-samoa-football-island-17-09-2010/.

Perez, H. (2005). "How to Rehabilitate a Mulatto: The Iconography of Tiger Woods." In *East Main Street: Asian American Popular Culture*, ed. S. Davé, L. Nishime, & T. G. Oden. New York: New York University Press.

Picca, L. H., & Feagin, J. R. (2007). *Two-Faced Racism: Whites in the Backstage and Frontstage*. New York: Routledge.

quanimal. (2012, February 7). "Jeremy Lin, the NBA, and Hegemonic Masculinity." *BTG*. Retrieved December 10, 2012, from http://btg.bobngo.com/?p=206.

Prashad, V. (1998). "Crafting Solidarities." In *A Part, Yet Apart: South Asians in Asian America*, ed. R. Srikant & L. D. Shankar. Philadelphia: Temple University Press.

Regalado, S. (2012). *Nikkei Baseball*. Urbana: University of Illinois Press.

Rhoden, W. C. (2006). *Forty Million Dollar Slaves: The Rise, Fall, and Redemption of the Black Athlete*. New York: Crown.

Shah, N. (2001). *Contagious Divides*. Berkeley: University of California Press.

Smith, A. (2005). *Conquest*. Boston: South End Press.

Thangaraj, S. I. (2012). "Playing through Difference: The Black-White Racial Logic and Interrogating South Asian American Identity." *Journal of Ethnic and Racial Studies*, 35 (6), pp. 998–1006.

———. (2013). "Competing Masculinities: South Asian American Identity Formation in Asian American Basketball Leagues." *South Asian Popular Culture*, 11 (3), pp. 243–255.

———. (2015). *Desi Hoop Dreams: Pickup Basketball and the Making of Asian American Masculinity*. New York: New York University Press.

Torre, P. S. (2010, February 1). "Harvard School of Basketball." *Sports Illustrated*. Retrieved December 10, 2012, from http://sportsillustrated.cnn.com/vault/article/magazine/MAG1165302/3/index.htm.

Trujillo, N. 2000. "Hegemonic Masculinity on the Mound." *In Reading Sport: Critical Essays on Power and Representation*, ed. S. Birrell & M. MacDonald. Boston: Northeastern University Press.

Uperesa, F. L. (2014). "Fabled Futures: Migration and Mobility for Samoans in American Football." *Contemporary Pacific*, 26 (2), pp. 281–301.

Uperesa, F. L., & Mountjoy, T. (2014). "Global Sport in the Pacific: A Brief Overview." *Contemporary Pacific*, 26 (2), pp. 263–279.

Wonsek, P. L. (1992). "College Basketball on Television: A Study of Racism in the Media." *Media, Culture and Society*, 14, pp. 449–461.

Yu, T. (2012, February 21). "Will Jeremy Lin's Success End Stereotypes?" *CNN.com*. Retrieved December 10, 2012, from http://www.cnn.com/2012/02/20/opinion/yu-jeremy-lin/index.htm.

Wang, O. (2012, March 6). "Living with Linsanity." *Los Angeles Review of Books*. Retrieved December 10, 2012, from http://blog.lareviewofbooks.org/post/18846363359/living-with-linsanity.

Wierenga, J. (2012, February 15). "Jeremy Lin: Why Every American Should Be Rooting for Linsanity to Last." *Bleacher Report*. Retrieved December 10, 2012, from http://bleacherreport.com/articles/1067330-jeremy-lin-why-every-american-should-be-rooting-for-lin-sanity-to-last.

Wright, R. (2012, February 14). "The Secret of Jeremy Lin's Success?" *Atlantic*. Retrieved December 10, 2012, from http://www.theatlantic.com/entertainment/archive/2012/02/the-secret-of-jeremy-lins-success/253051/.

Yang, J. (2012, February 15). "Will Lin-sanity Tame Tiger Moms?" *New York Daily News*. Retrieved December 10, 2012, from http://articles.nydailynews.com/2012-02-15/news/31064980_1_gie-ming-hoop-dreams-brother.

Zaldivar, G. (2012, February). "Jeremy Lin Is Modern-Day Hero America Loves." *Bleacher Report*. Retrieved December 10, 2012, from http://bleacherreport.com/articles/1059364-jeremy-lin-is-modern-day-hero-america-loves.

Zirin, D. (2012, February 7). "Feel the Lin-sanity: Why Jeremy Lin Is More than a Cultural Curio." *Nation*. Retrieved December 10, 2012, from http://www.thenation.com/blog/166161/feel-lin-sanity-why-jeremy-lin-more-cultural-curio#.

AFTERWORD

"Competing against Type"

LISA LOWE

The lithe, petite Japanese American figure skater, born with club feet, becomes an Olympic gold medalist through extraordinary discipline and hard work. We are riveted by the meteoric rise of the lanky, understated Taiwanese American "underdog" point guard, who scores 38 points against Kobe Bryant and the Lakers. A muscular Chinese American female martial artist fearlessly kicks, strikes, and punches another woman. Tears stream down the faces in the crowd, as they cheer for the victory of the passionate Filipino boxer who declares his Christian faith. The bespectacled, unflappable South Asian immigrant champion spells her final word, "guetapens," correctly, making her parents and grandparents very proud. These figures are familiar in the repertoire of the U.S. sports imagination, demonstrating the degree to which Asian Americans have not only competed successfully, but to which Asian immigrants are becoming significant participants in U.S. public culture itself.

Yet far from celebrating Asian American involvement in sports as evidence of integration into liberal democratic society, the essays in this volume have treated Asian American sporting cultures *critically*, and examined sports as key sites of socialization, assimilation, and national belonging. A form of popular culture in which discipline, force, and control are dramatized and spectacularized, sport is a platform for the practice and performance of everyday life; it offers a place to examine power, privilege, interests, and dominance. Boxing matches, baseball games, basketball tournaments—these are the *lingua franca* of American social life; they are mass-mediated performances, informed by myth, narrative, and melodrama, as well as national ideas about race, gender, ability, celebrity, and embodiment. Sports not only capture public attention, many are commodified entertainments to be consumed, instantly streamed, reported, blogged, satirized, and live-tweeted across a wide array of print and electronic venues.

This volume's essays in cultural criticism have examined how Asian American sporting cultures—from playing, competing, and participation to spectatorship and fandom—convey and contest normative values of American nationalism and patriotism. Many consider how sports practice and sports consumption are central activities within the social reproduction of racial, class, and gender hierarchies within the United States, and furthermore, within the expansion and maintenance of U.S. empire in Asia and in the Pacific Islands, which has given rise to much of the postwar and Cold War Asian immigration.[1] In this way, the volume contributes to a critical examination of sporting cultures as "racial projects" in which one may examine the dynamic negotiation, production, and transformation of racial meanings.[2] Put otherwise, Asian Americans' engagement with sports, as players or fans, constitute contradictory social sites within a complex, shifting racial capitalist order, a terrain on which racial formations are made and remade in ways that transform access to representation and social spheres. Asian American inclusion in sports should not be understood as an unequivocal sign of either social and political belonging or resistance. Rather, as a number of the essays observe, the representations of the entry of Asian Americans into sports may often confirm liberal multiculturalism, and at times, engage and renew racist, Orientalist, or "model minority" stereotypes. When triangulated with blackness and whiteness, the media representations of Asian Americans in sports can reiterate the familiar racial logics of white supremacy. In his contribution, for example, Oliver Wang observed that Jeremy Lin's stature—and body—became sites through which commentators sought to work through Asian race, racializations, and racial stratification in relation to U.S. whiteness and blackness. Stanley Thangaraj elsewhere has observed that the black-white racial binary that operates in the U.S. racial order "is simultaneously *insufficient* and *critical* to identity formation for South Asian Americans [who] do not transcend the black-white binary but rather directly involve and reconfigure this normative racial logic."[3]

At the same time, when Asian Americans in sports are constructed as racially different than black and white Americans, the "difference" is never exclusively *racial*. The volume observes that the social difference that is understood as "race" is always articulated with other axes of distinction, from nationality and religion to gender, sexuality, and embodiment. If sport is arguably one of the most racialized and gender-policed arenas of American society, the entrance of Asian Americans into different sports reconfigures race, class, and gender norms. In some cases, when Asian ethnic groups form their own leagues, as with the Hmong American football discussed by Chia Youyee Vang, athletic performance can provide a "counter-space" to express ethnic, regional, class, political, or religious differences from other Asian groups, as well as resistance to mainstream American notions of patriotic citizenry, patriarchal family, or normative gendered embodiment. In others, Asian ethnics may choose sports like ping pong or badminton, outside of the mainstream. Pawan Dhingra examined spelling bees as the "brain sport," that is, an alternative arena in which South Asian American youth compete according to "sports logic," even as their gender performances do not conform to those associated with the masculinity or femininity prescribed by American sports. Likewise, while many Asian American women athletes conform to Orientalist "types"—of diminutive physical beauty, work ethic, and family life—in their essay, Jessica Chin and David Andrews discussed Asian women fighters involved in the full contact sport of mixed martial arts as challenging racial and gender norms. Asian Americans in sports cultures can be read critically for what they tell us about not only race and racial difference in the United States, but moreover, about national belonging, gendered embodiment, sexual normativity, ethnicity, and religion, as well as the histories of U.S. empire, racial capitalism, and the "war on terror."

If we consider sports as a global conveyor of U.S. norms, values, and cultural hegemony to many parts of the world, it is evident that American sporting cultures—including brands, icons, and celebrities—have a forceful presence in Asia even before immigrants arrive in the United States. American sports are imported and consumed by Asian participants in global capitalism, well before Asians become Asian Americans. Furthermore, several essays in the volume have treated sports as a medium of U.S. imperialism in Asia and the Pacific Islands. Sport, like education and the military, has been historically an important means to foster loyalty, masculinity, and the deep attachments of colonized subjects to empire. Ryan Reft observed that Filipino soldiers played on U.S. Army and Navy teams, and sports like baseball and basketball served as cultural media that transformed war rivalries into domestic competitions, popularizing the alleged superiority of American masculinity, competition, and modernity, which rationalized U.S. rule. This idea resonates with Fa'anofo Lisaclaire Uperesa's work on American Samoans in U.S. football. While sports involve rigorous exercise regimens, surveillance, and physical discipline to produce docile bodies, Uperesa argued that football involves not merely the subjection of the colonized men, it also permits creative use of the body, a chance to escape routines of everyday life, and the means to maneuver within constraints of being player commodities; football may provide a path out of poverty, and in the context of a global sporting market, it may raise the status of Samoa within U.S. imperialism.[4]

An earlier Asian American studies and ethnic studies paradigm often defined race and racial formation in terms of people's political and economic *exclusion* from the U.S. nation-state, as noncitizens and as racialized immigrant labor. One of the most important contributions made by this volume on sports is that it suggests that we must revise the paradigm for studying Asian Americans to consider the racializing operations of *inclusion*, as well as *exclusion*. The conversion of Asians into citizens within the U.S. state, and into normative multicultural workers and consumers within domestic and global capitalism, constitutes a violence of inclusion, rather than only exclusion. For example, Shalini Shankar's recent work on Asian American advertising considers "racial naturalization" as a process by which Asian Americans form not only a "niche" market targeted by corporations, but Asian Americans are themselves recruited as "experts" with specific cultural and linguistic knowledge that is used to tailor advertising.[5] Asian Americans within consumer capitalism are often asked not only to commodify their "race," but they sometimes become the agents for the reproduction of multicultural capitalism itself. One way of discussing this violence of inclusion is to consider the shifts in racial capitalism that have occurred during the twentieth century: while the liberalism of national capitalism during the first half of the century focused on expanded production through racialized labor and civil rights, the neoliberal globalized finance capitalism of the second half of the century innovated export production, manufacturing, and marketing, secured and accomplished by the U.S. militarism and the carceral state.[6] Contemporary globalization involves *both* capital expanding and profiting in new ways from regional economic divides in the aftermath of colonial divisions of the first and third worlds, *and* the invention and multiplication of new sites, new media and practices, for the purposes of capital accumulation. Sports, and the expanding range of sports industries, are certainly a guide to these patterns within which the articulation of race and capitalism have shifted. Furthermore, Asian Americans in sports may be seen as one index of this violence of inclusion that accompanies the expansion of racial capitalism. With globalization, new categories of privilege and abjection confuse the former racial groupings traditionally studied by ethnic studies: "black," "white," "Asian," "Latino," "Muslim," and "Arab" are complex, shifting designations that include wealthy and poor, men and women, LGBT and queer, citizens and nonnationals, and so forth. Transnational migration from Asia, Africa, Latin America, and the Middle East, and the intersections of race with gender, sexuality, class, and region, exceed the formerly U.S.-centered paradigm of race and racism, especially when the globalization of capitalism accelerates and rearticulates the divides between rich and poor in the developed and developing worlds. As Jodi Melamed puts it, "with white supremacy and colonial capitalism giving way to racial liberalism and transnational capitalism and, eventually, to neoliberal multiculturalism and globalization. . . . Race continues to fuse technologies of racial domination with liberal freedoms to represent people who are exploited for or cut off from capitalist wealth as outsiders to liberal subjectivity."[7] U.S.-led empire is implemented not only through militarism and capitalism, but also through its moral instruments and ideological powers: humanitarian discourses of rescue, benevolence, and human rights; the partisan languages of "us" and "them," "good" and "evil," "free" and "violent"; and the patriotic fervor of sports fandom, spectatorship, and consumerism. Sport is the theater for the formation of national insiders and outsiders, heroes and villains, and all of the essays in *Asian American Sporting Cultures* present astute observations of the roles that Asian Americans play in this public staging of our times.

NOTES

1 On the relationship of Asian immigration to U.S. war and empire in Asia, see Jodi Kim, *The Ends of Empire: Asian American Critique and the Cold War* (Minneapolis: University of Minnesota, 2010).

2 Michael Omi and Howard Winant, *Racial Formation in the United States*, 3d ed. (New York: Routledge, 2014); Ben Carrington, *Race, Sport, and Politics: The Sporting Black Diaspora* (London: Sage, 2010); Ben Carrington, "Sport Matters," *Ethnic and Racial Studies*, Vol. 35, No. 6 (June 2012): 961–970.

3 Stanley I. Thangaraj, "Playing through Differences: Black-White Racial Logic and Interrogating South Asian American Identity," *Ethnic and Racial Studies*, Vol. 35, No. 6 (June 2012): 988–1006, p. 989.

4 Fa'anofo Lisaclaire Uperesa, "Seeking New Fields of Labor: Football and Colonial Political Economies in American Samoa," in *Formations of United States Colonialism*, ed. Alyosha Goldstein (Durham, NC: Duke University Press, 2014), pp. 207–232.

5 Shalini Shankar, *Advertising Diversity: Ad Agencies and the Creation of Asian American Consumers* (Durham, NC: Duke University Press, 2015).

6 Catherine Lutz writes that as of late 2008, official records report over 150,000 troops and 95,000 civilians massed in 837 military facilities in 45 countries and territories; yet even these official numbers are misleading, because they exclude not only the massive buildup and troop presence in Iraq and Afghanistan, but also leave out secret or unacknowledged facilities in Israel, Kuwait, the Philippines, and other sites. Lutz, "U.S. Military Bases on Guam in a Global Perspective," *Asia-Pacific Journal: Japan Focus*, July 26, 2010, http://www.japanfocus.org/-Catherine-Lutz/3389/article.html.

7 Jodi Melamed, "From Racial Liberalism to Neoliberal Multiculturalism," *Social Text*, Vol. 24, No. 4 (Winter 2006): 1–24.

ABOUT THE CONTRIBUTORS

DAVID L. ANDREWS is Professor of Physical Cultural Studies in the Department of Kinesiology at the University of Maryland, College Park. His research critically examines the contextually contingent organization, representation, and experience of physical culture. His publications include *The Blackwell Companion to Sport* (edited with Ben Carrington, 2013) and *Sport and Neoliberalism: Politics, Consumption, and Culture* (edited with Michael Silk, 2012).

CONSTANCIO R. ARNALDO, JR., is Visiting Assistant Professor of Asian American Studies at Miami University. He has written about Manny "Pac-Man" Pacquiao and Philippine cultural transnationalism in *Crossroads: Asian Americans and Popular Culture* (New York University Press, forthcoming).

CHRISTINA B. CHIN is Assistant Professor in the Sociology Department at California State University, Fullerton, where she is working on a book manuscript that examines the construction and negotiation of racial identities, gender roles, and ethnic community building within community-organized Japanese American youth basketball leagues.

JESSICA W. CHIN is Associate Professor in the Department of Kinesiology at San José State University. Her teaching and research interests include sociocultural analyses of sport and physical activity. She is particularly interested in critical examinations of the active female body and its use in the negotiation of power and identity in various sporting contexts. Her recent lines of research focus on the diverse experiences of hazing and initiation among women in collegiate athletics and popular representations of Asian American female athletes in nontraditional sporting spaces.

PAWAN DHINGRA is Professor and Chair of Sociology at Tufts University. He is the author of *Life Behind the Lobby: Indian American Motel Owners and the American Dream* (2013) and *Managing Multicultural Lives: Asian American Professionals and the Challenge of Multiple Identities* (2007). He is also co-authoring a textbook entitled *The Sociology of Asian Americans*.

J. JACK HALBERSTAM is Professor of English and Director of the Center for Feminist Research at University of Southern California (USC). He is the author of many books including *Female Masculinity* (1998), *In a Queer Time and Place* (New York University Press, 2005), *The Queer Art of Failure* (2011), and *Gaga Feminism* (2013).

DAVID LEONARD is Associate Professor and Chair in the Department of Critical Culture, Gender, and Race Studies at Washington State University, Pullman. He is the author of *After Artest: The NBA and the Assault on Blackness* (2012) and *Screens Fade to Black: Contemporary African American Cinema* (2006), and co-author with C. Richard King of *Commodified and Criminalized: New Racism and African Americans in Contemporary Sports* (2012).

LISA LOWE is Professor of English and American Studies at Tufts University, and a member of the consortium of Studies in Race, Colonialism, and Diaspora. She is the author of *Critical Terrains: French and British Orientalisms* (1991), *Immigrant Acts: On Asian American Cultural Politics* (1996), and *The Intimacies of Four Continents* (2015).

RYAN REFT has a PhD in U.S. Urban History from the University of California, San Diego, writes for KCET (Los Angeles), co-edits the blog Tropics of Meta, and teaches history at the University of Colorado Denver, University of Maryland University College, and Northern Virginia Community College.

SHALINI SHANKAR is Associate Professor at the Department of Anthropology at Northwestern University, and the author of *Desi Land: Teen Culture, Class, and Success in Silicon Valley* (2008) and *Advertising Diversity: Ad Agencies and the Creation of Asian American Consumers* (2015).

STANLEY I. THANGARAJ is Assistant Professor of Anthropology at the City College of New York. He is the co-editor of *Sport and South Asian Diasporas* (2014) and the author of *Desi Hoop Dreams: Pickup Basketball and the Making of Asian American Masculinity* (New York University Press, 2015).

CHIA YOUYEE VANG is Associate Professor of History at the University of Wisconsin, Milwaukee. She is the director of the Hmong Studies program. Vang is the author of *Hmong America: Reconstructing Community in Diaspora* (2010) and *Hmong in Minnesota* (2008).

OLIVER WANG is Associate Professor of Sociology at California State University, Long Beach. He writes extensively on race and popular culture for NPR, the *Los Angeles Times*, and KCET's ArtBound and wrote the essay "Living With Linsanity" for the *Los Angeles Review of Books* in March 2012. He is also the author of *Legions of Boom* (2015).

INDEX

acculturation, sports as vehicle of, 58–64, 70, 205
African Americans: Asian Americans in relation to, 82, 87–88, 103, 133, 158, 222–23, 226–34; Filipinos and, 44–46; hypermasculinity of, 127, 135, 224–25; Pacific Islanders in relation to, 236–37; racial binarism concerning, 1–3, 45, 46, 103, 248. *See also* blackness
Air India, 142
Alger, Horatio, Jr., 79, 106, 221
Ali, Muhammad, viii, 109
Alien Land Laws, 26
Amaker, Tommy, 44
American Dream, 77, 79–81, 83–84, 88, 106, 221–22, 237
And1 basketball, 44
Anderson, Benedict, 109
Anderson, Eric, 235
Andrews, David L., 13, 88, 249
Aoki, Guy, 87
Appadurai, Arjun, 55
Archetti, Eduardo P., 211
Arigo, John, 44
Arnaldo, Constancio R., Jr., 12, 45, 46
Arroyo, Gloria Magcapal, 114
Arum, Bob, 109
Asian Americans: African Americans in relation to, 82, 87–88, 103, 133, 158, 222–23, 226–34; and basketball, 37–47, 190, 206; and citizenship, 26–27; heterogeneity of, 5–7, 156; immigration of, 24–27; invisibility of, 111, 181, 192, 205, 230; masculinity of, 133–34, 154, 158, 204, 222, 224–25, 230–34; as model minority, 13, 46, 77, 80, 82, 86–87, 127–28, 132–33, 156–58, 191–92, 199, 226–28; as perpetual foreigners, 2, 34, 35, 103, 157, 180; as racial category, 5, 152; racial status of, 1–3, 15–16; sexuality of, 47; and sport, 11, 203–6, 225–26; stereotypes of, 47, 89, 108, 133–34, 153, 156–58, 193, 233
Asian American women, 13–14; and basketball, 38, 40; Hmong sport participation, 211–14; in mixed martial arts, 161–73; as model minority, 134; and race, 164–72; sexuality of, 158–59, 168; in sport, 134; as sport spectators, 68–69; stereotypes of, 134, 154–59, 164–72, 205; in stereotypical feminine sports, 159–61
Asians, stereotypes of, 29, 46
assimilation, 102–3

Barker, Barbara, 81
Barrera, Marco Antonio, 107, 114
Barthes, Roland, 62–63
Bartholomew, Rafe, 43, 45
baseball: Asian Americans and, 37–47; and civilizing mission, 23–24; Indians and, 56, 60, 66–67; international tours, 32–33, 36–37; invention of, 28; in Japan, 28–33, 35–36; Japanese Americans and, 30–34, 37; and masculinity, 29; in the Philippines, 23–24; in postwar years, 34–37; U.S. servicemen and, 24, 28

basketball: Asian Americans and, 37–47, 190, 206; Chinese Americans and, 38; Filipinos and, 41–46; Indian Americans and, 131; integration of, 3, 4; Japanese Americans and, 14, 38–40, 180–93; Linsanity, 75–92; and masculinity, 38, 42; in postwar years, 37–47; women playing, 38, 40
Basketball Association of America, 4
Baszler, Shayna, 164–65
Bederman, Gayle, viii
Belasco, Nic, 44
Bell, James Franklin, 23
Ben & Jerry's, 84
Bend It Like Beckham (film), 136
Beran, Janice, 42
Beverly, Patrick, 90
Bilas, Jay, 44
Birrell, Susan, 55, 70
blackness: Lin and, 82, 85, 87–88, 231–34, 240; Te'o and, 236–37, 240
black-white dichotomy, 1–3, 45, 46, 103, 248
Blinebury, Fran, 91
body: Asian, 190; Asian American female, 134; ideals of, 1; Indian-American, 132–33; Pacquiao and, 106, 109–10; spelling bees and, 139
Bourdieu, Pierre, 132
bowling, 60–61
Bowron, Fletcher, 34
boxing, 110
Boyd, Todd, 231–32
Brilliant, Mark, 46
Brooks, Charlotte, 35
Bruce, Toni, 103

Cai, R., 169
California: baseball in, 30–32; race in postwar, 34–35, 37, 39
California Fruit Growers Exchange, 31–32
Cameron, Alex, 146
capitalism. *See* consumer capitalism

Cariaso, Jeff, 44
Carpio, Bernardo, 116
Carr, David, 84
Carrington, Ben, 2
Castro, Alvin, 44
Catholicism, 42–43, 106, 116
celebrities. *See* sport celebrities
Central Intelligence Agency (CIA), 201
Cepeda, Esther, 83–84
Chillar, Brandon, 130
Chin, Christina B., 14, 37, 40
Chin, Jessica W., 13, 249
Chinese and Chinese Americans, 26, 38
Chinese Exclusion Act, 26–27
Chou, Rosalind, 227
Christianity: muscular, 23, 106; Pacquiao and, 106–7, 109, 115, 120n5. *See also* Catholicism
Chua, Amy, 86
citizenship: Asian Americans and, 26–27; sport and, 1, 5, 10
Clifton, Nate "Sweetwater," 3
Clottey, Joshua, 104
Cold War, 27, 36
Coleman, Chris, 215
Community Youth Council (Los Angeles), 39
competition: academic, 127; spelling bees as, 136–39
Constancio, Arnoldo, Jr., 162–63
consumer capitalism, 152–53, 250–51
Cordona, Mac Mac, 44
Cortez, Mike, 44
Cott, Nancy F., 26
cricket, 55–57, 64, 65, 130, 131
C2 Education, 142, 146

Dalrymple, Timothy, 229, 231
Davé, Shilpa, 3
Delaney, Tim, 203
Delgado, Richard, 76–77
Desai, Jigna, 3
Dhingra, Pawan, 13, 249

DiMaggio, Joe, 30
discrimination. *See* racism, discrimination, and exclusion
Domingo, Charisse, 117–18
Dominican Republic, 32
Doubleday, Abner, 28
Duncan, Arne, 82

Eastwood, Clint, 202
education, sport in relation to, 204–5. *See also* spelling bees
Ellis, Rosell "Roe," 45
El Paso Shoe Store Zapatores, 32–33
empire. *See* U.S. Empire
Eng, David L., 204, 215
Engel, Jen Floyd, 86
England, 111–12
equality, 24, 79
España-Maram, Linda, 4, 112, 204
Espiritu, Yên Lê, 202
ESPN (television network), 140–41
ethnicity. *See* race and ethnicity
E. W. Scripps Company, 145–46
exclusion. *See* racism, discrimination, and exclusion
Executive Order 9066, 4, 33

Fajardo, Kale, 116, 118
Falgoust, J. Michael, 229
fandom. *See* sport spectatorship
Far Eastern Games, 43
Farred, Grant, 233
Feagin, Joe, 227
Fight Girls (television show), 165
Filipino Repatriation Act, 41
Filipinos and Filipino Americans: and African Americans, 44–46; assimilation of, 103; and basketball, 24, 41–46; and citizenship, 27; immigration of, 24, 41, 108; invisibility of, 111; masculinity of, 42, 43, 108; and nationalism, 43, 103, 104, 109–18; and Pacquiao, 102–19
flag football, 212–14

Fletcher, Thomas, 55
football: flag football, 212–14; Hmong Americans and, 199, 206–9; Indian Americans and, 67, 130; and masculinity, 234–36
forever foreign. *See* perpetual foreigners, Asian Americans as
Freeman, Hadley, 87
Frey, Jinh Yu, 164–65
Friedman, Andrew, 25
Friends of Richard, 39
Fuji Athletic Club, 30
Furukawa, Tets, 34

Gandhi, Mohandas, 64
Garcia, Ceferino "Bolo Puncher," 3
Gardena, California, 37
Gay, Jason, 84
Gems, Gerald, 32, 42
gender: Asian Americans, 29, 133–34, 158–59, 189–91; professional basketball and, 47; spelling bees and, 137–39; and sport, 134–36
generations, relations between, 64–69, 186–89
Gentlemen's Agreement, 27
globalization, 251
golf, 67, 214
Gomes, Catherine, 169
Goodwin, Lonnie, 32
Gran Torino (film), 202
Gulati, Sunil, 130
Guthrie-Shimizu, Sayuri, 24, 36, 37

Hagiya, Jamie, 38–39
Halberstam, J. Jack, 10
Hall, S., 153
Harada, Tsuneo "Cappy," 35–37
Haria, Yoshi, 39–40
Harmon, Dick, 226
Harris, Darla, 165
Hart-Celler Immigration Act, 25, 41, 57
Hartmann, Douglas, 2

Hatton, Ricky "The Hitman," 111–13
Hawai'i, 30, 32
Hennessy, 107
Hewlett-Packard, 107
Hironoshin, Furuhashi, 36
Hiroto, Russ, 39
Hmong Americans, 14–15, 199–203, 206–16; as antithesis of model minority, 94n28, 200, 202; contributions to U.S. society of, 202–3; and ethnic sports tournaments, 209–15; and football, 199, 206–9; and high school football, 207–9; identity formation of, 211, 214; refugee experience of, 201–2; stereotypes of, 200; and U.S. Empire, 200–203; women's sport participation, 211–14
Hodgkin, G. B., 32
Holiday Bowl, in Crenshaw, California, 39
homoeroticism, of sports culture, 223–24
Hsu, Hua, 91–92
Hurt, Byron, 239
Hutchins, Andy, 223, 239
hypermasculinity: of African Americans, 127, 135, 224–25; Asian Americans and, 190–91

identity formation: of Hmong Americans, 211, 214; of Japanese Americans, 186–89; in popular culture, 8–9
Ileto, Reynaldo, 116
imagined communities, 109–10, 207, 209
immigration: and acculturation, 58–64, 70, 205; Asian Americans, 24–27; and assimilation, 102; Filipino Americans, 24, 41, 108; Japanese Americans, 27, 30; sport spectatorship and, 53–70; Vietnamese Americans, 25
imperialism. See U.S. Empire
Indians and Indian Americans: demographic characteristics of, 132; masculinity of, 134–35; as model minority, 132–33; and spelling bees, 127–29, 136–48; and sport, 127–36, 143; and sport spectatorship, 53–70
intergenerational relations, 64–69, 186–89
internment camps, for Japanese Americans, 4, 33–34, 38–39, 184–85
Invicta, 163, 170
Irie, George, 32
Iriye, Akira, 29
Issei, 31, 183

James, LeBron, 78
Japan: baseball in, 28–33, 35–36; imperialism of, 29, 33
Japanese Amateur Athletic Union, 184
Japanese American Citizens League, 184
Japanese Americans: and baseball, 30–34, 37; and basketball, 38–40; identity formation of, 186–89; immigration of, 27, 30; internment of, 4, 33–34, 38–39, 184–85; youth basketball leagues, 14, 180–93
Japanese Athletic Union, 184
Jeffries, Jim, viii
Jesus, 115, 116
Jianlian, Yi, 231
Johnson, Jack, viii
Joo, Rachael M., 55, 59
Jordan, Michael, 186, 221
Joseph, Janelle, 54, 64
justice, in underdog stories, 79, 82–83

Kang, Jay Caspian, 46, 76, 81, 89, 232
Karen, David, 132
Kawai, Y., 157
Kerrigan, Nancy, 160
Kian, Edward M., 235
Kim, Claire Jean, 103
King, Jamilah, 229
Kobuki, Yoshio "Kokomo Joe," 3
Kondabolu, Hari, 143–44
Korean Americans, 7
Kramer, Paul, 23
Kwan, Michelle, 153, 159–60

L.A. Nippons, 30, 32, 33
Laos, 201
Lazarus, Mark, 226–27
Lee, Bruce, 8
Lee, Choua, 202
Lee, Erika, 27
Lee, Jerry, 207
Lee, Sammy, 35
Legit Misfitz, 45
Leonard, Andrew, 229–30
Leonard, David, 15, 87, 153
Leung, Maxwell, 80, 82
Levy, Abe, 227
Lim, Thea, 111
Lin, Jeremy, ix, 6, 9, 12, 14, 15, 46–47, 69, 75–92, 106, 129, 153–54, 206, 221–22, 224, 226, 228–34, 240, 248
Linsanity, 12, 75–92, 206; American values present in, 80–81; growth of, 75, 78; meaning of, 88, 91–92, 153–54, 221; race as component of, 80–88, 231–34; stereotyping in, 82, 84, 85; as underdog story, 78–89
Lipinski, Tara, 160
Liu, Eric, 81
Lloyd, Earl, 3
Long Beach Press (newspaper), 35
Los Angeles Lakers, 186
Lowe, Lisa, 5, 6, 10, 25
Lowe, Zach, 77
Lupica, Mike, 79–80

Ma, Sheng-Mei, 171
Madigan, Tim, 203
Mahankali, Arvind, 142, 144
Manalansan, Martin, 5
Mannur, Anita, 227–28
Marbury, Stephon, 46
Markham, Jesse, 117
Marquat, William, 35–36
Márquez, Juan Manuel, 104
marriage. *See* out-marriage
martial arts. *See* mixed martial arts
Martin, Janet, 163–64

masculinity: Asian American, 133–34, 154, 158, 190–91, 204, 222, 230–34; baseball and, 29; basketball and, 38, 42; boxing and, 110; Chinese American, 38; female MMA fighters and, 163–64; Filipino, 42, 43, 108; football and, 234–36; Indian American, 134–35; of Lin, 222, 224, 230–34; of Pacific Islanders, 224–25; Pacquiao and, 107–9; sexuality and, 223–24; sport associated with, 134–35, 222–24, 235; of Te'o, 223–24, 236–39
MastiSpell bee, 128
May, Reuben, 2
Mayweather, Floyd, Jr., 85, 113
McDonald, Mary, 55, 70
McGrady, Tracy, 46
media sport, 55
Mei Wahs, 38
Melamed, Jodi, 251
men. *See* masculinity
meritocracy: minorities and, 87; spelling bees as, 146; sport as, 9, 11, 16, 107, 110, 136, 146, 240; United States as, 25, 80
Messner, Michael, 234–35
Metropolitan Life Insurance, 142, 146
Mexican Americans, 31–32, 39
microaggressions, racial, 189–92
militarization, 24–25, 27
Miller, Willie, 44–45
Ming, Yao, 129, 228, 229, 231, 233
Misaka, Wataru "Kilo Wat," 3, 4, 6, 233
missionaries, 23
mixed martial arts (MMA), 13–14, 161–73
model minorities: and the American Dream, 80; antitheses of, 82, 87, 94n28, 200, 202; Asian Americans, 13, 46, 77, 80, 82, 86–87, 127–28, 132–33, 156–58, 191–92, 199, 226–28; Asian American women, 134; bodies associated with, 133; gendered construction of, 133–34; Indian Americans, 132–33; Japanese Americans, 14; Lin as instance of, 85–87; Pacquiao as instance of, 107

Monterey Park, California, 37
Morales, Erik, 107, 114
Moua, Charly, 199
muscular Christianity, 23, 106

Nakamura, Miriam, 164
Nakamura, Tadashi, 40
Nakase, Natalie, 40–41
Nandur, Kumar, 140
National Basketball Association (NBA), 45, 47, 80–88, 222
National Football League (NFL), 130, 145, 222
nationalism: Filipino, 43, 103, 104, 109–18; and imagined communities, 109–10; spelling bees and, 146–47; sport and, 147
NBA. *See* National Basketball Association
Negro League, 31, 32
neoliberalism, 144–47
NFL. *See* National Football League
NFL Play 60, 145
Ng, Konrad, 78
Nguyen, Dat, 227
Nguyen, Mimi, 3, 8
Nike, 104, 106–7, 112–15, 230
Nisei, 31, 33, 35, 183
Nisei Athletic Union, 186
Nishime, Leilani, 3
North South Foundation (NSF), 128, 140, 141, 145

Obama, Barack, 141
O'Doul, Lefty, 36
Omachi, George, 33
Omi, Michael, 2
Oren, Tasha G., 3
Orientalism, 29, 154–59, 162
out-marriage, 41

Pacific Coast League, 30
Pacific Coast Youth (PCY) basketball league, 181, 186–91
Pacific Islanders, 14–15, 94n28, 224–25, 236–40

Pacquiao, Manny "Pac-Man," 12–13, 102–19
Page Act, 26–27
Palin, Sarah, 83
Palreddy, Soumya, 204
Pan, Arnold, 90
Park, J., 155
pasyon, 116
PCY. *See* Pacific Coast Youth (PCY) basketball league
Peek, Ali, 44
Perez, Hiram, 227
perpetual foreigners, Asian Americans as, 2, 34, 35, 103, 157, 180, 185
Perry, Matthew, 36
Philadelphia Royal Giants, 32
Philippines, 12; baseball in, 23–24, 27; basketball in, 41–45; and British imperialism, 111–13; nationalism in, 43, 103, 104, 109–18; Pacquiao as symbol of, 113–18; and U.S. imperialism, 23–24, 27, 41–43, 108–9. *See also* Filipinos and Filipino Americans
Philippines Basketball Association (PBA), 43–44
Phillips, Brian, 79
Plessy v. Ferguson (1896), 1
postracial society, 107
Potter, David M., 79
Prashad, Vijay, 156, 228
Protestantism, 42

race and ethnicity: black-white dichotomy in, 1–3, 45, 46, 103, 248; capitalism and, 152–53, 250–51; female MMA fighters and, 164–72; Linsanity and, 80–88; microaggressions based on, 189–92; national ideals of, 1–2; NBA and, 80–88; sport and, 135, 248; and sports tournaments, 209–15
racism, discrimination, and exclusion: in Asian American basketball, 39; Asian Americans, 87, 189–92; in baseball, 30; created in sport identity formation, 8–

9; Japanese Americans, 183–84; Korean Americans, 35; Mexican Americans, 39; sport as remedy for, 63–64
Rafu Shimpo (newspaper), 31
Reft, Ryan, ix, 11, 183, 250
refugees, 201–2
Regalado, Samuel, 4, 33
Rizal, José, 116
Roach, Freddie, 114
Robinson, Jackie, 1, 34
Roherback, D. W., 27
Roosevelt, Teddy, 28

Said, Edward, 154–56
Sakuma, Sakata, 29
Samoans, 15, 236–40
San Francisco Chronicle (newspaper), 38
San Miguel Brewery, 107
Sansei, 186
Santa Ana Register (newspaper), 35
SASB. *See* South Asian Spelling Bee
scholarship, racial logics in, 2–4
Scripps National Spelling Bee, 128, 140–41, 145–46
Seau, Junior, 226–34
segregation. *See* racism, discrimination, and exclusion
Semenya, Caster, viii
sexuality: Asian American, 47, 158–59, 168; Chinese, 26, 38; Filipino, 27; masculinity and, 223–24; Te'o and, 238–40
Shankar, Shalini, 11–12, 250
Shigeru, Mizuhara, 36
Shriver, Jenny Liou, 164–65
Simon, Mark, 80
Singh, Vijay, 69, 129
soccer, 130, 211–12
softball, 60
Sony Television, 142
South Asian Americans, 7
South Asian Spelling Bee (SASB), 128, 141–42
spectatorship. *See* sport spectatorship

Spellbound (documentary), 138, 146
spelling bees, 13, 127–29, 136–48; and the body, 139; coaches for, 139–40; as competitions, 136–39; costs of, 146; and gender, 137–39; liminal character of, 147–48; and nationalism, 146–47; neoliberal logic of, 144–47; sponsors of, 142, 145–46; sport in relation to, 127–28, 138–45; televising of, 140–41, 143; training tools for, 140
Spoelstra, Erik, 41
sport: bodily ideals of, 1; education in relation to, 204–5; masculinity associated with, 134–35, 222–24, 235; meaning of, 77; and national citizenship, 1, 5, 10; nationalism and, 147; neoliberalism and, 144; parent attitude toward, 204; societal role of, 203; spelling bees in relation to, 127–28, 138–45
sport celebrities, 12–13, 152–53
Sports Illustrated (magazine), 199
sport spectatorship, 53–70
Stein, Leland, 82
stereotypes: Asian Americans, 47, 89, 108, 133–34, 153, 156–58, 193, 233; Asian American women, 134, 154–59, 164–72, 205; Asians, 29, 46; Chinese Americans, 26, 38; female MMA fighters, 163–64; feminine sport cultures, 159–61; Hmong Americans, 200; Lin as subject of, 82, 84, 85; reinforcement of, 153
Stoler, Ann Laura, 23
Sunkist, 31–32
Suzuki, Ichiro, 229

Taiwan, 29
Tan, Michael, 43
Tebbit, Norman, 55
Tengen, Ty, 117
tennis, 57, 61–62, 67, 214
Te'o, Manti, 15, 221–24, 226–28, 236–40
Thangaraj, Stanley, 46, 54, 191, 248

Tokyo Giants, 33, 35, 36
Tong, William, 80
top spin, 215
Tork, 58–59
Torre, Pablo, 84–85
Touchdown Media, 142
Townsend, Raymond, 233
Tu, Thuy Nguyen, 3, 8
tuj lub (top spin), 215
Turner, Victor, 60
Tydings-McDuffie Act, 24, 41
Tyson, Mike, viii

Uchiomo, Bobby, 39
The Ultimate Fighter (television show), 162
Ultimate Fighting Championship, 162
underdogs, 77–89, 106
Uperesa, Fa'anofo Lisaclaire, 236, 250
U.S. Empire: Asian American encounters with, 6–7; Hmong Americans and, 200–203; Japan in conflict with, 33; Philippines and, 23–24, 27, 41–43, 108–9; sport as instrument of, 23–29, 249–51
Uyematsu, Amy, 46

Vainuku, Soma, 238
Vang, Chia Youyee, 14–15, 249
Vang, Elliot, 207–8
Vang, Marilyn, 213
Veeramani, Anamika, 136
Vietnamese refugees, 25
Vietnam War, 200–202
Vogel, Frank, 41
volleyball, 211
Vue, Charlie, 207

Wada, Fred, 36
Wahs, Mei, ix
Walia, Rahul, 142
Wallace, Tim, 54
Walters, Rex, 233

Wang, Oliver, ix, 12, 106, 234, 248
War Brides Act, 24
war on terror, 5, 7, 107, 249
War Relocation Authority, 33–34
Washington, Robert, 132
Waterson, Michelle, 164–68, 170–71
Wheaton, Belinda, 103
White, Dana, 162
White, Dorset, 58–59
Whitlock, Jason, 85
Wie, Michelle, 129, 153, 159–60
Wilkins, K., 155
Willard, Michael, 33
Williams, Serena, ix
Williams, Ted, 30
Winant, Howard, 2
WNBA. *See* Women's National Basketball Association
women: in nontraditional sports, 163; stereotypical sports for, 159–61. *See also* Asian American women
Women's National Basketball Association (WNBA), 47
Wong, Helen, 3, 38
Wong, William Woo, 3, 38
Woods, Tiger, 129
World Wrestling Federation, 62–63
wrestling, 62–65, 130

Yamaguchi, Kristi, 153, 159–60
Yang, Erick, 207
Yellow Peril, 108, 132, 199, 225
Yep, Kathleen, ix–x, 2, 4, 38, 203–4, 206
YMCA, 2, 42
Yomiuri (newspaper), 36
Yonsei, 186
YWCA, 42

Zeitchick, Dave, 207–8
Zhizhi, Wang, 231
Zimmerman, Jonathan, 86
Zirin, Dave, 233–34
Zuffa, 162